T0322786

ALCHEMY

Brian Clough & Peter Taylor
at Hartlepools United

CHRISTOPHER HULL

The
History
Press

Jacket Illustrations:
Front: *Northern Daily Mail*
Cartoons graciously provided by North News & Pictures Ltd

First published 2022

The History Press
97 St George's Place, Cheltenham,
Gloucestershire, GL50 3QB
www.thehistorypress.co.uk

© Christopher Hull, 2022
Map illustrated by Rick Britton; © Christopher Hull

The right of Christopher Hull to be identified as the Author
of this work has been asserted in accordance with the
Copyright, Designs and Patents Act 1988.

All rights reserved. No part of this book may be reprinted
or reproduced or utilised in any form or by any electronic,
mechanical or other means, now known or hereafter invented,
including photocopying and recording, or in any information
storage or retrieval system, without the permission in writing
from the Publishers.

British Library Cataloguing in Publication Data.
A catalogue record for this book is available from the British Library.

ISBN 978 0 7509 9959 5

Typesetting and origination by The History Press
Printed and bound in Great Britain by TJ Books Limited, Padstow, Cornwall.

Trees for LYfe

CONTENTS

PART III: THE SUMMER OF '66

PART IV: THE 1966/67 SEASON

CONCLUSION

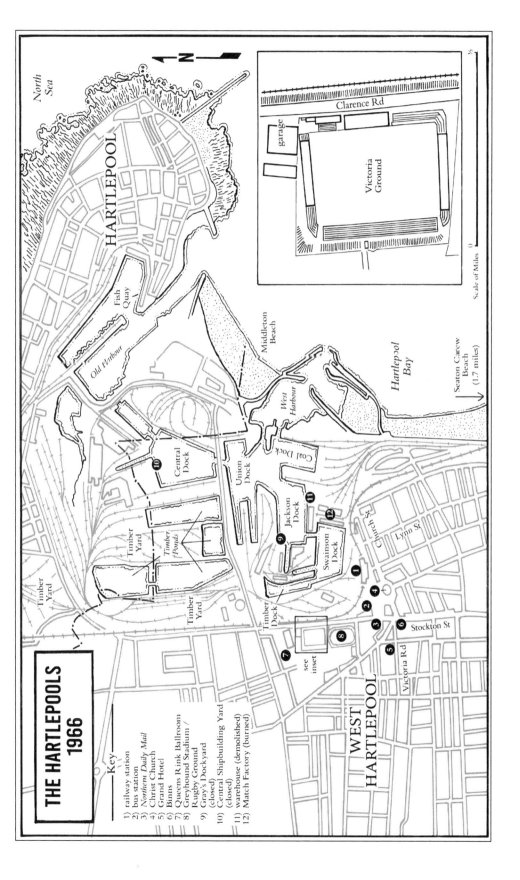

THE HARTLEPOOLS 1966

North Sea

HARTLEPOOL

Fish Quay

Old Harbour

Middleton Beach

West Harbour

Hartlepool Bay

Seaton Carew Beach (1.7 miles)

Central Dock

Union Dock

Coal Dock

Timber Yard

Timber Ponds

Jackson Dock

Swainson Dock

Timber Yard

Timber Dock

Church St

Lynn St

Stockton St

Victoria Rd

see inset

WEST HARTLEPOOL

Clarence Rd

garage

Victoria Ground

Scale of Miles

Key

1) railway station
2) bus station
3) *Northern Daily Mail*
4) Christ Church
5) Grand Hotel
6) Binns
7) Queens Rink Ballroom
8) Greyhound Stadium / Rugby Ground
9) Gray's Dockyard (closed)
10) Central Shipbuilding Yard (closed)
11) warehouse (demolished)
12) Match Factory (burned)

INTRODUCTION

PROLOGUE

1 May 1993

The final whistle is about to blow on Brian Clough's twenty-seven-year management career. In the Premier League's inaugural season, a home defeat condemns Nottingham Forest to the First Division. Just days from retirement, Clough suffers his first-ever relegation as player or manager. Sporting his trademark green Umbro sweatshirt, he slurs his words in post-match interviews. Worn down by alcoholism and stress, red blotches speckle his face. Clough begins the banter cheerful but ends it tearful. His verdict on relegation? The team and their manager were 'not good enough'. He thanks the men behind the microphone for their professionalism over the years, while they salute him for entertaining us. The BBC's Barry Davies, himself a legend, receives a hug and a kiss.

The end resembled the closing scene in a Shakespearean tragedy. Two lead roles had been central to the football drama, but Clough played out its fifth and final act alone.

As a pair, Brian Clough & Peter Taylor were household names in British football from the late 1960s until the early 1980s. Their characters and talents chimed to produce inimitable chemistry and amass trophies. When they were firing on all cylinders, the effect was magical. In five years at Forest from 1976 they won two League Cups, the First Division Championship, and back-to-back European Cups. In similar fashion, they steered Derby County from the lower reaches of the Second Division to the First Division Championship in 1972. The Clough & Taylor brand was synonymous with transforming underperforming teams at unfashionable clubs and turning them into serial winners.

But when the two elements of the formula were apart, there was no spark of chemistry. For example, Clough never fully committed to Brighton &

Hove Albion in the years between managing Derby and Forest in the East Midlands. The pair barely made an impression at the south-coast club. And when Clough went it alone during forty-four infamous days at Leeds United in 1974, the results were disastrous.

Yet when they were together and in top gear, as at Derby and Forest, nobody could hold a candle to them. Brian Clough was the charismatic half of the double act. Due to regular television appearances, his nasal Yorkshire drawl was seared into the national consciousness. When he spoke, the public listened. In his own mind and the minds of many listeners, he spoke truth to authority. But for others, his big-mouth brashness and overconfidence were a turn-off.

Peter Taylor was seven years his senior, but nowhere near as telegenic. Away from the limelight in which his partner basked, he was the more ambitious and strategic-thinking man. He also liked to gamble, literally and metaphorically, trusting his instincts to take a punt. His eye for talented players and bargain buys, as well as horses, was second to none. Together, the Clough & Taylor brand was as complex and balanced as a fine blended whisky, but not to everyone's taste.

Before they first hit the big time at Derby, the pair served their joint-managerial apprenticeship at the base of the football pyramid. During a nineteen-month baptism of fire at the Cinderella club of North-East football, they tackled all manner of challenges and difficulties. The club had never won promotion and lay next-to-bottom of the Fourth Division. It had applied for re-election to the Football League in five out of the previous six seasons. With few pennies to rub together, its council-owned ground was one of only two in the league without floodlights.

Clough & Taylor's rocky journey to the top of the football tree therefore began at its very bottom.

1

HERO TO ZERO

December 1962

Beginning on Christmas Eve, a Siberian anticyclone joined freezing air from the North Pole to inflict one of the harshest ever winters on Great Britain. The Big Freeze of 1962–63 held the country in its icy grip until March, with -20°C temperatures and 15ft snowdrifts paralysing everyday life. For weeks on end, no number of braziers, groundsmen's pitchforks or bales of straw could prevent decimation to the Football League programme.

Boxing Day's fixture list suffered nineteen postponements and another three abandonments. Matches called off included Middlesbrough v Norwich on Teesside. Sunderland's home fixture up the North-East coast only survived thanks to Wearside's proximity to the relatively temperate North Sea. Despite the referee deeming the half-frozen pitch playable, however, a pre-match hailstorm left it more treacherous still.

Wrapped up against the rotten weather, the fans streaming through Roker Park's turnstiles were full of expectation. Sitting second in the Second Division, Sunderland's promotion hopes were pinned on the red-and-white-striped no.9 shirt of their plucky goal-a-game striker. Ahead of the match he was seen dancing on the balls of his feet in the stadium's foyer, describing the goals he'd score. With a record of twenty-four goals in twenty-four games that season, few questioned his cocky self-confidence.[1]

The game against Bury, the best attended in the country, started brightly for Sunderland. Their first big moment of excitement came in the 16th minute, a dress rehearsal for the calamity to come. Bury goalkeeper Chris Harker upended their star centre-forward Brian Clough as he pounced on a cross, only for Charlie Hurley to skew the resulting penalty wide.

Recollecting the second and far more pivotal 27th-minute incident three decades later, Clough explained: 'I'd got my head down into the penalty area chasing a bad ball into the box … The goalkeeper came out a bit barmy. Anyway, I went over him and I did my knee and I did my big head … and I finished up in the infirmary in Sunderland.'[2]

Veteran North-East football correspondent Doug Weatherall remembers the Boxing Day game as if it was yesterday:

> I can see him now on the icy ground, watching the ball over his shoulder. Brian's weight was behind him as he was stretching. The advancing goalkeeper had his weight forward and there was a terrible collision.[3]

He crawled through the slush on all fours, slumped on his backside in the six-yard box, and pounded the pitch with his right palm. Everyone packed into Roker Park knew it was a bad one.

A photo sequence told the story the next day under the headline: 'The clash that could cost Sunderland promotion.' 'Clough, his face twisted in pain, lies helpless on the muddy carpet of Roker Park'; 'The crowd falls silent as the St John Ambulance Brigade volunteers carry the injured leader from the field.'[4] While the 1–0 home defeat to Bury was Sunderland's first in thirty-two league games, the fans had lost much more than a football game.

The deathly hush that rippled through the Boxing Day crowd suggested their promotion hopes had shattered like falling icicles from the Clock Stand roof.

Among the crowd that fateful afternoon was a sport-mad and music-loving 13-year-old schoolboy living in West Hartlepool. He'd saved up his pocket money to travel up the North-East coast to Seaburn near Roker by train. John McGovern rubbed elbows on the terraces to catch a good view of the action. Like other supporters at the Fulwell End, he was 'gobsmacked' by the turning point on 27 minutes that transformed the game's festive atmosphere into that of a wake. After departing early to catch a less crowded train home, other passengers on the station platform enquired about the score. Sunderland were losing, he told them, but much more ominously, 'I think Clough's broken his leg.'[5]

Fast-forward three years, and the roles of player and onlooker would be reversed. Without knowing it, the 42,407 Boxing Day fans on Wearside had witnessed a key career- and life-defining moment for Brian Clough. He'd play again, but surgery on medial and cruciate knee ligament damage in the 1960s was not what it is today.

When McGovern met Clough face to face in 1965, it was for a practice game at the ramshackle Victoria Ground, home to Hartlepools United Football Club. (The club would lose its extra 's' after the amalgamation of The Hartlepools – Hartlepool and West Hartlepool – in 1967). The league's youngest manager, Brian Clough, alongside assistant manager Peter Taylor, recognised a gem who'd play under them for many years to come. Brian Clough and John McGovern's joint football journey therefore began on Boxing Day 1962, with the mud-spattered striker rueing his ruined right knee.

2

'BORO DAYS

In Brian Clough's eyes, his Mam kept the cleanest front step on their street. The street was Valley Road on Middlesbrough's Grove Estate. He was closer to his mother than his father, a sugar boiler in a local sweet factory and a Middlesbrough FC season ticket holder. In the football-obsessed North East, Brian and his father stood on Ayresome Park's terraces to worship Teesside heroes George Hardwick and Wilf Mannion, famed for his inimitable body swerve.

Sally (known as Sal) and Joe Clough instilled discipline in their children and a love of family life. Liver and onions was a teatime favourite, and there was no TV. Just a wireless, a gramophone and a piano. His Mam, who ruled the roost, spent many hours at the mangle, where Brian often helped her with the sheets.

Born in 1935, Brian was the fourth eldest of six boys along with two sisters. Typical of the day, the six brothers slept three-in-a-bed and were never cold. They all shared errands, while their parents scrimped and saved for the two-week family holiday to Blackpool every summer.

Academically, his brothers and sisters outperformed him. Indeed, a lifelong sense of inferiority arose from him failing his eleven-plus, the only sibling to do so. He cried on hearing the news. While they progressed to grammar school, he attended the local non-selective secondary. He left without any O- or A-levels, a fact he often mentioned in later life when boasting about the silverware he won as a football manager. In his mind, medals and trophies trumped paper qualifications.

Young Brian had a burning ambition to get picked for every team but struggled for selection at Marton Grove Secondary Modern. Resentment at being overlooked smouldered within him. It didn't help that he was a small child who only spurted upwards from the age of 16 to reach 5ft 11in. His first love was cricket and the Yorkshire and England opening batsman Len Hutton. But his brothers' preference for a different sport turned him into a football fanatic who drove himself to outcompete them. There were always pairs of football boots hanging behind their coalhouse door, and constant debate about who was the best player. For a time, four Clough brothers – Desmond, Billy, Joe and Brian – played for Saturday/Sunday afternoon village team Great Broughton in the Cleveland League. This left their mother with a large pile of muddy kit to wash every weekend. His other hobbies included collecting birds' eggs, hunting out the best conkers, and climbing trees to pick apples and pears from the posher areas of Middlesbrough.[1]

Brian stood out with schoolteachers for his strong opinions on any given topic. Yet despite his cockiness and lack of academic prowess, the school made him head boy, an honour that brought him immense pride. The pleasing taste of authority, wearing a head boy's cap and instructing his fellow pupils, stayed with him.

He left school at 15 to start an apprenticeship as a fitter and turner at the massive ICI plant in Billingham, racing there on a bike with dropped handle-bars and narrow tyres. But his lack of dexterity meant he was unsuited to the work, and an underground tour of an anhydrite mine terrified him. ICI made him a junior clerk, but he was little more than a note-carrying messenger boy who progressed to filling out overtime sheets.[2]

A schoolteacher's recommendation led Brian to start playing for Middlesbrough FC's junior side. Yet no sooner had he progressed from ama-teur to professional at 17½ years old then he was called up for two years of national service in the Royal Air Force. Posted to RAF Watchet in Somerset, he could barely have been any further away from the North East, although test match cricket on the wireless provided a pleasant distraction. He played football for his station side on Wednesdays and Saturdays but bristled at never being picked for the RAF national team.[3]

On returning to Middlesbrough, it took far too long in Clough's mind for him to become a first-team regular. He made his first-team debut against Barnsley on 17 September 1955 and scored four goals in nine games that season. What he termed his 'Golden Year' of 1956/57 made him a regular first-teamer and built his reputation as a prolific sharpshooter. He also gained notoriety as a bighead and a loudmouth. He just couldn't refrain from call-ing out his fellow players' shortcomings, particularly their frailties in defence. In Brian's opinion, and he said so, there was no point in him banging in a hatful of goals up front if they were leaking them by the sack load at the back. Until they resolved the problem, he asserted, 'Boro would be perennial under-achievers in the Second Division.

In a situation that would play out again at Sunderland, Clough made few friends in the Middlesbrough dressing room. After initial difficulties establishing himself in the first team, his goalscoring prowess cemented his position in 'Boro's forward line. The one real friendship he did develop was with a goalkeeper seven years his senior who arrived on Teesside in 1955 after ten years at Coventry City, nine of them under the influential manager Harry Storer.

Born and brought up in Nottingham, Peter Taylor arrived at 'Boro with his young family and soon began to mentor Brian Clough. He couldn't understand why his new younger acquaintance was not a regular in the first team given his goalscoring ability. 'This fair-haired boy of 20 was the greatest player I had ever seen. I knew then that he must find success,' Taylor said later. With a keen eye for football talent, developed under Storer, Taylor persuaded 'Boro manager Bob Dennison to give his cocky colleague more opportunities in the first team. Like most of his football-related judgements, Taylor was spot on.

Bachelor Clough and family man Taylor hung out together. The junior partner made regular visits to Taylor's home, where they'd spend endless hours discussing football. They travelled top-deck on buses to take in countless matches around the North East. The pair talked tactics and honed a joint philosophy about how the game should be played, and how managers should manage.

Under Storer at Coventry, Taylor had studiously observed how his manager spotted and acquired talented players, often at bargain prices. And furthermore, he learned from him how to discern and exploit their best attributes. Storer was not a man to suffer fools in his dressing room or in the boardroom, and liked the game played hard.[4] Taylor had become a disciple of Storer at Coventry, as Clough would become a disciple of Taylor at Middlesbrough. His new friend became his champion in the 'Boro dressing room. Beyond his footballing nous, Taylor also made Clough laugh with his observational dry wit. Furthermore, he told him to his face when he was wrong.

In 1957, Clough began to date a local girl he met at the Rea cafeteria, a regular player hangout for a milkshake and a chat. Brian considered himself the luckiest man in the world to have met her, and after two years of courting he married Barbara in 1959. Like Peter Taylor, she was able to keep him on an even keel, at least most of the time.

On the one hand, Clough had good reason to be cocky. His goalscoring record was phenomenal and the statistics spoke for themselves. In four consecutive seasons at Middlesbrough he scored more than forty goals. In the 1957/58 and 1958/59 seasons he was literally a goal-a-game striker, with stats of 42/42 and 43/43 games to goals respectively. Two of his goalscoring records still stand today, perhaps never to be surpassed. In total, he scored 251 league goals from 274 starts. Only three weeks before his life-defining injury, Clough had completed the fastest 250 goals in league football. Like his record in reaching 200 goals, it still stands. Among this goal frenzy, he scored eighteen hat-tricks at Middlesbrough and Sunderland. In addition to these, he scored four goals on five occasions at Middlesbrough, and once bagged five goals in a 9–0 hammering of Brighton at Ayresome Park in August 1958.

Clough was renowned as a fox in the 6-yard box, pouncing on any sniff of goal. He'd often pick up the ball in midfield, distribute it accurately to either wing, to dash forward into the open space for a quick return.[5] The near post was his main bread and dripping.

There is one large caveat to these records, however. All Clough's goals, bar one, were scored in the Second Division. The lingering question is why no First Division club bought him if he was *that* good, and why he won just two full England caps. He would have told you that it was due to the rank bad judgement of First Division managers and England team selectors. According to Clough, and some agreed, England played him in the wrong position or in the wrong formation. Others reckoned his lack of progression up the league and at international level had a lot to do with his oversized head and salty tongue.

As well as possessing an uncanny ability to score goals, he also excelled in rubbing up people the wrong way. In a notorious episode at Middlesbrough, for example, most of his teammates signed a round-robin requesting that the club withdraw the captaincy from him. Instead of shooting his mouth off, Clough shot a hat-trick in their next game to help sink Bristol Rovers 5-1. Manager Bob Dennison quipped that his players should repeat the round-robin if it was going to have that effect.

Doug Weatherall had attended a game at Carlisle and stayed the night in the town. He was supposed to cover a game at Workington the next day when his office called and instructed him to get over to Teesside and cover the story.

Doug sped to Clough's house in Middlesbrough, but on his arrival spotted a car belonging to Len Shackleton, a former Newcastle and Sunderland footballer and now working for the *Daily Express*. Derrick Hodson was there too, working for the same newspaper. They had unfortunately beaten Doug to scoop the headline story that Clough was requesting a transfer. Nevertheless, when Doug asked Clough out of his rivals' earshot how the episode made him feel, he lamented, 'It's broken my heart.'[6]

Clough carried the hurt for another two years before ending his playing days at 'Boro. After a sixteen-day summer cruise in the Mediterranean with his wife Barbara, their ship docked at Southampton early one morning, where the suntanned Sunderland manager Alan Brown awaited them. With the two North-East clubs having already agreed a deal, he'd interrupted a holiday in Cornwall to try and seal it. It took the two men just six minutes to shake hands on Clough's salary. A month after Peter Taylor departed for Port Vale, a transfer fee of £45,000* took the prolific centre-forward up the A19 from Teesside to Wearside in July 1961.

---

* Readers interested in modern-day equivalent prices should use www.bankofengland.co.uk/monetary-policy/inflation/inflation-calculator

3

NEVER GIVE UP

The Cloughs slid into personal hell on Boxing Day 1962. Following his injury, Brian found himself in Williamson Ward 2 of Sunderland Accident Hospital. Even his wife Barbara was unable to visit him, as she was confined to bed at home with flu.[1]

The couple's friend Doug Weatherall saw him the day after his injury and immediately enquired, 'What's the score Brian?'

'They tell me that everything in my knee's gone.'

When Doug described the injury to Newcastle United's physio, his verdict was 'he's finished'. According to Doug, however, 'Brian never admitted that his career was over'.[2]

Barbara did eventually visit her husband four to five days later, only to inform him she'd suffered a miscarriage. Brian was unaware she was even pregnant. With stitches from cracking his head on the icy pitch, to having his entire leg in plaster from ankle to groin, it had turned into a joyless Christmas. When he was ready to leave hospital, Alan Brown gave him a lift home and literally carried the player on his back from the car door to the threshold of his club bungalow on St Nicholas Avenue. Clough admitted he was not the easiest husband to live with during this period, resting his shattered knee on the cushions of their red G Plan settee.[3]

In early 1963, the Big Freeze led to so many P-P (postponed) entries in weekend fixture lists that the three main Football Pools companies – Littlewoods, Vernons and Zetters – set up a Pools Panel for the first time. The six-man team of experts met behind closed doors to decide who would have won the matches had they been played. The BBC announced their guesstimates on live television.

Elsewhere, the Big Freeze paralysed roads, railways and airports. Snowploughs, shovels and rock salt attempted to get the country's lorries, trains and planes moving again. But that was cold comfort for the nation's farmers, who struggled to get their produce out of the frozen ground. A vegetable shortage resulted, and the price of cabbages, carrots and potatoes shot up.

Upon seeing Clough's injury on Boxing Day 1962, Alan Brown had immediately deemed the situation hopeless. Yet neither manager nor club physio John Watters could tell Clough because it would have 'shattered him'. They judged he needed at least a sliver of hope to cling onto over the difficult months that followed.[4]

Brown thus paid more attention to the psychological blow suffered by his star centre-forward. In the next day's newspaper, he declared 'this COULD be a long one'. While stressing it was 'a big blow' to the club and its fans, he underlined that 'the player is suffering more than we are'.[5]

He did his utmost to soften the blow by driving Clough hard to recover from crippling injury, despite the futility. Brown had been through the same sad process before. As a trainer at Sheffield Wednesday, he'd had to tell Derek Dooley his career was finished after the centre-forward broke a leg playing at Preston. More tragically still, Dooley had to have his leg amputated.[6]

On the weekly *Football Echo*'s front page ten days after his injury, Clough thanked the legions of Clock Standers and Roker Enders, etc., who had sent messages of encouragement to him. His 'secretary' – his wife Barbara – had answered them all.[7] But he sounded much less chirpy two weeks later: 'The thought of being out for the season has brought hours of depression. It would be wrong for me to say otherwise. I was enjoying my football more than at any time in my career and beginning to feel that Sunderland could take on anybody.'[8]

By the time they removed his leg plaster in late March, Clough was still top scorer in the league, despite not having played for three months. He was relieved to see the back of the cast, and the *Echo*'s front page pictured him completing a giant jigsaw alongside Barbara at home.[9] Two months later his crutches had given way to sticks, and his depression to determination. But hard work alone would not compensate for his crippling knee injury.

Renowned as an arch disciplinarian with a soft underbelly, Alan Brown drove Clough hard during his convalescence. In late June, Clough was leaving his car at home to walk to Roker Park to regain fitness on its terracing and perimeter track.[10] He sprinted up and down the fifty-seven steps of Roker Park's terracing, often with Brown in tow for moral support. He used a diminishing pile of forty football boot studs to keep count, and even chased pigeons to gain fitness. Alone, he sprinted up and down Seaburn's Cat and Dog steps on repeat, never doubting he'd make a full recovery.[11]

His period of convalescence reinforced Clough's respect for the Northumbrian's ironclad rule. It was indeed the lean and upright Brown who taught Clough most about discipline, applied to the individual and to his teams. The player admitted to being frightened of a manager whose 'bollockings' he defined as being worth ten from anybody else. Instead of tearing a strip off players, he tore off their entire shirts.[12] According to Doug Weatherall, Corbridge-born Brown was 'the most formidable manager' he ever met. 'Anybody who can deal with Alan Brown,' he told me, 'can deal with any other manager.'[13]

Clough revered Brown like a subordinate does his commanding officer. Indeed, Brown ran his teams like a sergeant major does a parade ground. He was the dictator that Clough aspired to be. In time, others would consider Clough's supreme confidence – as they did Brown's – as arrogance spilling over into conceit.

Brown had dropped two severe 'bollockings' on Clough's head on his first day of training at Sunderland. Firstly, for speaking to a friend at the training ground perimeter fence in the morning; and secondly, for enquiring about the England cricket team's test match score at Roker Park in the afternoon. After a good start on the pitch, his new manager then dropped him from the first team for being a 'a little stale' while praising the way he reacted to it. In Clough's opinion, he was 'the man with the firm hand but warm heart'. According to him, for 'all his outward toughness […] there's no manager more human, more discerning than Alan Brown'.[14]

After a playing career as centre-half for Huddersfield, Burnley and Notts County, Brown had entered the police force before returning to football as a coach and then manager. He had dragged Sunderland's reputation out of the mire following a corruption scandal in the late 1950s in which the club was heavily implicated and made a scapegoat. They had for years bent the rules by making illegal indirect payments to their players when a maximum wage existed for professional footballers.[15] Thenceforward, Sunderland's board of directors were renowned for caution and penny-pinching.

Meanwhile, Brown was known as a harsh disciplinarian with a strong moralistic bent. He had a fixation with players' personal conduct. For example, he frowned on players smoking and drinking, and abhorred them 'boozing' in public. He had zero interest in the permissive society of the 1960s. Above all, he inculcated self-discipline in his players. Rarely did they step out of line, and when they did, they felt his wrath. Furthermore, he involved himself in his players' problems, however small. Called the 'The Iron Man' of football by the British tabloids, and 'the Bomber' by his players, he led by example through full application to the job in hand and attention to detail.[16]

Come December 1963, it appeared to be all over for Clough's football-ing career. Sunderland's *Football Echo* correspondent Argus (a nom de plume) affirmed there had never been more than 'an outside chance' that their free-scoring centre-forward would recover from the worst type of knee injury that could befall a player. As others before him had found, there was 'no comeback' from such ligament damage. His had been a 'brave battle', but it was never more than 'a forlorn hope'.[17]

Medical experts advised Sunderland that if Clough attempted to play football again, another tackle could turn him into a cripple. But as the *Echo* affirmed, the experts' most difficult task was 'convincing Brian'. Asked if he should defy doctors' orders, Alan Brown counselled that 'they know best'.[18]

On the one hand, Clough seemed resigned, saying, 'I've tried for a year to beat the injury. Now I'm told it's hopeless.' Apart from his delicate knee, he was perfectly fit and training with the rest of the team, and kicking balls 'just as hard, just as accurately as ever'. He had insured himself for £1,500 against a career-ending injury and stood to collect £500 from the players' union insur-ance fund. But that was small compensation for a player many rated as the best centre-forward in Britain. Clough lamented, 'Football to me wasn't only my career. It was my whole life.'[19] It wouldn't solve all his troubles, but Sunderland had promised him a testimonial game.

Meanwhile, Brown appeared to offer a valedictory on his playing career: 'Clough's great goal-scoring record speaks for itself. His greatest asset? His confidence. His belief that no matter how things were going against him he would get a goal. This is a rare quality. He also has a unique style.'[20]

Walter Turnbull joined in too, writing that his early retirement would be 'a great loss to the game', while hoping he'd find another outlet in the sport for his 'unbounded enthusiasm'.[21] At the same time, legendary Newcastle striker 'Wor Jackie' Milburn lamented the 'cruel blow' that had deprived modern-day football of one of its 'greatest' centre-forwards. He deemed him 'a soccer addict who lived for football'.[22] Alan Brown's apparent final verdict was that: 'This truly is a great tragedy for all of us.'[23]

On reading news of his early retirement from the game, the Richmond (Yorkshire) division of the Labour Party asked Clough if they could put his name forward for nomination as candidate. It wasn't the most enticing offer because Richmond was one of the safest Tory seats in the country. And it wasn't the first time he'd been asked to go into politics. Even when playing at Middlesbrough, he had been approached about being a town councillor. The *Sunday Mirror* described Clough as 'an able speaker'. And whether it was judo, snakes and ladders, or soccer, he always played with 'a tremendous killer instinct' but 'with scrupulous fairness'.

He didn't enter the cut-and-thrust of politics, despite the temptation to do so. What he was certain about was that the suspense and agony of sitting on the sidelines was destroying him. He told the newspaper: 'I wait in the treatment rooms as the lads trot along the corridor to take the field at five minutes to three. The sound of those studs shuffling along the concrete pulls my heart out.'[24]

With time on his hands and strong opinions to voice, *The People* newspaper knew a good thing when they saw it and published a series of three weekly articles by Clough. The now apparently retired loudmouth of football did not hold back. In fact, he gave his critics both barrels.

The headline of the first two-page spread described him as 'soccer's odd man out [and] the Goal King with a grudge'. For starters, 'Mr Goals' demanded to know why he'd been cold-shouldered by the England selectors when he was soccer's 'most consistent scorer' and 'banging in the goals left, right and centre'. He neglected to mention at this point that all these goals had been scored in the Second Division. Apparently, there had been 'half a million fans screaming "Clough must play for England"'.

He couldn't get over how 'bitter' he felt, although he did recognise he'd been tagged 'a difficult character, a big head … [and] a bad mixer'. Clough recounted an England training camp at Roehampton when a party of England players had organised a shopping trip to Central London. Clough and fellow north-easterner Bobby Charlton had decided to watch birds nesting in a local wood instead.[25]

The second article began by proclaiming, 'I hope the England selectors read this.' You can be sure they did, and that they didn't forget the experience quickly. Again, he couldn't fathom why he hadn't been picked more for England.

When it came to the round-robin episode at Middlesbrough, he cited some (from the majority) who'd signed it:

'Brian howls at me on the field.'

'He doesn't mix with us in card schools at away matches.'

'He doesn't act like a captain.'

What they had failed to understand, apparently, was that everything he said was 'in the heat of the moment and forgotten immediately'.[26] It might have been instantly forgotten by Clough, but was forever remembered by those at the sharp end of his tongue.

In the third article, meanwhile, he asserted that people simply misunderstood him. Rather than wanting to run the show, as he had at Middlesbrough, he preferred 'a tough guy for a boss'. Be it Brown at Sunderland, Stan Cullis at Wolves, or Harry Storer at Derby, he respected sternness. In fact, seeking Storer's advice, the Derby manager had advised him to join Brown at Sunderland.[27]

While the three weekly articles did nothing to endear him to his fellow players or the England establishment, who he had already antagonised in the extreme, they did demonstrate an aptitude for courting controversy and getting his message out. Newspapers weren't shy to give him column inches, and the public was keen to read what he said.

Despite missing Clough's goalscoring prowess, Sunderland still got within a whisker of promotion in the 1962/63 season. They missed out on goal average, with Stoke City crowned Second Division champions on 53 points, and Sunderland placed third behind Chelsea on 52 points apiece. While both rivals had performed similarly at home, Sunderland's defence had shipped more goals and points playing away from Roker Park. Up to the First Division steamed Stoke and Chelsea, while Sunderland stayed put. Would Clough's missing goals have made the difference? The only thing we can be sure about is that Clough himself would have thought so.

Sunderland prospered during the 1963/64 season, despite Clough's continued absence. Yet after finally achieving promotion in April 1964, the resignation in July of Alan Brown after seven years at the club to take over at Sheffield Wednesday came as a hammer blow to Sunderland supporters.

Eight months after medical experts had advised Clough to pack in the game, fresh opinion on his fragile knee left the decision with Clough. His last word deemed that he re-signed for Sunderland and began pre-season training alongside the rest of the team in the summer of 1964. Hovering over the question of his return to action was insurance compensation to the tune of the £40,000 that was due to the club should he take early retirement.[28] On reporting back for pre-season training, Clough declared himself 'as fit as a fiddle and rarin' to go'. He'd been training alone at Roker Park thus far, but now led colleagues on 2-mile runs and strenuous workouts 'without raising a sweat'.[29] Cloughie refused to call it a day.

With his hopes raised of a return from the ashes to wearing the Sunderland no.9 shirt again, Clough turned out on the cricket oval for a Footballers & Sportswriters XI v Wearmouth XI match. He opened the batting with a knock of 32 runs before being stumped. With ball in hand, he took one wicket for 32 runs.[30] Meanwhile, the local press talked up the possibility of him returning on the football pitch. 'Can Clough confound medical opinion and conquer an injury which has put many a top man out of the game for good?' one newspaper asked.[31]

Another local headline declared: '45 minutes from truth: Brian Clough's biggest gamble.' Only Clough could know the tremendous risk he was taking, the report suggested.[32] When he appeared for a second-half appearance in a pre-season friendly against Huddersfield, 'sentiment ran wild' among the near-25,000 Roker Park crowd. Wild cheers erupted every time he touched the ball in his first comeback in the second half of a friendly against Huddersfield. There was no doubt he could still play football, the *Sunderland Echo* affirmed, but could he perform at the top level?[33] The player himself moaned he had scarcely got a kick of the ball, but left the next step to Sunderland's directors.[34] And it was the Sunderland directors rather than the club's manager who would decide Clough's fate in a board meeting on 19 August 1964. It was also the directors who decided team selection, and that was because Sunderland were still without a manager at the start of the 1964/65 season. The club were back where they wanted to be in the First Division but had yet to find a replacement for Alan Brown.

Clough's first competitive game was against Grimsby Reserves at Blundell Park, hitting the goal trail again on 78 minutes with a low free kick from 20 yards. During a fifteen-minute spell, the *Sunderland Echo*'s reserve-team correspondent Vedra judged that he looked like the player who was 'terrorizing Second Division defences' twenty months previously.[35] His first competitive appearance at Roker Park, on 29 August 1964, swelled the attendance to five times its normal size. Clough 'thrilled' fans with a 'vintage' hat-trick, 'toying with' and tearing through the opposing defence, although it did belong to Fourth Division Halifax Town's Reserves.[36] Despite the lowly opposition, Clough declared himself 'ready for First Division football'.[37] Yet he was running a dire risk every time he played football. Nothing more than nylon stitches attached his severed knee ligament to the bone.[38]

Nine months after his declaration that he would never play again, and having 'never stopped hoping and fighting' to build up strength in his injured knee, Clough's fourth and largest step was his return to first-team action at home to West Bromwich Albion on 2 September 1964.[39] Yet there was a serious danger of over-hyping his return. The *Daily Mirror* declared that the Sunderland goal ace 'written off' by doctors after a serious knee injury was now making a miraculous comeback.[40] In what was his first ever appearance in the First Division, a 52,000 crowd saw him make an encouraging comeback in a 2–2 draw, adopting his favourite near-post position, showing much of his 'former dash and fire', and cracking a shot against the base of the post.[41]

Three days later he spearheaded Sunderland's attack at home to a Leeds United side featuring Norman Hunter, Jackie Charlton and Billy Bremner.

After a corner kick, Clough celebrated scoring with a header into an empty net from under the bar in the 51st minute. In a 3–3 draw, it was his first ever goal in the top division and his last in professional football.[42]

In his next and final game, Sunderland came from behind again to salvage a draw at home to Aston Villa. Yet the *Echo* correspondent judged that neither Johnny Crossan nor Brian Clough 'made any real impression' in attack. It was 'uphill all the way' for Clough. While carrying the sympathy of the crowd, he was 'lacking his old pace and power'.[43] In Argus's opinion, Clough hadn't convinced and still had a long way to go. Sunderland's directors had rushed him into the side on the strength of a good performance against Halifax Town Reserves.[44] Argus reaffirmed his position the next day too, describing how they'd recalled Clough too soon, when 'the pace and power which one made him the most feared leader in the game is no longer at his command'.[45] He'd thus made three first-team appearances in the First Division, and Sunderland had drawn all three.

Sunderland's directors dropped Clough for their next game at Arsenal on 12 September 1964, and he stayed out of the side. *The People* forecast two weeks later that he'd played his last game for Sunderland, with the club about to agree liability terms with their insurers. It turned out they'd jumped the gun by several weeks.[46]

4

ON THE SCRAPHEAP

Dropped from the Sunderland team, the man whose ambition had been to score more goals in the First Division than Everton legend Dixie Dean had found a new vocation by October 1964. Megaphone in hand, he was pictured canvassing for the Labour Party in Sunderland South.[1]

In November, the insurance company that had four months earlier decided it would not be unreasonable for him to play again, asked their London specialist to re-examine Clough's knee.[2] Now that it had been tested in competitive football, he travelled down to the capital with club physiotherapist John Watters.[3] The verdict was negative, so adding a definitive full stop to a brilliant but truncated football career.

Sunderland needed the £40,000 insurance cash to buy a new centre-forward. Despite all the huff and puff and dreams of returning to spearhead Sunderland's forward line, Clough had played his last game in professional football.

The bombshell decision left Clough embittered and sent him into a tailspin of resentment and self-pity. Fortunately, a stroke of good luck and judgement soon dragged him out of despair. It resulted from Sunderland's directors finally appointing a new manager. Former Middlesbrough defender and captain George Hardwick gave up his job with an oil company to return to full-time football in the North East.[4]

Like most football managers, he hit the ground running and shuffled his coaching and playing staff. Interviewed decades later, Hardwick affirmed that Clough was causing 'all hell in Roker Park' when he arrived. He was 'bitter and twisted' about not playing and 'hated everybody in sight'. The crocked star forward would stand in the tunnel as ex-colleagues jogged onto the pitch, barking in their ears, 'Who the bloody hell are you? You can't play. You should never be in this team.' And according to Hardwick, the sulky ex-player told the directors equally 'how useless they are'. The new manager soon hauled Clough into his office and warned him, 'No more trouble from you.' The newly retired player would have to work for his salary, considering he possessed more than enough knowledge of football to run a bunch of kids. The new manager put him with the third-string 'A' team. It was the lucky break he needed. A gleeful Clough placed his hand on Hardwick's shoulder and exclaimed, 'Hey boss. You'll do for me.'[5]

In such a way, the gentlemanly Hardwick did his former fan at Ayresome Park the best turn possible. Instead of allowing him to mope around the corridors of Roker Park, he gave him a new lease of life, something to keep his mind and mouth occupied in a constructive rather than destructive way. Clough would now train the apprentice professionals and part-timers of Sunderland's Northern Intermediate League youth team. His first game with new duties was an FA Youth Cup second-round game on Monday, 7 December 1964.[6] At home to Darlington, 17-year-old 'Little Bobby' Kerr starred in an 8–1 demolition of their regional rivals.

The opportunity was the perfect outlet for Clough's pent-up energy and theories about football. He discovered an innate talent to teach, and a renewed fondness for being in charge. Out went repetitive physical exercise in training, and in came more ball work. Instead of running lap after lap, five- and six-a-side games became the order of the day at their Cleadon training ground. Preparation for matches was key. His own sweat-drenched involvement meant that he and the players sparked on the same wavelength, and ensured they reached their peak on match days, not in training two days earlier. The young players' positive response to Clough's coaching confirmed what he knew already – that players under his charge listened to what he said, and he excelled in such a role.[7]

Sunderland youth player John O'Hare, later to play again under Clough at championship-winning Derby County and Nottingham Forest, remembers how his arrival was 'a breath of fresh air' that transformed their training. Before Clough it had all been about 'running half-laps'. But their energetic new coach concentrated on 'sharpness, reaction, quick thinking'. John says the youth team players 'had a lot of time for him'.[8]

The results of his efforts were impressive. In a remarkable season, Clough and Bill Scott guided Sunderland's youngsters to the semi-final of the FA Youth Cup, developing and nurturing stars of the future such as Bobby Kerr, John O'Hare, Colin Suggett and Colin Todd. Later in his management career, of course, Todd would play under Clough at Derby.

On the way to the semi-final, Sunderland Youth handed out a rare thrashing to Newcastle Youth in the third round and stormed through to the quarter-finals with a fine 3–1 triumph over Leeds United.[9] Sunderland's team was the youngest they had ever fielded in the competition. Everton Youth, the recognised best side and eventual winners of the FA Youth Cup, defeated the especially youthful Sunderland over two legs in the semi-final.[10]

On Hardwick's advice, Clough trained for an FA coaching badge at Durham, but disagreed with the Football Association man running the course. Clough took pleasure in telling and showing long-ball theorist Charles Hughes that he was wrong. For example, Hughes insisted the forehead be used when heading the ball into the net. Clough countered that any part of the head or indeed body could be used to score a goal, so long as you stuck it in legally. According to Clough, the others on the course listened to him and not to Hughes.[11] But then he would say that, wouldn't he. Suffice to say this early brush between Clough and the FA did not go well. It was indicative of what became a near whole management career of conflict with the Football Association. And a lifetime of rubbing people up the wrong way.

Clough was a Marmite character, both loved and loathed by different people. Or by individuals in equal measure but on alternate days. While he thrived in his youth team role, his inability to button his lip continued to antagonise his former first-team playing colleagues and the suits in the boardroom.

His good fortune under Hardwick turned to bad luck when Sunderland sacked the manager at the end of the 1964/65 season, despite them finishing fifteenth in the First Division, seven points safe from relegation. Clough approached his successor Ian McColl to confirm he'd be continuing his work with the youngsters after the Scotsman took over in May 1965. The new manager used the excuse that Sunderland's directors weren't keen for him to carry on. Clough believed, instead, that McColl wanted his own men around him.[12] But Hardwick bore out McColl's version of events when he said, 'The directors would not accept him. They just would not accept him.'[13] Clough soon followed Hardwick out of Roker Park. And the club's insurers finally paid out £40,000 to Sunderland in insurance liability on their retired striker. In the football edition of snakes and ladders, Clough was back at square one.

The twin physical and psychological blows hit him like a steam train. Indeed, he only accepted his career was over when medical opinion and Sunderland football club made the decision for him two years after his injury, in November 1964.

On Michael Parkinson's weekly Saturday evening TV chat show in 1973, Clough confessed that Sunderland 'was life to me. They were life to me.' When informed there was no longer room for him at the club he loved, he admitted to Parky, 'It kind of shattered me for a period of time. It broke me up.'[14]

The whole basis of his earning power, his fame, his outward and self-respect, and most importantly his ego, had evaporated. His bad footballing break left him broken-hearted. Without wanting or being able to admit it, he'd been scratching on football's scrapheap for two years. At 30 years old, not only was his footballing career over, but he'd been sacked from his first coaching role in the game. He'd proved his ability both on and off the field, but his mouth was his undoing. Football was all Clough knew and excelled at. Indeed, football was all he was skilled in.

5

THE FEAR

Clough touched rock bottom in the summer of '65, just as the sixties entered their most swinging phase. The retiree player and sacked coach only felt like swinging out against the world that had dealt him such cruel blows. By his own admission, he 'went berserk for a time … drank heavily and was hell to live with'. He didn't act 'very manly' and 'nearly went off the rails'.[1]

He later confessed, 'In the North East you have this fear of not having a job … And I had this fear of being unemployed … And I can't do very much else apart from work in football.'[2] Adding to his worries, he had another mouth to feed. His wife Barbara had given birth to their first child, Simon, in June 1964. And she'd now fallen pregnant again. Indeed, the summer of 1965 was – in his own words – 'when the fear crept in'.[3]

Clough found solace but no cure in drink and song. His most cherished crooners were The Ink Spots and Frank Sinatra. He spent many hours that summer listening to Ol' Blue Eyes and mowing the lawn. The newly retired ex-striker might have visualised the Wembley pitch as he did so, set to host the World Cup Final in July 1966. His love affair with football had only been partly consummated, and he'd spend the rest of his life compensating for things that never quite were.

Given his unique Jekyll & Hyde character, Clough had few friends in the Sunderland dressing room, and even fewer in its boardroom. But he did have a sea of compassionate admirers among the club's fans.

At a loss and with time on his hands, Clough became involved with those organising and playing for the local trainee teachers' football team. Grant Shearer, President of the Athletics Union at Sunderland Teachers' Training College and in his final year as a trainee teacher, approached George Wardale to be their football team coach. Instead, they got Brian Clough to coach three sessions for them in September 1965. According to Grant, when he'd arrived from his hometown of Carlisle to begin his studies, 'Clough was a god' on Wearside.[4]

Grant, 22 years old at the time, is perceptive when describing the Clough that he first got to know in the summer of 1965. Clough would invite Grant and his fellow trainee teacher Russ Postlewhite to his bungalow on St Nicholas Avenue on Sundays to watch *Shoot*, the weekly TV football highlights programme. He'd tell them, 'Come around on Sunday and tell me how the team has done.' His dedicated wife Barbara, nicknamed Squibs, would get a brew on, while 15-month-old Simon made himself heard.[5]

Grant describes Clough as a complex character, who came across as straightforward and down to earth. Beneath the bluster was a bright and kindly man. But he held certain rigid beliefs and was completely intolerant in some aspects of his life. He used to berate Grant for drinking, for example. And while very knowledgeable about football and cricket, he was very opinionated and often harsh about certain players' and managers' attributes. For example, Grant questioned Alan Brown's lack of trophies, but Clough fired back, 'Look how many future managers have played under him as players.' He defined himself as a socialist, but Grant categorises his politics as working-class conservatism. His overriding values were those of aspiration and hard work.[6]

Given what had happened to Clough prior to their meeting, Grant describes him as 'very bitter' about his injury. They'd sometimes meet Clough at the nearby Barnes Hotel for a Sunday roast. He recalls one occasion when the ex-player drove 200 yards from his home in his carpet slippers and his entrance separated the throngs of AFC Sunderland-worshipping lunchtime drinkers like Moses' parting of the seas. Served immediately at the bar, Clough ordered an orange juice.[7]

Russ Postlewhite recalls the digs where he and Grant lived on Barnes Park opposite a children's hospital. Their young landlady, Mrs Mason, was married to a largely absent seagoing engineer, their home providing board and lodging to students such as themselves. They returned one afternoon to find Mrs Mason breathless through excitement. She'd answered a knock on the front door only to find local football hero Brian Clough on her front step. Starstruck, Mrs Mason relayed his message to her two lodgers: 'Tell the boys, suited and booted and down my house by seven o'clock.' They'd often arrive at his bungalow and enquire, 'Where are we going Brian?' They'd drive to venues such as Newton Aycliffe Boys Club and rub shoulders with Sunderland's reserve team players. The events were often football talk-ins, where oddly, Sunderland first-team players were largely absent.

But wherever they went, there were packed and eager-to-listen audiences. Clough was a terrific speaker and those in attendance were either transfixed or roaring with laughter. On other occasions the boys would simply babysit for Brian and Barbara Clough, although he'd rarely tell them where he and his wife were going out. Russ says they 'got on well' with Clough. 'He used us, but we didn't mind.' After all, he introduced them to some big-name people, including football players.[8]

Sunderland had promised Clough a testimonial. To avoid a boring 'milk-and-water friendly', he planned a Tyneside versus Wearside battle in what he pledged would be his final appearance in a Sunderland shirt, and promised, 'I will referee. I will linesman. I will help sell the programmes. But no one will see me play in a match again.'[9]

Clough set about assembling the best players possible for his send-off game. Yet if he expected any charity from ex-playing colleagues, little was forthcoming. Years of rubbing people up the wrong way meant that the crocked centre-forward encountered a wall of coldness. When he came to call in favours, despite the tragic ending to his career, he found he was a Billy Few Mates.

One shining example was Sunderland left-back Len Ashurst. Clough blamed his ex-colleague for the 'bad ball' he'd been chasing when he smashed into the outrushing Bury goalkeeper on Boxing Day 1962. Roughly a month before the testimonial game, Ashurst had walked out of a Sunderland Rotary Club event at the Barnes Hotel. Salty-tongued Clough turned a speech into a 'tirade' in which he 'slammed' Ashurst and each first-team player in turn by listing all their faults.

When the request arrived to play in his testimonial, Ashurst refused it, and several teammates followed suit. This forced Clough to offer them 'a tenner' cash-in-hand appearance money – a 'bung'.[10] Four days before the 27 October game, he was still finalising the line-ups.

It was during these weeks that two job offers determined Clough's new career path. One came from West Bromwich Albion to coach their juniors, although that would mean a move away from his native North East. The other came about thanks to ex-Sunderland legend and *Sunday People* back-page columnist Len Shackleton. Bradford-born 'Shack' was a kindred spirit, who took on the football establishment as he'd taken on hapless defenders. Like Clough, he was bitter and outspoken about England selectors who'd awarded him only five caps. Most notoriously, his cynicism-filled 1955 book *The Clown Prince of Soccer* had a chapter headed 'The average director's knowledge of football', consisting of a single blank page.[11]

The accepted version of events is that football fixer Shack brokered Clough's first managerial appointment. Either he suggested to a club chairman that Clough fill his vacant managerial post, or he persuaded Clough to apply for it. Or possibly a combination of the two. George Hardwick said he also put in a word for his former coach. Whatever the sequence, there were 'hints' that a job at North-East football's poorest relations 'could be his if he cares to go for it'. He was due to have informal talks with their chairman.[12]

A crowd of 31,898 crammed into Roker Park on Wednesday, 27 October, to pay tribute to one of their own. One local newspaper paid homage to 'the greatest post-war goal machine the game has seen'. For another he'd been the 'terror around the six-yard line'.[13] A Sunderland XI faced a Newcastle United Select XI composed of United's defence and five guest stars. These included Arsenal's George 'Geordie' Armstrong and George Eastham (a former United player), as well as Liverpool's Ian St John. Sunderland's former Irish international Ambrose Fogarty travelled to watch the game but became a last-minute replacement when Mike Hellawell suffered a stomach upset. The Newcastle XI trounced the Sunderland XI 6–2, but the result was irrelevant. As were Clough's two goals, the second a generous late penalty gift from the referee. The more important business took place after the game.

In the ground's crowded refreshment room, Sunderland chairman Syd Collings announced that Clough had accepted the vacant manager's position at Hartlepools United. The Football League's newest and youngest manager then declared in his own imitable way: 'If you want to see some good stuff from Saturday onwards, get yourselves down to a little place called Hartlepools. It won't be a little place for very long.'

His bragging then extended to telling Collings: 'We will be meeting you three seasons from now.'

'In which division?' the quick-witted chairman fired back.[14]

We can assume that the tongue-in-cheek and immodest Clough was planning three successive promotions from the Fourth to the First Division. Yet his immediate task would be keeping Hartlepools in the Football League. He'd coached Sunderland's youth team but had agreed to take on football's toughest assignment with zero management experience.

But Clough wasn't daft. He'd pondered all available lifelines before taking the job. Len Shackleton's offer and advice had been the first. Given a 50/50 choice between coaching youngsters at West Bromwich Albion or being top dog at Hartlepools, he'd chosen his native North East. Straight after his testimonial – and Clough being Clough – he felt no need to ask the audience. Given the scale of the challenge, his most vital lifeline was phoning a friend.

PART I: HARTLEPOOLS

6

THE HARTLEPOOLS

To outsiders, myth and stereotype have long defined Hartlepool, the town's current name. The most enduring and amusing legend dates to the Napoleonic Wars of the early nineteenth century and goes something like this. Locals spotted a French naval ship floundering off the coastline and rushed to the beach, where they discovered its surviving mascot among the driftwood. Suspecting and even believing the monkey dressed in a mini navy uniform to be a Frenchman and a spy, they hauled the accused to the town square, found him guilty after a summary trial, and hanged him. There's no evidence at all to prove the story, but it has clung like a limpet to everything and everybody linked to Hartlepool. Hence the epithet Monkey Hanger, for natives of the town and long-suffering supporters of its local football club.

Another tall but much more recent tale involved Peter Mandelson, the local Labour Party MP (1992–2004). Many regarded the so-called 'Prince of Darkness' in Prime Minister Tony Blair's New Labour government with suspicion, including the townspeople he represented. Trying to get down with the locals, he supposedly visited a Hartlepool chip shop, mistook the mushy peas in Styrofoam for something more exotic, and ordered a guacamole garnish for his fish and chips. The urban myth gained traction due to cynicism about the media Svengali's metropolitan image. Many felt that Party HQ had parachuted Blair's close ally into a safe (at the time) Labour seat. The prime minister's own safe constituency was just 13 miles away in Sedgefield.

What *was* true, however, was Mandelson's support in 2002 for a directly elected mayor in the town. But he hadn't counted on local monkey business. As a lark, the cheeky chap who dressed up as Hartlepool United's matchday monkey mascot decided to run as a mayoral candidate. H'Angus the Monkey campaigned on a slogan of 'free bananas for schoolchildren'. Against initial odds of 100–1, he won. The result provoked belly laughs across the country and acute embarrassment for Mandelson. Duly elected as mayor for Hartlepool, the prankster peeled off his monkey suit and slipped on the mayor's robes. The episode highlighted locals' acid humour and distrust of new-fangled ideas.

The quirky town also inspired the long-running newspaper cartoon Andy Capp: a flat-cap-wearing northerner and his headscarf-wearing wife Florrie (Flo). Their West Hartlepool-born creator Reg Smythe (1917–98) partly based the characters on his parents. His father was a shipyard worker, and Reg left school at 14 to work as a butcher's errand boy. After time spent unemployed, he served for ten years in the Northumberland Fusiliers, seeing active service as a machine-gunner in North Africa during the war.[1]

From his first appearance in the *Daily Mirror* in 1957, working-class Capp was never without a tab (cigarette), until both the author and his character quit the habit in 1983. Andy's cap was always pulled low, both obscuring his eyes from readers and giving him a narrow view on the world. Smythe found inspiration for Andy Capp from an experience he had as a boy alongside his father on the terraces of their local football club, Hartlepools United. Evidently distracted from the action on the pitch, he noticed a fellow spectator removing his cap to a coat pocket.

'Mister, it's started to rain,' Reg pointed out. The man said he knew.

'But … it's started to rain – and you've taken your cap off,' Reg insisted.

Staring down at young Reg, he responded: 'You don't think, do you, that I'm going to sit in the house all night wearing a wet cap?'

Insular in the extreme, and devoted to booze, darts and pigeon racing, his idle male chauvinism jarred with the later advent of political correctness. While his wife wore curlers and wielded a rolling pin, Andy often knocked her about.[2] In the new climate, there was nothing slapstick or funny about domestic abuse and Flo's black eye. Although by 1965 the domestic violence had already started to diminish or was obscured in a dust cloud.[3] The couple's relationship developed into one that was more mother and child than husband and wife. Andy turned shorter, too.[4]

While Smythe didn't like his creation Andy, he confessed to mild admiration:

I might have two [drinks] with him, but I don't think I'd have three, because Andy's the kind of man – a little man – who gets a bit funny when he's had a few. You've always got to be careful with the small man in a bar, not the tall man.

Reg preferred Flo for her sense of humour, essential to abide her husband.

Smythe returned to Hartlepool in 1976 after enduring London's rat race and human coldness for thirty years. He found the local mindset unchanged, and The Boilermakers' Club still a great hangout for a pint and to eavesdrop on idle chatter for his cartoon. He always defended his hometown from detractors. For him, Hartlepool was 'a lovely place to live … [with] the sea on the front door [and] the country on the back door'. Unlike Londoners, Hartlepudlians were 'very kind' and 'very very soft'.[5]

Andy Capp's 'waster' image struck a chord with foreign and UK readers alike. At the time of Reg Smythe's death from lung cancer in 1998, the series was syndicated to 1,700 newspapers in fifty-two countries and read by 250 million people. The little waster was renamed Tuffa Viktor in Sweden, Andre Chapeau in France, Angelo Capello in Italy, and Willi Wakker in Germany. He gave the impression that the British working man spent half his life in the pub, the betting shop, and the dole office.[6] It was a stereotype that was hard to shake off.

The Hartlepools were still separate towns in 1965: the original headland fishing port of Hartlepool, and the Victorian new town of West Hartlepool – forged by the Industrial Revolution. Together they were the Hartlepools, and hence the extra 's' added to the name of the local football club.

Like the North-East settlements of Chester-le-Street and Hetton-le-Hole, which still maintain their hyphens today, the Norman French 'le' distinguished Hart-le-Pool from the neighbouring inland village of Hart. The 'Pool' suffix referred to the sheltered seawater bay that lay below the hook-shaped limestone headland of Hartlepool. Until the nineteenth century this peninsula with its natural harbour was little more than a port of around 900 inhabitants, many of them fishermen with a reputation for hard work.

Two miles to the south, and removed from the Borough of West Hartlepool's industrial areas, lay the seaside resort of Seaton Carew. It boasted a promenade and village green, an amusement park with rides and sideshows, an open-air skating rink, putting and bowling greens, a paddling pool, and two caravan sites. Not to mention stretches of sand, beaches and sand dunes, used over decades for training by the players of Hartlepools United. To the south, across the mouth of the River Tees, the cliffs of North Yorkshire; and to the north the Headland (Hartlepool) with lighthouse, breakwater and harbour entrance.[7]

The seagulls dominate the pigeons for the bronze heads of two nineteenth-century industrialists in central Hartlepool. The statues belong to Ralph Ward Jackson and Sir William Gray, two Victorian-era gentlemen who literally put West Hartlepool on the map by building railways and docks.

The Stockton-to-Darlington railway had given the Industrial Revolution fresh impetus when it carried the world's first passengers and freight by steam traction in 1825. There had always been an abundance of coal in County Durham's coalfields, but the challenge was getting it to the consumer. Railways solved the issue, and the naturally sheltered port of Hartlepool was the perfect outlet for locally mined coal.

Unlike ports on the shallower Tees, ships could sail into Hartlepool, load with coal brought by rail, and depart the very same day. There was initial cooperation between competing railway companies as they connected inland coalfields with the coast. They transformed a 'pool' of sand dunes and water-logged ground into the Victoria Dock in 1840. But bitter quarrels ensued, leading Stockton solicitor Ralph Ward Jackson to dump ballast from collier brigs on sand-hills and marshes to the south of Hartlepool and construct the West Dock. The neighbouring town of West Hartlepool had been born, as well as over a century of local rivalry, resentment and bickering between the two separate towns.

The picks, shovels and sweat of an influx of workmen and navvies dug and laid further docks and railways. Timber for pit props was imported, sawn up at dockside, and transported by rail to support the mineshafts of County Durham's pits. In the other direction, wagons carried extracted coal from the pit head for distribution by ship up and down the North Sea coast.

Further construction of piers and harbour works converted more areas of swamp and rabbit warrens into a bustling coal port. Shipowners favoured West Hartlepool over rivals on Wearside and Teesside due to its speedy turnaround and cheaper port duties. Its docks boomed to make it the principal North-East coastal port by 1860. By the 1880s, its seven docks, two tidal basins and four timber ponds made it the third busiest port in England after London and Liverpool.[8]

Other coal-related industries developed too. The first ship was built in 1837, and the Hartlepool Iron Works – with foundry and forge – opened the following year to build locomotive engines. William Gray and Company Limited grew from 1862 to become one of the country's leading shipbuilding, marine engineering and repair establishments. Steam power replaced sail power in the 1870s and '80s, but shipbuilders in the Hartlepools moved with the times as wooden hulls turned to iron, and iron to steel.[9] Coal, shipbuilding and iron became mainstay industries of the two towns.

From about 7,500 inhabitants in 1854, West Hartlepool's population quadrupled during the next twenty-five years. When Queen Victoria celebrated her Golden Jubilee in 1887, more than 50,000 people lived in the new town.[10]

The shipbuilding and ship-owning companies were targets for enemy action in the First World War of 1914–18. A squadron of German warships bombarded the Headland in December 1914 to inflict heavy casualties. The disruption to world trade from the war and an economic slump in the early 1920s initiated a steady process of decline in local shipbuilding. Meanwhile, depression in the 1930s inflicted severe hardship on the Hartlepools, as both factories and shipyards laid off workers.

Heavy engineering and the coal industry in the North East revived during and after the Second World War. But subsequent nationalisation of the coal and railway industries led the National Coal Board to initiate a profit-led system. By the 1960s, there had been a shift in national fuel policy to prioritise oil over coal production. Mining jobs reduced by two thirds between 1957 and 1974, from 150,000 to 50,000. Fewer mines and miners meant less coal passing through the Hartlepools.

The once thriving port and local industries entered a spiral of decline in the second half of the twentieth century. Starting in the 1960s, long-established basic and heavy industries began to diminish and disappear.

Foremost among them was shipbuilding, which ended when the yards of William Gray & Company Limited closed in 1962 after exactly 100 years of existence. Gray's had previously won the 'blue ribbon' six times for the highest output of new tonnage in the country. The company's remaining 2,000 workers, from a once 5,000-strong labour force, clocked off for the last time.[11] A whole legacy of traditions and specialist skills amassed over 125 years disappeared, dealing a bitter blow to the pride and prestige of the Hartlepools.

In 1963, social campaigner and future Labour MP Jack Ashley produced and directed a BBC documentary about unemployment in West Hartlepool. It depicted a town where rumours about worker lay-offs had turned out to be true. The documentary described idle berths leading to idle machines, and idle men to less bustle at dockside. Instead of clocking on at factory or shipyard, thousands of unemployed were now signing on at the labour exchange. Men's pride in work had turned into the humiliation of queuing for dole money, as livelihoods and prospects of new work disappeared. As well as interviewing locals in their homes, the documentary filmed a good deal of social drinking and singing in smoke-filled bars and working men's clubs.[12] Critics, including locals, attacked an overly depressing portrayal of West Hartlepool and its people.

In this period too, Lancashire-born *Guardian* chief features writer Geoffrey Moorhouse described 'an almost continuous degradation ... along the coastal strip from Hartlepools to South Shields'. As he drove along 'the tortuous, narrow A19' between Teesside and Tyneside, he spotted warnings at regular intervals of 'likely subsidence' from mine workings. The well-travelled journalist described 'desperate' pit villages at the bottom of steep banks, 'with a slag heap or two for company'.[13]

The Hartlepools in the 1960s were also an ideal subject for British photojournalist Don McCullin, renowned for his impactful images of war and urban strife. His series of black-and-white photographs of West Hartlepool in 1963 included a sea coal gatherer balancing sacks of coal on his bicycle saddle; a man leaning into the wind, hands stuffed into the pockets of his overcoat; a headscarfed mother pushing a large pram. Their backdrop included cooling towers and horizontal palls of smoke from industrial chimneys, a low sun punching a hole through steam from a train locomotive, and waste ground with half-collapsed wooden-stake fencing.

More than a decade before their Hollywood blockbusters *Alien* (1979), *Blade Runner* (1982) and *Top Gun* (1986), North-East brothers – and future movie directors – Ridley and Tony Scott shot the experimental black-and-white film *Boy and Bicycle* (1965) in and around West Hartlepool. In different years, they both studied at the town's College of Art. Using a clockwork Bolex 16mm cine-camera borrowed from the Royal College of Art in London, Ridley directed his brother Tony pedalling down streets and along the coast, expressing a stream of teenage thoughts and frustrations.

Accompanied by a John Barry music score, we see – and hear about – Double Diamond Club ('It's the beer men drink'); Embassy cigarettes, Player's ('Player's Please'), Senior Service, Wills 'Gold Flake', Nelson tipped, Woodies (i.e. Woodbines); Trebor chocstix (3*d* each), hotpot and sago. The twenty-eight-minute film ends near Seaton Carew Amusement Park. Ridley Scott used the same central element in 1973 to shoot his iconic Hovis 'Boy on the Bike' TV commercial. Its brass music indicated it was somewhere up north, but the cobbled hill of thatched and stone cottages was really Shaftesbury in Dorset.

Despite economic downturn in the 1960s, production of medium and heavy steel plates continued at the South Durham Steel & Iron Company. Its North and South Works were located at Hartlepool and Greatham respectively. Meanwhile, the works of Richardsons Westgarth (Hartlepool) Limited covered 25 acres and employed 2,500 workers. They manufactured a range of engineering products, particularly in power generation.[14]

There were two dock systems at the Hartlepools – the tidal Victoria Dock and Old Harbour, and five enclosed docks and basins: North Basin, Central Dock, Union Dock, Coal Dock and Jackson Dock. Twenty-two quayside cranes stood over them, handling imports for northern industries and coalfields such as iron ore, timber, butane gas, wood pulp, hardboard and paper. Exports included magnesite, liquefied chemicals, steel manufactures, limestone, machinery, coal and coke. County Durham coal arrived in bottom-door discharge train wagons and was loaded into ships via coaling staithes. Most of it was carried down the North Sea coast to electricity generating stations in the south. One belonged to the Ford Motor Company at its Dagenham Works in East London.[15]

Service depots for new North Sea oil exploration and drilling platforms had already occupied some of the space vacated by declining coal exports. But fishing was unlikely to recapture its pre-war days when 100 boats filled Fish Quay on Victoria Dock. The herring drifters had long since moved south to Scarborough and Whitby.[16]

Ralph Ward Jackson had dreamt of West Hartlepool as an eastern seaboard rival to the great port of Liverpool on Merseyside. But by 1965, industries in the town he'd founded – and its twin Hartlepool – were past their peak.

Nevertheless, dockside cranes and steam locomotives were still conspicuous features of the docks and railways next to the Victoria Ground. Knocking on its official entrance door in October '65 was Brian Clough, also in dire need of resurrection.

7

LITTLE TOWN BLUES

Before association football, cricket and rugby football had been played on land owned by the North Eastern Railway Company to the north of Christ Church, adjacent to the railway and the docks on Clarence Road. West Hartlepool Rugby Football Club transformed it into a sports ground in the 1880s and named it in honour of Queen Victoria and her jubilee year. When they turned insolvent in 1908, the newly formed Hartlepools United Football and Athletic Club occupied their place. In such a way, a football club founded in the Edwardian era made the Victoria Ground its home.

At the mid-point of the First World War, a fleeing German Zeppelin found itself under attack from a British single-engine biplane late on the evening of 26 November 1916. As it fled towards West Hartlepool's docks and relative safety over the North Sea, the Zeppelin jettisoned its remaining bombs. The Victoria Ground's tiny stand took a direct hit from the final bomb, blasting large chunks of its woodwork over Clarence Road and onto the railway line. The airship – with its nineteen-man crew – soon burst into flames and nose-dived into the sea a mile from the coast.[1]

The stand was not –'owing to an oversight' – insured. Through the Foreign Claims Office, the club demanded a sum of £2,055 15s from the German government.[2] Despite repeated claims, the German Kaiser refused to pay a single *pfennig* in compensation for the half-destroyed stand. A 'temporary' wooden replacement stood for nearly seventy years until the Valley Parade fire disaster at Bradford City finally condemned it to demolition in 1985.

Hartlepools United initially played in the North Eastern League until their election into the Football League's newly formed Third Division (North) in 1921. Almost from the outset, the club struggled to stay afloat financially. Meanwhile, local rivals Durham City lost their league status in 1928 (replaced by Carlisle United), and Ashington in 1929 (replaced by York City).

The 'Pools were never cash rich, and managers made do on a shoestring budget. Townspeople criticised directors for making money out of the club, but the opposite was true. They kept the club ticking over and were always disappointed when local businessmen didn't contribute more.[3] Some club officials stayed in post for decades.

West Hartlepool Rugby Football Club reformed to play on land next to their old ground on Clarence Road from 1912, and it became a shared sports arena in 1938. The newly named Greyhound Stadium added bigger stands, a totalizer board, and a surrounding dog track. For years, their football neighbours exercised on its rugby pitch in the middle to preserve their own.

Average league attendances across the country hit an all-time high during the post-war austerity years of the late 1940s and 1950s. Following its regular resumption in the 1946/47 season, football attracted seas of cap-wearing supporters to follow their folk heroes in baggy shorts from packed terraces. It was the final era of Bovril, Oxo and Ovaltine pitch-side and stand-roof advertising, when fans collected cigarette cards with drawn coloured images of their favourite stars. In the 1950s, cricket meant Denis Compton, motor racing meant Stirling Moss, and Stanley Matthews epitomised football.

Coinciding with these golden years of British football, the thirteen and a half years that 'the maestro' Fred Westgarth managed the club from 1943 to 1957 marked the high-water mark for Hartlepools United. After a leg injury ended the former County Durham miner's football playing career, he climbed the management pyramid from non-league South Shields and Ebbw Vale to professional Luton, Stockport, Carlisle and Bradford City.

They were lucky to have such a well-known and widely respected figure. Fellow managers often turned to Fred due to his great experience and wide contacts in the game.

In building teams, this master of brevity was famed for his 'get them for nowt and sell them for big money' approach. He was from the tough, old school of managers, an arch disciplinarian in the dressing room who insisted his players shun cowardice and take a chance. 'I'll bet Fred is laying down the law,' fans would say at half time. Many stories circulated, and football pressmen gratefully lapped them up. Although famed as a teetotaller, Fred liked a flutter, and would 'tic-tac' collective dog-winning bets to his players on the pitch. One of his greatest friendships in football was with Arsenal manager Tom Whittaker (1947–56), with whom he held hours-long Sunday telephone chats to discuss 'yesterday's' action.[4]

Westgarth built up the 'virtually derelict club' from scratch after the war and led their first challenge for promotion. The 1956/57 season was their league and cup pinnacle, but tragedy struck before Christmas. After receiving a plum FA Cup third-round draw at home to Manchester United, the charismatic Geordie collapsed following a match. Their longest-serving manager was thus absent from the most important and best-attended home game in the club's history in January 1957.

Nobody gave them a cat in hell's chance, but Fred's team went down fighting against the Busby Babes in a pulsating 4–3 home defeat. He died a month later aged 69, with 'Pools sitting pretty atop the Third Division (North). At the season's end, Derby County pipped them to the championship and the only promotion spot. A much darker human shadow fell over the whole of English football almost a year to the day after Westgarth's death, when eight Manchester United players perished in their prime in the Munich Air Disaster of February 1958. It wiped out the core of Matt Busby's dream team.

It was downhill all the way for Hartlepools following Westgarth's reign. They failed by two points to finish in the top twelve of Third Division (North) when the two regional divisions disappeared at the end of the 1957/58 season. The whole inaugural Fourth Division season in 1958/59 was a seat-of-the-pants ride, in which they narrowly avoided re-election.

The club's finances suffered in parallel. Even during the halcyon Westgarth years of regular 7,000–10,000+ home attendances, the club made a profit in just one of his final six seasons in charge (1951/52). It was the first time in the club's history that turnstile takings alone had produced a positive balance sheet. Before, they'd always relied on selling players or a cup run to make a profit. If it was any other business, the chairman judged, 'it would be imprudent to carry on'.[5]

Crowds of 10,000 were regarded as the minimum to keep the wheels turning in 1954. But their average league attendance fell from 9,225 in the 1956/57 season to 3,646 three years later. There was constant debate about the 'missing thousands'. The financial losses were such that directors went cap-in-hand to one of their two supporters' associations. To ensure the club's survival, funds raised for ground improvements were dedicated to day-to-day expenses.[6]

The team sunk like a stone to endure a run of woeful seasons from 1959 to 1964. Chairman Harry Sargeant lamented the club's remarkable slide in fortunes within just two years of Westgarth's demise. From competing for Second Division status, the team's forwards had now 'forgotten how to score', while its defenders depended 'far too much on offside tactics'. The club was losing money heavily and only fundraising donations were keeping 'the flag of League soccer flying' in the town.[7]

Football's popularity was past its peak as it entered a new decade. League attendances dropped from 41.3 million in 1948–49 to 27.6 million by

1964–65. Following years of rationing and economic austerity, a newly affluent society became more discerning about spending leisure time and greater disposable income. Cars, televisions and even foreign holidays had become more affordable, and the public was less disposed to watch football in discomfort and in all weathers.[8] At Hartlepools, underperformance and consistently poor results were added drags on Victoria Ground attendances.

Re-election to the Football League had operated since the 1880s. In the newly formed Fourth Division, teams finishing in the bottom four were obliged to go cap-in-hand to the Football League Annual General Meeting (AGM). Every June, fellow clubs either voted for them to remain in the League or for an aspiring non-league club to replace them. Many viewed the procedure as an old pals' act, and the league as a closed shop.

The re-election system meant Hartlepools United needed every possible friend in the early 1960s. Thankfully, they had William Shakespeare on their side. Since 1949, Club Secretary Frank Perryman had maintained a Christmas card list of ninety-one other league chairmen. Every year he'd cherry-pick quotations from the playwright's comedies, histories and tragedies to create a card for them all. From *Henry VI Part III*: 'Now join your hands, and with your hands your hearts.' The mailing list and accrued goodwill came in very useful when writing re-election begging letters to the chairmen every summer from 1960 to 1964. They competed against non-league aspirants like Oxford United, whose glossy circulars carried photographs of their very eligible ground.[9]

After avoiding re-election by four points in the 1958/59 season, the rot properly set in the following year when 'Pools finished rock bottom with 27 points. Manager Ray Middleton found it impossible to replicate Westgarth's magic and decided to 'give way to somebody else' at the end of October 1959.[10] They tasted victory just twice before Christmas in the 1960/61 season and ended it second bottom.

A thirteen-game winless run contributed to them finishing second bottom again in the 1961/62 season. Manager Bill Robinson sportingly accepted the sack in June 1962, recognising that the players' skill 'was not sufficiently augmented by zest and resolution'.[11]

Given the consistency of their failure, Hartlepools became punters' favourites in the Football Pools. Predicting their defeat on weekly coupons was often a nailed-on cert.

'Pools surpassed themselves in 1962/63 during a seventeen-match winless run of five draws and twelve defeats. They won just seven league games all season, finishing seven points adrift and plumb bottom of the Fourth Division. After winning only once during the opening eleven league games of the 1963/64 season, their final league table position improved by a single place to finish second bottom again. Their record in the five seasons from 1959 to 1964 was plainly abysmal. They were without doubt the worst team in the Football League.

The fear of demotion and/or extinction was keenly felt. North-East neighbours Gateshead weren't re-elected in 1960 and Peterborough United were voted into the Football League. Accrington Stanley resigned due to financial insolvency in March 1962, after which Oxford United replaced them.

Given that the holed ship Hartlepools United slammed into the quay so consistently, it was the captain at the helm who took it in the neck. After Westgarth's long reign, the Victoria Ground became the place where management careers went to die, or where they refused to take off. A revolving turnstile clicked new managers out just as quickly as it clicked them in. The post possessed a night-follows-day inevitability, where failure might as well have been listed in the job description.

Poor performances on the pitch were mirrored by the club's poor finances off it and the tumbledown Victoria Ground. More in hope than anything, the board often announced plans to improve the Vic so fans would 'cease to be ashamed' of it. Yet it was the Supporters' Association who raised funds to repair the gale-damaged main stand. [12] Opening rear shutters for winds to waft through didn't always prevent roof panels blowing off.

The club's finances stayed on a shaky footing, and Secretary Perryman was forever cheese-paring. Before the Second World War, West Hartlepool Corporation had purchased the whole of the Mill House site from the London & North Eastern Railway, selling the Victoria Ground section to the club in 1949. But to ease a debt of £16,300, the club sold the ground back to the council for £10,000 in a moment of desperation in 1961, retaining an 'option' to buy it back. The club had gone from homeowner to council tenant, paying an annual subsidised rent. [13]

A little-known requirement of the council's rental lease agreement was that 'Pools needed to remain in the Football League. Should the club ever fail to be re-elected, they'd not only lose their league status, but the ground they called home. [14]

When it appeared that matters couldn't get any worse, Sunday newspaper *The People* published an exposé of bribery in football, alleging that three Hartlepools players had taken money to lose a match in May 1963. [15] Captain and centre-back Ken Thomson was accused of throwing three away matches in the 1962/63 season. He claimed he'd never 'thrown a game', but simply bet on matches they were 'certain to lose'. Studying the evidence, a QC at the

Nottingham Assizes trial asserted, 'What a dismal record. What a team this must have been.' Found guilty on two out of three match-fixing charges, both 4–1 defeats, Thomson received a life ban from football.[16]

Ex-Sunderland centre-forward Bob Gurney was another who failed where his predecessors hadn't succeeded. He recognised on taking the job that confidence was low, and it would be 'a big struggle', but was sure 'the circle will turn'. He survived nine months and one re-election before the club announced it was 'dispensing with his services' in January 1964.[17] Gurney didn't want to sling mud, but revealed how the new chairman had signed Ambrose Fogarty and Terry Francis without consulting him.[18] After their re-election at the league's AGM in June 1963, he declared, 'there must – and I emphasize must – be no repetition.' The vote announcement had given him 'butterflies' in his tummy.[19] Club officials suffered more butterflies in London the following June.

The annual spectre of re-election hung over the club's league status like an executioner's axe, following the dismal seasons of 1959/60, 1960/61, 1961/62, 1962/63 and 1963/64. Yet each June, their death sentence – and council eviction – were commuted.

The 'tall, fiery, intimidating' Alvan Williams, 'with hands as big as spades', managed to finally halt the rot. Promoted from trainer-coach to manager without a contract in February 1964, the panatela-smoking Welshman lacked games to avoid re-election that first season but did achieve mission-near-impossible the next. Working fourteen-hour days, sometimes longer, the local paper reported how there were 'no evenings at the fireside for Mr Williams' as he scoured the country for talent in his Jaguar.[20]

On the crest of an early wave in the 1964/65 season, gates increased from 6,000 to beyond 10,000, as 'Pools soared to eighth in the Fourth Division by early October. It was like the good old days under the team that Fred built. Unfortunately, the undefeated home record of Alvan's team then hit a brick wall. A straight run of six defeats in seven games plunged them to twenty-first in the table and a sub-5,000 crowd a month later. In little or no time 'the usual moans and groans had begun'. Fans lamented, 'That's the last three 'bob they're getting from me,' and, 'I've never seen anything like it.'[21]

From the Wash to the Mersey, Williams sought a sharpshooter to boost his team's firepower. By April 1965, Alvan had led 'Pools to escape re-election for the first time since 1959. There was a local civic reception to celebrate the rare escape. Players pricked cocktail sausages and raised their glasses. The mayor declared that after five years in the doldrums, local workers' output had also improved.[22]

With a near miracle accomplished, however, their young Welsh manager scarpered south to manage Southend United instead. With no contract, he was free to go. After a long pursuit, and working alongside the chairman, his final task before his 3 June departure was to sign Bolton-born centre-forward Ernie Phythian from Wrexham for £5,000.[23]

Increased optimism led to increased prices. In the 1965/66 season, adults would pay 4s on the terraces and 6s in the main stand (season tickets were £4 10s and £6 10s respectively). Matchday terrace prices were 1s 6d for boys and 2s 6d for OAPs.[24] Alternatively, you could sneak through a hole in the fence from the Greyhound Stadium.

The local football correspondent reported how the club had been 'flooded out' with thirty to forty applications for the vacant managerial post. Several were from well-known personalities. They included Gateshead manager Bobby Mitchell, a former Scottish international and FA Cup winner at Newcastle. Former 'Boro manager Bob Dennison was mentioned, although he was unlikely to abandon Hereford of the Southern League. And there was a certain Brian Clough, 'freed' by Sunderland and wanted by Darlington. His experience would be 'a tremendous asset' to any club.[25]

The board plumped for Morecambe player/manager Geoff Twentyman, a farmer's son from Cumberland. The former Carlisle and Liverpool centre-half (170 appearances) and Ballymena United player/manager (three years) was a declared admirer of Bill Shankly's management methods. He'd played under the tenacious Scot for two years at Carlisle but departed Anfield before Shanks arrived there in 1959. In Twentyman's last week of summer work before occupying the hottest management hotseat in the country, he was out collecting eggs from various farms. He'd work at 'Pools without a contract.[26]

Geoff Twentyman managed just four months, including two summer months and the opening fourteen games of the 1965/66 season. His 'quiet, methodical, rational approach' earned the respect of players, fans and reporters.[27] But while Williams had drawn up the anchor, Twentyman let it slip again to the ocean floor. One bright moment during his brief tenure was a League Cup second-round tie away to Don Revie's Leeds United, in which 'a half-strength Goliath defeated a full-strength David'. A late spate of goals from mighty Leeds – including Norman Hunter, Jack Charlton and Johnny Giles – sunk 'Pools 4–2.[28]

A few weeks before he was 'relieved of his duties', they'd gone down 2–1 at home to Chesterfield. 'I hope you're not going to write a big report about that lot,' a fan moaned to the man from the *Northern Echo*. Jack Fletcher's 'dismal story' described the team's 'weary, dispirited air' and a 'slow handclap' that spread around the ground in the second half.[29]

Even so, dismissal came as a shock to Twentyman when he opened his post and read about it. 'I don't want any fuss' was his immediate reaction. And there wasn't any. A run of five games had produced one goal, one point, and a dismal slide down the table. According to the local newspaper, his team's 'lack of fight' meant it crumpled every time it conceded a goal.[30] Twentyman departed with 'Pools next to bottom of the Fourth Division.

Reigns of managers prior to Clough & Taylor's arrival were therefore as follows:

Fred Westgarth (1943–57): **died** after 13 years and 6 months
Ray Middleton (1957–59): **resigned** after 2 years and 5 months
Bill Robinson (1959–62): **sacked** after 2 years and 7 months
Allenby Chilton (1962–63): **sacked** after 8 months
Bob Gurney (1963–64): **sacked** after 9 months
Alvan Williams (1964–65): **resigned** after 1 year and 4 months
Geoff Twentyman (1965): **sacked** after 4 months

In such a way, Hartlepools United found themselves scratching for a new manager yet again in October 1965. A build-up of problems that month provoked 'a major crisis' at the club. The chairman had resigned again, citing ill health. Trainer Peter Gordon was about to depart to re-join ex-'Pools manager Alvan Williams at Southend. And there was 'unrest among the players'. The entire defence was already up for sale when the goalkeeper slapped in his own transfer request.[31] They had troubles, and they were multiplying.

Managerless 'Pools lost their next game at home to Barnsley, and for the second time in three games, had a player sent off. 'It would have been more fun at a funeral,' said the *Northern Echo*. The irony of the second half was that 'the more Hartlepools tried, the less likely they seemed to succeed'.[32]

The new incumbent would be taking over a near impossible job, perhaps the hardest in football. Their first objective would not be success, but avoidance of failure; not promotion, but escaping re-election. Yet to achieve merely that was a mammoth task.

Like the coal-burning smoke that drifted over West Hartlepool, an existential threat hovered over the club. Next to penniless, it struggled to stay afloat. The squad was a ragtag collection of players, most of them acquired on free transfers. They were leaking goals at the back and misfiring up front.

Among fans, year-on-year poor results had led to low expectations and world-weariness. The air of pessimism and cynicism was hard to shake off.

A good run was the only way to bring 'em in. Yet bad results produced smaller crowds, and reduced gate receipts meant less scope to improve the team. Crises on and off the pitch were a permanent pathology, as the club lurched from one setback to another.

Turmoil in the boardroom was matched by unrest in the dressing room. A new manager's backside would barely warm the dugout before it was booted like a defensive clearance onto Clarence Road. To take on the manager's job at Hartlepools United was to gullibly go where all others – bar Westgarth and Williams – had failed before. Gloom and doom reigned over the Cinderella club of North-East football, where re-election was a state of mind.

Clough, soon joined by Taylor, therefore waded into a sea of challenges. Perhaps the biggest was their 5ft 4in challenge. With a surname as short as he was tall, he drove a two-tone sand-over-sable Rolls-Royce Silver Cloud.

8

V FOR VICTOR

By the 1960s, football shorts were shorter and less baggy, and experiments with silk had been abandoned. Cotton shirts and crewnecks were back in, and nylon was making inroads during the season's warmer months. Socks were now manufactured from stretch nylon, making them lighter and more durable.[1] A neater two-bar feature at the top had mostly superseded the fashion for hoops.

Shin pads were slimmer and more essential than ever, given that roughhouse tackling was in vogue. Boots were lighter, more flexible, and finished below the ankle. Moulded rubber and interchangeable screw-in studs (made of plastic, rubber and alloy steel) had largely replaced leather studs.

Branded boots included the Lawrence Blue Streak, the Adidas La Paz and La Plata, the J. Greaves Italian, the '66 by Simlan, and the Super Stylo Matchmaker ST5.

Laced leather balls with pig's bladders had long since disappeared. Balls featured recessed air valves, and lamination prevented soaking and additional dead weight. The novelty of floodlights from the mid-1950s brought in white leather balls, more visible than brown. Orange was the colour when slipping and sliding in the snow.

Liverpool set a few cultural trends in the 1960s. In music, the port city twisted and shouted to the Merseybeat scene and The Beatles. On the football terraces, Scousers swayed in unison to sing 'Ee-aye-addio, Tommy [Smith]'s our laddie-o'. Supporters around the country aped them with their own club songs.

Years of campaigning by Jimmy Hill, Fulham inside-right and chairman of the Professional Footballers' Association (PFA), led to abolition of the maximum wage in 1961. A new substitute law for the 1965/66 season meant a no.12 could replace an injured player in league matches for the first time. The law was extended to include the FA Cup the following season.

The mangle, to which Clough and his Mam became so attached in Middlesbrough, was becoming a domestic appliance of the past. Yet despite more affordable televisions and better TV programming on Saturday after-noons, many thousands still stayed loyal and devoted to the People's Game. It wasn't just a matter of comfort and easy consumption.

One might ask why 'Pools fans, albeit in reduced numbers, continued to endure the ritual humiliation on Saturday afternoons. One north-eastern paper defined the team in 1965 as 'consistent tail-enders', bringing 'extra deri-sion on a town which was till recently a music-hall joke'.[2]

Well, there was the sense of belonging and identity for a start. English clubs were usually named after their location, including the odd-sounding Hartlepools United (representing both West Hartlepool and Hartlepool). Following outsiders would break the powerful link between self and place.[3] Bigger teams existed in the North East, long considered a cradle of foot-balling talent and therefore a 'Hotbed of Soccer'. But the trophy haul of Middlesbrough, Newcastle and Sunderland was hardly overwhelming. Since the war, Newcastle had won three FA Cups, in 1951, 1952 and 1955. Their sole piece of league silverware was the Second Division Championship in 1965. The trophy cabinets at Ayresome Park and Roker Park remained bare.

To stand in all weathers watching a team of underperformers fail yet again is not everybody's idea of a fun-packed afternoon. It reeked of fortnightly penance, an exercise in self-flagellation. Furthermore, fans were spending their hard-earned pennies for the privilege.

But football and fandom are worlds all their own, where sanity and rational-ity are forgotten by sane and rational people. The sport provided a pressure valve, an outlet to vent one's spleen, the opportunity to behave as one cannot behave at home. On the Victoria Ground terraces, according to the *Mail*, 'a man knows his football and argument is part of the day's entertainment'.[4]

For 90 or so minutes on a Saturday, fans were put through the wringer, experiencing everything from euphoria (e.g. a home goal) to dysphoria (i.e. unease or general dissatisfaction with life). Following 'Pools offered escapism of sorts, from home life, from work, or the dole. But if weekday existence was already a struggle, that struggle was mirrored on the pitch.

Come rain or come shine, and no matter how consistent the failure, a hard-core of thousands kept turning out. Owner loyalty to this rescue dog was like a love-is-blind infatuation, an unbreakable marriage vow. For richer but mostly for poorer. In sickness and seldom in health. Till death them do part.

Variables that made for uncertainty of outcome included the performance of players and referees, the weather, the state of the pitch, and the quality of the opposition. And therein a glimmer of hope, however forlorn.

Devotion was literally blind in the case of superfan George McKenzie from South Shields. Despite losing his sight during the Second World War, he attended all home reserve and first-team matches. His buddy Bob Blaine provided a bespoke running commentary for each game.[5]

With low expectations, the best fans could hope for was maximum effort, an occasional win, a few draws, and dignity in defeat. Following a team of perennial under-achievers had bred cynicism and arch criticism, leaving the Victoria Ground's leaky main stand and terraces awash with droll comments and fatalism.

Images from the era show terrace supporters in anoraks, a sheepskin jacket, donkey jackets, overcoats and duffle coats. Puffs of ciggy, rollie and pipe smoke waft in the air. Headwear includes trilbies, homburgs, fedoras, school caps, bobble hats and flat caps. A few carry a canvas-covered knapsack or haversack. Some sport hand-knitted striped scarves, mufflers, rosettes, pin-badges. Younger supporters perch on the perimeter fence clasping rattles and autograph books.

The club's pocket-sized 5½ x 4⅜in official programme consisted of sixteen pages and cost 4*d*. Its cover carried a black-and-white team or action photo courtesy of the *Northern Daily Mail*. Half its content was advertising: Maurice hairdressing salon, Murray Street, 'Plain or fancy – zingy or zany'; 'After the match drop in for a snack at Bianco's', Whitby Street; 'Get United with a Strongarm!' the local Cameron's Brewery beer. Page 4 carried the manager's 'Victoria Ground Chatter'. The facing page contained Pen Pictures (but no photos) of the opposition, followed by a 'Roll Call' of home players' appearances and goals. The double-page centre spread carried home and away team formations on a splash of lime green. Fixtures and results came next, and finally the Fourth Division league table and Half-Time Scoreboard – A to N.

During the five-minute interval, two men emerged with a box and a page of scribbled notes to hang large white numbers on the half-time scoreboards at two corners of the pitch. Programme in hand, you matched the lettered fixtures to the sets of numbers, and hey presto, you had fourteen running scores from around the country. A wooden tea-hut at the Town/Greyhound Stadium End served a decent brew. Tea only, mind, no coffee. Like the cinema, a lad (rather than a lass) sold Mars bars and Fry's chocolate from an usherette tray at the pitch perimeter. After its own stop-start lap, the charity collection blanket sagged with coins lobbed from the crowd. Loudspeakers on the main stand

and end-terrace roofs crackled with music on vinyl, and announcements that few could hear or comprehend.[6] You could always count on a poorly timed bronchial cough.

The pitch's notorious 'hump' on the edge of the Rink End penalty box didn't make for a level playing field. It delighted home fans but befuddled opponents when the ball sprang off the hump in such variations as the leg-break and the yo-yo.[7]

On request, the Headland to Church Street bus slowed down on Clarence Road to give upper-deck passengers a bird's-eye view of the game. And above the Victoria Ground, the squawking seagulls, always the seagulls. Circling, swooping, and diving for crusts.

Less raucous on Saturdays was the cacophony of trade and industry beyond Clarence Road – the hiss and puff of steam locos hauling coal wagons, the screech of steel wheels on steel rails. Mixed into the dockside din, the sawing of unloaded timber into pit props. More distantly, the clang and clatter of the dock cranes, and coal slipping from train wagons into staithes, and from staithes into colliers. The intermittent and familiar *brr-brrr* riveting of steel plates was no more. The last shipyard had fallen silent in 1962.

The local newspaper in the Hartlepools was the *Northern Daily Mail*, belonging to Portsmouth and Sunderland Newspapers. One of its two sister papers was regional neighbour the *Sunderland Echo*, while its other sister lived at the opposite end of the country – *The Evening News*, Portsmouth.

A large white building with various annexes housed the *Mail*, opposite West Hartlepool bus station, halfway between the train station and the Victoria Ground. It was a hive of activity. Teleprinters in the roof of the building spewed out news from around the country and the world. Sub-editors wrote the headlines and shaped copy from on-the-ground reporters.

Its sports desk consisted of two men. One was the football correspondent who reported on the games and behind-the-scenes stories of Hartlepools United. Like many counterparts up and down the country, he wrote under a pseudonym. For decades, it was Sentinel who wielded the pen and notepad – and Imperial Model T typewriter – behind all 'Pools-related news at the *Mail*.

The highlight of the week for football fans in towns and cities around the country, and for those with a stake in the Football Pools, was Saturday evening's football edition. These titles became known for the colour of the paper they were printed on, e.g. *The Pink 'Un* and *The Green 'Un*.

Sunderland's *Pink 'Un* turned white due to a shortage of pink paper in 1913. It turned blue after the First World War and reverted to pink when Sunderland defeated Preston North End in the 1937 FA Cup Final. Like their fans, it turned white on the team's first relegation in 1958, turned blue on beginning life in the Second Division, and was tinted pink on promotion back to the First Division in April 1964.[8]

A distinctive feature of the *Northern Daily Mail*'s pink *Football Mail* edition was the caricature figure of the flat-capped docker on its cover page, swinging from a suspended timber pit prop. Late each Saturday he indicated with outstretched right hand and thumb the Hartlepools United result. Thumb up and a smile for a 'Pools win, hand level for a draw, and thumb down with a frown for defeat.

The mechanics of football journalism had come a long way since carrier pigeons used to rush results from football grounds to newspaper offices. Production of late Saturday afternoon football editions had become a well-oiled operation thanks to technological advances and decades of practice. Young Scottish reporter (and later BBC TV correspondent) Bill Hamilton was Sentinel in the 1964/65 season and detailed the process for me.

First link in the chain was the Victoria Ground press box, situated at the back of the post-First World War wooden stand. It didn't have an enclosing glass screen but did possess an old oak door that opened onto a very ordinary bench. A locked Bakelite phone in its far corner gave Sentinel direct connection to the *Mail* office a few hundred yards away. Common to all press boxes, it possessed a baseboard for visiting teams' reporters to plug in the jack of a locally hired phone and file copy to their local sports paper. Reporters for Saturday evening editions would phone their office roughly every ten minutes to dictate a rolling print commentary to a copy typist.[9]

Sentinel would pick up a second phone belonging to the Press Association (PA) two minutes before the end of the game. He'd relay the final score the second the final whistle sounded, and along with incoming results from grounds around the country, the PA would transmit them by teleprinter to the BBC, ITV and every daily paper in the country. Millions of Football Pools punters could then check results against their coupons from the comfort of their armchairs.[10]

The only regulars in the Victoria Ground press box were Sentinel of the *Mail* and Jack Fletcher of the *Northern Echo*, the regional morning paper based in Darlington. Originally a native of Skegness, Fletcher's reporting was more leisurely due to a later deadline. The *Echo* published his match report on Monday, giving him until Sunday afternoon to dwell, go over his notes, perhaps develop a new angle, and type up and file his match report. Others in the press box were non-regulars, i.e. a reporter covering the visiting team, and the occasional freelancer.

Later Sentinel incumbent Arthur Pickering (late 1969–early 1980s) told me that the *Mail*'s always reliable copy typist was Gwen Hilton. A common spanner in the works was a late goal that changed the result, forcing a quick re-draft of the already prepared opening paragraph. An office-based sub (sub-editor) would need to rewrite the headline, too.[11]

Subs polished the dictated commentary into a finished article in the adrenaline-filled *Mail* building. Their next step was to insert their copy into a pneumatic air-tube system for speedy despatch to the composing room. Composers set it into type on a linotype machine, the first stage in a process known as 'hot metal' typesetting. Slugs of type were then assembled into full pages on 'the stone' – a large flat table covered with edged metal sheets.[12]

These composed pages were transferred to the foundry. Here the convex steel plates were cast and then gently lowered onto the drums of a great dinosaur of a rotary printing machine in the basement. Within half an hour of the final whistle, the football edition was rolling hot off the presses, stacked into stringed and wrapped bundles, and loaded into the *Mail*'s own vans for distribution to newsagents and street corner sellers around the two towns. Other vans sped to the outlying districts and colliery areas of County Durham. Meanwhile, eager boys grabbed their loose bundles of warm *Footy Mail*s to shift on foot in local streets and pubs.[13]

'Follow the 'Pools Home and Away in the *Football Mail*. Every Saturday, 4*d.*' The *Mail*'s pages were quickly absorbed and equally absorbent. After all, today's sports news was the following Friday's fish and chip paper. Between grease marks and splashes of vinegar in August and September 1965, takeaway diners might have spotted two picture stories as they handled a hot saveloy or delved for scraps. Brian Clough had been in town, coaching on a soccer course sponsored by West Hartlepool Education Authority. In a group chat before lunch at Brierton School, Clough sported a zip-up training top with a large V on the front. He smiled at the Hartlepools United chairman, who smiled back. Between them, with his hands in his pockets, and looking like he was chewing a wasp, was manager Geoff Twentyman.[14]

Therefore, two months before taking over at the Victoria Ground, Clough and the club's chairman had already met. Clough had of course applied for the earlier managerial vacancy now filled by the more experienced Twentyman. Two games into the new season, a home win and an away defeat, it was perhaps too early for the chairman to be having second thoughts.

Clough was in town again less than a month later, this time to raise money for his 27 October testimonial through a 'Golden goal scoop'.[15] The *Mail* pictured him on the Victoria Ground pitch before the highpoint of Twentyman's short reign – a 5–2 home victory on 18 September over Newport County. His team would lose four of their next five league games.

The club chairman looked on as the ex-England and Sunderland centre-forward drew a name from a wire globe tombola, for a different competition to his own. The following day, the chairman handed Mrs Pounder the keys to her shining £500 vehicle, first prize in the Auxiliary Association's car draw. A month earlier, rubber-legged comedian Max Wall had made the original draw, but it hadn't gone to plan. The winning ticket owner felt he couldn't accept the prize, and it was no laughing matter. The club's celebrity guest had randomly picked the name Ernest Ord.[16] He happened to be the 'Pools chairman.

PART II:
THE 1965/66 SEASON

9

PHONE A FRIEND

The former star striker had left the limelight of Roker Park to enter a Victoria Ground without lights, where football obscurity loomed. A few hours before the announcement that Clough had taken the Hartlepools job, reserve team manager Bill Heselton and long-serving director Stanley Metcalfe both resigned. For years, Heselton had struggled to patch together eleven players for the reserves every Saturday. Timber merchant Metcalfe cited 'personal reasons'.[1]

That same week, The Beatles visited Buckingham Palace to collect their MBEs from the Queen. Partnered by actor Terence Stamp, model Jean Shrimpton – aka 'The Shrimp' – attended Derby Day in Melbourne, Australia. She debuted a white minidress, the prelude to the epochal miniskirt, a full five inches above the knee. Moors murderers Ian Brady and Myra Hindley were in custody after killing a fifth child in their July 1963 to October 1965 torture and murder spree. Knotty Ash-born comedian Ken Dodd was spending a fifth week at no.1 with his hit single 'Tears'.

In local news, yobs hacked out 'VANDALISM' in foot-high letters on a Seaton Carew bowling green. Their spelling was impeccable, but the calligraphy was a bit rough at the edges. Meanwhile, a teenager struck Rolling Stone Mick Jagger with a coin at Stockton's ABC Theatre. Holding a bandage over his right eye, the lead Stone carried on swinging and singing.[2]

Brian Clough's management career began at 11 a.m. on Friday, 29 October 1965. He'd signed a two-year contract on an annual salary of £2,500, making him one of the Fourth Division's highest-paid managers. At 30 years old, he was the youngest in the Football League. He gave short shrift to Sentinel's first question about aspirations: 'I am aiming to win on Saturday, and win the following Saturday. Then you can come back and ask me the same question, and you will get the same answer.'

No tactics were laid down in stone, but he was aiming 'to cut out the rough play' that had seen the team receive three red cards in the previous four games. Regarding the various managers who'd passed through the club in recent years, he simply added, 'All I know is that I am here and still in football, and they are not.'[3] To pull away from the bottom of the Fourth Division they just needed 'the right spirit' and 'the right blend'. He'd be introducing his own methods and they'd play his way.[4] He spoke like Frank Sinatra.

Right-half Barry Ashworth recalls how Clough breezed into the Victoria Ground's home dressing room on day one, made straight for the long bench table at its centre, and rested a raised foot on a strut. The rookie manager then ran an index finger across the table and checked it for grime.[5]

Barry Ashworth – like Ernie Phythian – was an Alvan Williams recruit and had played the final eleven games of the previous season. Another recent squad addition was 22-year-old left-back Brian Drysdale, a free transfer from Lincoln City in summer 1965. Born and brought up in Wingate, Country Durham, Brian wanted to be a coal miner or a footballer as a schoolboy. He realised the first ambition when he spent a year down the local pit aged 16. In a family of six boys, four of them worked down the mines.[6]

He'd only just made his full debut when Clough walked into the club. Ahead of a First Team v Reserves practice game, the new manager instructed him, 'I want to see the winger in Row F, young man.' Drysdale nodded without knowing for sure what his new manager wanted. Nevertheless, he kept tight with the winger for the whole game, never letting him out of his sight. He thought he'd performed well and was chuffed when Clough told him afterwards, 'Well done, young man.'[7]

'Pools fans reacted to 'chirpy' Clough's cocky declarations about soaring up the Football League in letters to the *Mail*. 'The best of British, Brian, you'll need it!' wrote one. Meanwhile, another judged their 'consistently bad team' was now beyond 'even a comedian's joke'. Sentinel agreed that given the struggling team's deplorable record over the last six seasons, many considered his mission one of 'salvation and rescue' from 'eternal damnation'.[8]

If anybody was up to the challenge, it was Brian Clough. In an early interview, he told the *Newcastle Journal* he was 'conceited' and liked 'being the boss'. If players would listen and accept what he said, they'd probably say he 'was right'. He might be the youngest manager in the country, but what did age matter if you could do the job? His management style would combine Alan Brown's 'strength', George Hardwick's 'charm', and Bob Dennison's 'patience'. He wasn't one for soccer clichés and would simply proceed from match to match as he'd gone 'from goal to goal'. When players and spectators saw that things were being run properly, he was in no doubt they'd come to watch Hartlepools.[9]

On Clough's first day as manager there was a further departure from the club. Centre-half Alan Fox had only missed one first-team game since arriving on a free from Wrexham in summer 1964, but he was off. Fox had been refused a transfer four times in the previous three months, but Clough accepted his further request immediately. It was so late in the day that Fox signed for Bradford City after being announced in the 'Pools squad to face them the following afternoon.[10]

In driving rain on a Valley Parade pitch covered in puddles, Clough's new team gave an encouraging performance of 'effort and endeavour', scoring away from home for only the second time that season in a 3–1 triumph. Only a post denied outside-left Jimmy Mulvaney a hat-trick in the closing stages of Hartlepools' first away win in '65/66. Albeit Bradford City were rooted plumb bottom of the Fourth Division, one place below them.

Left-half Eric Harrison, a summer 1964 season signing from Halifax Town, filled in superbly for Fox in the centre of the defence. For their opponents, Fox appeared 'unsteady and insecure' in an 'unhappy debut'.[11] His 'uncomfortable afternoon' went from bad to worse after the game when he asked Clough outside the dressing room for a lift back to the North East. Clough told him to take a run and jump but did give his wife Jean a ride back on the team coach. Fox travelled home alone by train instead.[12]

With soon-to-depart trainer Peter Gordon alongside him on the bench, Clough had managed the first game by himself, but he was not a lone ranger for long. Before accepting the job, he'd contacted his former 'Boro teammate and friend Peter Taylor, then manager of Burton Albion in the second tier of the Southern League. Len Shackleton claimed it was his idea that Clough 'fetch his mate' as soon as he was offered the manager's job. Shack sensed they'd both work better together, and Clough was so taken with the suggestion that he couldn't fathom why he hadn't thought of it himself.[13] As Clough recalled decades later, 'You need friends in this life and I needed one in particular at Hartlepools.' Persuading his old mate to join him in trying to transform 'a ramshackle, failing, totally skint football club called Hartlepools United' was his 'best piece of recruitment' ever.[14]

The pair hadn't spoken in about three years, so the summons came out of the blue. Clough rang Taylor and came straight to the point: 'Look. I've been offered the Hartlepool managership. If you come with me, I'll take it. If not, I won't.'[15] The proposition put Taylor in a quandary. Not only were Burton sitting top of the Southern League First Division, but he'd just signed a three-year contract and moved into a bungalow in Newhall with his wife and two children. Yet he was 'mad keen' to manage in the Football League. They agreed to meet halfway between the East Midlands and the North East to discuss the matter in person and plumped for the Chase Hotel opposite York racecourse.

Both their wives accompanied them, with 16-month-old Simon Clough also in tow. As Taylor put it, Clough's face 'reflected a dreadful year' in which both his playing days and Sunderland youth coaching job had ended. Taylor 'saw the drink in his thickened features' and realised he'd 'reached a dead end in his career'. Joining Clough as his assistant at Hartlepools would mean a £17 a week drop in wages and losing a £7 a week coaching at a local school. Despite that, and contrary to advice from his wife and close friends, Taylor trusted his instincts and shook on it.[16]

Why leave Burton Albion in the middle of one of their best-ever seasons? Taylor told the *Sports Argus* he'd 'always wanted to get back to full-time soccer'. Following his arrival three years earlier he had pruned the Burton squad down to four players and built it up almost from scratch with 'shrewd signings'.[17] A similar approach was required at Hartlepools.

What had really made up his mind? Sentinel asked Taylor the same question when he arrived at the Victoria Ground on Thursday, 4 November 1965, before dashing back to the East Midlands for a Burton Albion evening game:

> You may ask why a manager of a successful non-League club joins a struggling League side as assistant manager. The answer is that I want success and I know that under Brian Clough we will achieve that success. We were close friends at Middlesbrough, and I quickly learned to respect him both as a man and as a professional. I joined this club because of the man, and I know that together we can, and will, make something of the challenge here.

Clough also offered his tuppence-worth: 'He knows the game as well as anyone, and I am glad to have him here working with me.'[18]

The flame of alchemic reaction had been lit.

Accompanying ITV football commentator Brian Moore around his native North East to make a 1990 documentary, Clough recalled how 'having got the Hartlepools job, I was absolutely delighted and thrilled'.[19] Persuading Taylor to join him was the final link in a chain of life- and career-defining moments in the years from 1962 to 1965. Now they were together again, it was time to get to work.

Slumming it at Hartlepools United wasn't completely alien to Peter Taylor. He was born and brought up in The Meadows, a working-class area of

Nottingham, when the lace and coal mining industries, as well as the Raleigh (bicycles) and John Player (tobacco) factories, dominated the East Midlands city.

While not quite a spiv, he was certainly streetwise and something of a chancer. Taylor had an eye for life's opportunities and had developed another for good players. He also possessed a range of facial tics. They included squinting, pursing his lips, and rolling his tongue inside his cheek.

War and evacuation interrupted his teenage years. He progressed from goalkeeping for Forest Colts (youth side) to the Nottingham Forest first team (depleted by war service), augmenting his wages through bricklaying – his Plan B should his football career fail to flourish. Coventry signed the 6ft 2in goalkeeper in 1946, where he fell under the spell of its craggy manager Harry Storer. Taylor never set the world on fire as a goalkeeper. While his distribution was good, he went down in instalments for saves. During a period when barging the 'keeper into the net with ball in hand was seldom deemed a foul, he was risk-averse with crosses. In nine years at Coventry and six at Middlesbrough, he made a modest 86 and 140 appearances respectively in their no.1 shirt. His main football talent lay off the pitch, as Harry Storer recognised.

Clough appeared to take to football management like a duck to water. It helped that he came prepared. He'd not only enjoyed the experience of managing the Sunderland youth team, but had also been an observant player in the dressing room and on the training ground, mulling for years how he'd do the job. Along with playing partner Taylor at Middlesbrough, of course, they'd developed a joint footballing philosophy over afternoon milkshakes at Rea's Coffee Bar, and conversations late into the night at Taylor's home. Clough had cherry-picked the best qualities of managers he'd played under at 'Boro and Sunderland. He wedded these to his own special character traits. And together, they combined their best attributes and compensated for each other's weaknesses to produce a management alchemy that worked to magical effect.

Clough's first programme notes assured fans that his new assistant Taylor knew the game 'inside out'. They shared 'many ideas and theories' and were looking forward to tackling the job of putting the club 'back on its feet'. While there would be no rash promises, they were confident their new partnership heralded 'a new era' in the club's history. After a splendid win and just a week in the job, Clough judged the team was better than its league position indicated. Indeed, the current players were quite capable of improving the club's position.[20] With a little tinkering, therefore, things could only get better. Could they get any worse?

Even at the time, it appeared that Hartlepools had recruited somebody a bit special. The *Mail* said England's 'most prolific scorer' already carried an aura of 'being unique, an original'. This chap was no chip off any old block. Indeed, trouble and strife were 'no strangers to Brian Clough', particularly in his native North East. But he knew his own mind and wasn't afraid to speak it, no matter what people thought. Sentinel sought the views of somebody who knew him well, so asked Peter Taylor about his old mate and new management partner: 'You either like this man very much, or you dislike him, there is no in-between. If you like a man to be frank, outspoken, and honest, then you will like this man. If you don't, you won't get on at all.'[21]

The manager of whose attributes they were both in awe was Harry Storer. His knowledge extended well beyond football. For a start, he'd played first-class cricket, as an all-rounder for Derbyshire in the 1920s and '30s. Under his tough exterior, the blunt Storer could hold forth on economics, history and sociology. But psychology was his strongest suit, enabling him to read footballers' minds and deal with them. A lifelong dog lover, he held to the philosophy that 'it was not the dog in the fight but the fight in the dog that counted'. He could not abide cowardice, either moral or physical. Neither could he tolerate incompetent or interfering directors.[22]

Tactically, he believed a strong defence was the springboard of attack. He therefore expected players to run through brick walls for him, themselves, and the team. He was a classic wheeler-dealer when dismantling and assembling a team on the cheap. On scouting missions for new players, he preferred to watch them perform away from home. Once at home and three times away (in front of a hostile crowd) was the formula for judging a player's temperament and measuring the strength of his heart in battle.[23] These were all details that Taylor picked up observing Storer at Coventry. And it was Storer who first identified in Taylor an eye for spotting a good player, and a future for him in football management.

Much like the Alan Brown approach, therefore, Storer had a hawk's eye and a salamander's tongue for skivers and cowards. His dressing room was more like an army barrack room, such was the discipline and drill on display. Indeed, there was no room for shirkers under sergeant major managers like this pair. Brown and Storer wanted players to view them as 'hard but fair' disciplinarians, and for all concerned to know where they stood.[24] Their teams were built on discipline and solid foundations at the back.

Another trait that had developed among the post-war generation of football managers was contempt for outsiders.[25] Clough & Taylor shared this loathing of interference from non-football people they viewed as amateurs. Although a problem with this attitude was that football insiders (i.e.

ex-players turned coaches and managers) depended on outsiders (club directors) for their employment.

Clough's initial focus at Hartlepools was on '100 per cent effort' from the players, 'because football is just like life and hard work brings results'.[26] With the memory of Brown's bark ringing in his ear, full-on commitment ran through Clough like the letters in a stick of Redcar rock. The work ethic came from his mother and his Yorkshire upbringing. After his first game in charge he reported himself thoroughly satisfied with the players' effort, and how they'd fought for the whole ninety minutes.[27] He'd never let up on this aspect of their game.

Publicity was another innate Clough talent. This included a real gift for one-liners, which the footballing press lapped up. Again, he was no rookie when he arrived at Hartlepools in October 1965. He'd later say that he enjoyed his first taste of football journalism at Middlesbrough. A local editor there told him, 'You've got a thing for it.' At first, his wife Barbara (a former shorthand typist) simply turned what he said into something readable.[28] At Sunderland, several ghostwritten articles appeared under his name.

It also helped that by the 1960s, newspapers had become hungry for good football copy, and this extended well beyond quotes from players. The football manager now enjoyed greater prominence in the press than ever before.[29] In this regard, the 'instant quotability' of managers like Liverpool's Bill Shankly surely influenced him.[30] Clough had the utmost respect for the no-nonsense Scotsman.

Football had started to feature regularly on television too, both nationally and locally. For example, the BBC first broadcast *Match of the Day* in August 1964. And when footie on the box went into orbit at the turn of the 1960s and '70s, Clough's natural flair for the medium enjoyed a rocket boost.

Before then, at lowly Hartlepools United, Clough's media magnetism attracted TV cameras for his first ever home game as a football manager in November 1965.

10

BUCKETS & FEATHERS

The Victoria Ground's inner sanctum had been fashioned from two barrack huts at the end of the First World War. Their rear formed part of the ground perimeter, with wall flaps that opened onto Clarence Road. The wooden-slat structure with a pitched bitumen roof lay between the Rink End and the main stand, where the visitors' cramped dressing room was accommodated.

The treatment room in the hut complex contained an adjustable rubbing-down table and a floor-standing heat lamp. A corner cupboard stored an assortment of bottles labelled as oils, liniment and embrocation. Another hut section housed toilets, handbasins, and a ceramic-tiled bath filled from a water boiler into which seven players could squeeze.

Wooden benches ran along the long walls of the central changing area, with pairs of wall hooks at head height. Upright mechanical scales stood beneath a noticeboard where team sheets were pinned. A glass-fronted cigarette-vending machine was fixed to another wall. Electric cord-switch heaters hung from the ceiling at either end, with a long, strutted wooden table in the centre. Large, lidded wicker skips of playing kit were stored underneath, along with a few footballs. A rectangular green chalkboard with painted pitch markings lay flat on the table for tactical instruction. If required, plastic Subbuteo figures set out defensive, attacking and set-piece formations. A wide hinge-lidded wooden box with a carrying handle contained assorted bandages, an arm sling, a leg splint, fabric plasters, plastic tape, TCP liquid, Vaseline, smelling salts, pain-killers, a suture kit of needle and thread, pairs of scissors and tweezers.

Players hopped down two steps from the single exit/entrance door and within a few strides entered the playing area next to the home bench. Its corrugated steel rear curved forwards into a roof. The bench seated three, and Taylor's bucket and sponge rarely left its side. Like the barrack huts and main stand, its exterior was painted in forest green.

Geoff Twentyman's team began the 1965/66 campaign in a kit of royal blue jerseys with white round neckbands and cuffs, white shorts, and red stockings with white tops.[1] Gone were the vertical blue-and-white striped jerseys of Alvan Williams's reign.

Volunteer supporters had redecorated the home dressing room's interior in green and white. Another novelty for the 1965/66 season was the Junior Supporters' Club (JSC), with a club song – 'It's a long, long way to First Division'. Members sported a JSC badge and occupied a Boys' Enclosure on the Mill House/Rink End corner.[2] Despite its name, the enclosure – and the JSC – also admitted girls.

Comfort levels at the Victoria Ground had improved in small increments over the years, often in a two steps forward, one step back fashion. Much like German enemy action in 1916, a gale blew roofing from the main stand onto the railway line in January 1936. It also ripped off corrugated iron sheeting from the Town End terrace roof, erected just the season before.[3]

As with the Great War, the armed services requisitioned the Victoria Ground during the Second World War. Their tug-o'-war contests and other heavy-footed activities churned the pitch. The 600-seat 'temporary' main stand, with telegraph poles for main supporting columns, ended the war in a sorry state. Workmen had to repair it and replace all rotted timbers to make it safe.[4]

There was a positive legacy of these armed occupations, however. After the First World War, the aforementioned barrack huts had found their way to the Victoria Ground from a military base on the North Sands (by Hartlepool Golf Club). They were still being used as the home dressing room in the 1960s, before being replaced like for like after arson destroyed them in 1972, and were finally demolished in 1985, when other portable huts took their place.

Given Clough & Taylor's admiration for barrack room managers like Brown and Storer, they'd landed in fitting surroundings. It wasn't all fire and brimstone, however. They encapsulated their management philosophy as: 'Discipline, yes. Regimentation, no.'[5]

In the *Halifax Evening Chronicle* in 1951, Hotspur described 'the little bleak windswept Victoria Ground'.[6] That same year, a voluntary 'small band' of local steelworkers assisted members of the Supporters' Association to extend the Town End roof along the terrace's full width of 238ft.[7]

Matchdays apart, the wooden perimeter fence along Clarence Road was insecure. Courting couples from the adjacent Queens Rink Ballroom slipped in for late-night smooching in the main stand.[8] Workmen repaired and refit- ted the stand in the summer of 1954, only for a 73mph gale in December to tear 50sq ft of asbestos sheets from the roof and leave them shattered around the ground.[9]

Auxiliary Association funds upgraded the steep mud embankment on the long Mill House side to twenty-five steps of cindered terracing in the summer of 1957. Instead of 'shinning up' the sheer earth bank to the rear, up to 7,000 supporters could now enter from the ends of the 280ft-long terracing. Each cinder step was 14in wide, supported by pine risers and ash treads. Unfortunately, when winds whipped in off the North Sea, dust devils of cinders enveloped the fans. Asked by the *Mail* about the modest improvements, one concluded that the club 'wanted to go places'. Another was less overwhelmed, suggesting that concrete would be better than timber and cinders.[10]

On an early recce of the Victoria Ground in late 1965, Peter Taylor discovered a pile of poultry feathers in the wooden stand's rafters. It turned out that the ever-resourceful Fred Westgarth had kept bantam chickens at the ground, an additional sideline to football management. When describing his constant battles to keep the club afloat, Fred confessed to a reporter: 'I sometimes wonder whether it wouldn't be better to sack the players and use the dressing rooms to keep pigeons. It would be a lot less worry.'[11] Thankfully, Fred never did branch out to raising two breeds of plumed birds in the main stand.

Taylor claimed, only half tongue in cheek, that Jeyes Fluid was their biggest first season signing, suggesting they spent more on disinfectant than on players. The Victoria Ground was indeed a mess, but the new management duo ensured 'it was a clean mess'. While they splashed Jeyes on the drains they unblocked, the club 'leaked all over'. Drips even fell on their heads as they talked on the phone.[12]

Clough concurred, writing less than three years after they left the club about their time on 'Poverty Street'. He described buckets 'all over the place':

Scattered around the floor of the directors' room (a hut under the stand). And waiting to trip me up in the manager's so-called office. They were needed to catch the rain coming through the holes in the roof – and we seemed to have plenty of rainy days in Hartlepool. My first job nearly every morning was emptying those darned buckets, otherwise we would have been flooded out.[13]

Meanwhile, he'd describe the manager's office as no bigger than his downstairs toilet at home.[14] On 'the football breadline', they didn't know 'where the next shilling, let alone the next pound, was coming from'.[15] Right-back Stan

Storton says the Victoria Ground was 'a bit depressing'. It looked like 'it was falling to pieces'.[16]

One source of pride at the Victoria Ground was the pitch, 'the envy of most league clubs'. It always looked presentable and was a joy to play on, after groundsmen and volunteers seeded, cut and rolled the playing surface every summer close season.[17] Although it did have its notorious 'hump'.

Clough brought in Taylor as his assistant manager without telling the chairman, who was less than happy about it:

> Clough didn't consult me at all – just recruited Taylor off his own bat. It was bad enough giving *him* £40 a week, without having to pay someone else as well. I didn't want Taylor. I had no time for him, but I had to go along with it because I wanted Clough.[18]

They came as a package. To justify his wage, Taylor was designated trainer, i.e. the sponge man. While he had a great eye for football talent, he had no eye at all for physiology.

Indeed, Clough claimed there was nothing funnier than seeing Taylor act as 'bucket and sponge man': 'He knew nothing about joints, ligaments and tendons. If it couldn't be cured by sploshing a cold sponge on it and telling the injured player to "gerrup and gerron wi' it", he had no cure at all.'[19]

For example, when Bobby McLeod went down injured in one winter game, Taylor's no-frills treatment consisted of him loping across the pitch to empty a bucket of freezing water down the back of his neck. Players soon learnt through bitter experience not to go down injured.[20]

Taylor was the first to publish a book about their years together in football in the revealing and friendship-busting *With Clough by Taylor* (1980). For him, their biggest problem at Hartlepools 'was the chairman!' He repeated the oft-quoted falsehood that Ernest Ord had grown rich in the war, although it was true he'd made his money 'in clothing and trading checks'. Neither was there any reason to question Taylor's assertion that he 'disliked him from the start'.[21]

Clough was even less complimentary. He thought he'd agreed to work for 'one of the most evil men' he'd ever met.[22] For him: 'Ord couldn't have been a big man if he'd tried. As a bloke who was hardly tall enough to peer over the steering wheel of his Rolls-Royce, he was at something of a disadvantage.'

He'd later say that his career-long aversion to directors came from 'working for that horrible little bugger Ernie Ord at Hartlepools'.[23] But Clough – and

Taylor – were prone to exaggeration when it came to directors, particularly chairmen. Disdain for them was in their management DNA. As for Mr Ord, he hated being called Ernie. But newspapers and players and pretty much everybody called him Ernie nevertheless.

Ernest Ord (1909–90) was very much a self-made businessman. Born to humble beginnings in Crook near Bishop Auckland in County Durham, his life was a classic cabin-boy-to-captain story. He started work as an errand boy at a local shop aged 14. From there he transferred to its gents' outfitting department. At 20 he rose to assistant manager at their Durham City branch, being promoted six weeks later to relief manager with responsibility for Yorkshire, Lincolnshire and Northumberland. Within two years he became shop manager at their branch in Lynn Street, a main shopping thoroughfare in West Hartlepool.

Having learnt nearly everything about gents' tailoring, he opened his own outfitters shop in the Athenæum Buildings, also on Lynn Street, in 1934. Even after closing time at 7 p.m., Ord was often seen on Hartlepool and West Hartlepool's streets carrying a samples bag as he canvassed for customers. The business flourished, he enlarged the shop, absorbed Smith & Ivy ladies outfitters, and established The Welcut Tailors Ltd.[24] His rivals wondered where he sourced all his suit cloth from. He was rising at the crack of dawn every day to drive his Ford up and down the A19 to Leeds three times a day to fill his boot with rolls of the raw material. Ambitious and wily, Ord became very well acquainted with the Jewish business community in both Leeds and London.[25]

One well wide of the mark urban legend about Ord's wealth is that he made his millions during the Second World War, dealing in the black market. Another is that he owned Ord & Printing Ltd in West Hartlepool (printers of the Hartlepools United official club programme).

In truth, Welcut Tailors unveiled a new shopfront the day after war was declared, and Ord took on an extra job. Working both days and nights and hardly sleeping most of the week, engineering company Head Wrightson recognised Ord's leadership skills and promoted him to shop foreman within a month and to assistant works manager four months later.[26]

He focused all his energies on tailoring after the war and Welcut Tailors expanded to open branches in Darlington, Wallsend, Spennymoor, Stockton and Bishop Auckland.

Harris tweed, Donegal tweed, even Glencarrick thornproof tweed. Overcoats by Guard, Camart, Frame and Simon. Genuine Crombies, too. The Welcut Tailors Ltd: 'Tailored for business and pleasure.'[27]

During years when retail credit trading boomed, Ord had an eye for a good business opportunity. He'd seen how check traders kept increasing the discount he had to pay them for the right to accept their trading checks (an alternative to cash). He needed their business but warned them that one day, the boot would be on the other foot. He was good to his word when he founded the Hartlepools Mutual Trading Company in 1946. Ord made hay while the sun shone as his check-trading company boomed to open fifteen branches and become the biggest of its kind in the North East. He sold out to United Draperies in 1960 for 'several hundred thousand pounds', but continued as chairman of its subsidiary company with multiple branches.[28]

When a reporter from *The People* spent a few days in the Hartlepools in 1965, he was astonished by how many hard-up townsfolk survived on credit. Under the headline 'The Town that Lives on Tick', he described how buying on credit was the norm. Rather than cash, the 8in × 4in trading check was king – in values from £1 to £20. With a population of less than 100,000, there were 20,000 locals on the books of twenty-three local trading check suppliers. Credit agents made weekly calls at the homes of their low-income clients to collect £1 repayments. Interest on the checks could range up to 70 per cent on an annualised basis. Names went on a blacklist if you defaulted, but very few did because they were desperate for more checks. Meanwhile, for the privilege of getting their business, the many shops who accepted the checks had to allow the suppliers a discount of 11–12½ per cent.

This was only half the story, because checks couldn't be used to buy items like fags and booze. Middlemen therefore exchanged checks for cash, offering £15 for a £20 check, for example. There appeared to be as much bartering of checks as there was spending of them. And for this, even local vice was on tick (i.e. on credit). A prostitute approached *The People* reporter in the street and offered to accept a check instead of ready cash. According to his article, the Hartlepools lived 'in a rosy dream world of credit'.[29]

Evidently an ambitious man, Ernie Ord became a director of Hartlepools United Football Club in November 1951. Unlike his counterparts, he possessed significant financial means. Giving lie to any notion about deep pockets and short arms, he'd put his money where his mouth was. But his direct signing of new players ruffled managers' feathers. For example, Ord signed inside-forward Joe Scott from close neighbours Middlesbrough in early January 1959.[30]

He resigned as vice-chairman and director in April 1963 but returned as chairman after Norman Hope resigned the post two months later. A director for twelve years and chairman for three, Hope left to concentrate on his estate agency and auctioneering business. The *Mail* described a 'virtually bloodless' revolution and referred to Ord as the 'rebel director'. The *Northern Echo* called him the boardroom's 'stormy petrel'.[31]

Criticising past decisions, Ord said he'd often been left in a minority of one. For example, when the Hope-led board flogged the Victoria Ground to the Corporation in a moment of desperation in January 1961. It was like selling their 'birth right', Ord said. 'At £10,000 we didn't sell it, we gave it away.' And he'd only be happy when they bought it back.[32] That same year, club secretary Frank Perryman resigned after thirty-one years in post. He cited pressure of work and became vice-chairman. Accountant Bill Hillan (31) from Whitley Bay took over as secretary, based at his accountancy office seven minutes' walk from the ground on Victoria Road.[33]

New chairman Ord vowed to put more money into the club and run it his way. 'I shall do things first and argue afterwards,' he stated. 'We are either going to have a good football club – or not one at all.' Furthermore, he wouldn't be satisfied with Fourth Division football. He judged the two towns big enough to support life in the Second Division. Meanwhile, those who'd stuck by the club 'to watch rubbish' were 'heroes'. Ord knew all about putting goods in the shop window. If the football club did that, the customers would come. An early decision dispensed with trainer Ned Westgarth. Appointed by his manager father Fred eighteen years earlier, Ord said he was sorry, but it was 'results that count. The slate has to be cleaned.'[34]

That first summer, Ord ploughed money into oak panelling and a fitted carpet for a directors' new private room, a separate manager's office (for the first time), reflooring, repairing and redecorating the home dressing room, and painting the main stand green.[35]

The local businessman prided himself on making quick decisions. 'I'm a yes or no man. Come down and see me,' Ord told the *Mail*.[36] He might have been decisive, but he was also impulsive and 'a trifle superstitious'. On realising his first board meeting as chairman fell on 13 August, he rescheduled it.[37] A few months later, he put down a big marker when he negotiated the transfer of Eire international Ambrose Fogarty from North-East neighbours Sunderland. The outlay of £10,000 was unprecedented for Hartlepools United, the same sum paid by the council for the ground.

Dublin-born Fogarty had signed from Glentoran for £3,000 in 1957 and scored 44 goals in 174 appearances for Sunderland. For example, he'd played in the ill-fated Boxing Day game when Clough suffered his career-ending injury in 1962. At 29 years old, 'Amby' Fogarty was reluctant to drop down divisions to play for Hartlepools, so rebuffed Ord's first approach. But Alan Brown was keen to offload him and relations between player and manager became strained. He eventually signed for Hartlepools, and the Republic of Ireland called him up for the eleventh and final time, making him the only player in the club's history to win a full international cap.[38]

The Irishman was known for his craft, courage, and never-say-die spirit. Sentinel considered him just the type to flourish in the 'hurly-burly' of the Fourth Division. The club was to be congratulated for 'aiming so high'. Indeed, nabbing the 'Little Lion of Roker Park' was a coup. But it came as news to manager Bob Gurney and new trainer Alvan Williams when they entered the ground one morning. Neither was involved in his signing.[39]

By February 1964, eight months into his chairmanship, Ord said 'only a miracle' could save them from re-election. He described their latest perfor-mance as 'disgusting, the worst exhibition I've seen at the Victoria Ground'. He added that money came 'too easy' to the players.[40]

Out of the blue, and not for the last time, Ord quit as chairman 'due to health reasons' in October 1964. The board asked him to carry on, and in the absence of a willing replacement, he was soon persuaded.[41] That was a relief, because according to one regional newspaper, he was the driving force behind the club and practically its sole financial benefactor.[42]

During the pre-season build-up the following summer, he confessed that while business was his first love, football was his other passion. He watched training most mornings, worried what people wrote about the club, and ploughed his own funds into the team. His wife thought he should have more sense. But according to Ord, a chairman who isn't active in the day-to-day running of a club 'is no chairman at all'. For the 1965/66 season, he insisted players arrive in collar and tie to training and incentivised their pay packets to improve results.[43]

Like Ord, Clough & Taylor also saw themselves as decisive men. The pair were devotees of Harry Storer and his football commandments, including one about never befriending directors. Suffice it to say that friction between the headstrong pair and Chairman Ord was a foregone conclusion.

11

HOWAY, HOWAY, HOWAY

The team for the Bradford City match had been picked by the directors, so the 6 November 1965 fixture against Crewe was Clough & Taylor's first proper game in charge. Tyne Tees TV cameras were at the Vic to record for their forty-minute late Saturday evening *Shoot* soccer highlights programme.

Clough's instructions to left-back Brian Drysdale ahead of the game were to 'kick the winger into the docks'. 'My arse was making buttons,' the defender confessed, but he did what he was told.[1] After Crewe crashed an early effort onto the bar, Ernie Phythian shot his side ahead after 14 minutes and they never looked back. Ernie bagged a brace, as did Cliff Wright, his first an overhead kick. A pitch invasion by 'hordes of youngsters' greeted his second as they ran out 4–1 winners.[2] Howay for 'Pools!

Sentinel wondered if the win signalled 'a genuine revival' or was merely 'a convulsive jerk'. Jack Fletcher for the *Northern Echo* judged that confidence was contagious. Clough was 'a young man who is going places' and the manager's enthusiasm had rubbed off on the players. Nevertheless, ability 'to master the worst does not mean you can live with the best'. Crewe were also swimming near the bottom of the Fourth Division pond. Both press men heaped praise on Brian Drysdale, who with such studied passing and thoughtful play at left-back, 'would take some shifting from the side'. Other star performers were Eric Harrison at the back and Ernie Phythian up front.[3]

In Clough's eyes, the big difference in his first two games in charge was the team's 'willingness to fight the whole way'. As well as 'effort and endeavour', the side was now full of confidence. But after just two games, he wasn't getting carried away. Improvement would be 'slow and gradual', and although success would come, it would require time and patience from everybody.[4] Meanwhile, Chairman Ernie Ord was 'a bit disappointed' with the home attendance of 4,302.[5]

There was minimal scope for learning on the job, so Clough & Taylor hit the ground running. Several players who were there at the creation can vouch for that. Cliff Wright says he copped for an early rebuke from Clough thanks to their shared time together at 'Boro. Cliff had joined their ground staff at 15 and became an apprentice at 16. While he didn't play alongside Clough, he used to clean his boots. And he heard about internal ructions at Ayresome Park, where Clough was infamous for dominating team talks and being 'a gobshite in the dressing room'.

Early doors at the Victoria Ground, Cliff committed the cardinal sin of calling Brian by his first name. He soon got a 'tap on the shoulder' from Peter Taylor. 'The boss wants you in his office,' said the new number two. Facing Clough, the manager told Cliff straight, 'Thou don't call me Brian.' He was the 'boss', get it? Given a fine and with his short lecture over, it only remained for the boss to bellow, 'Now get out,' or fruitier words to that effect.

Unfortunately, over-familiarity struck again. The next time Cliff called Brian by his name the initial fine of a fortnight's wages was increased to three. He learned his lesson the hard way, through a lighter pay packet, and didn't make the mistake a third time.

According to Cliff, the new boss's mantra at Hartlepools was, 'You must conform.' Clough had himself felt the sting of Alan Brown's iron-clad rule at Sunderland. 'I never ever questioned his authority again,' said Cliff. 'I conformed. Never said another word against.' If you dared to, 'he would steamroller you. You were a goner.' Indeed, the knowledge that 'he was in charge' and 'you weren't to step out of line' was a constant during Clough's reign.[6] More fool you if you rowed against the tide.

Eric Harrison recalled Clough calling all the players together a couple of days after walking in. He demanded their 100 per cent commitment to the club. If there was anybody who wanted out, they should see him after training.[7] Brian Drysdale told me something similar: 'If you gave 100 per cent for Cloughie, he'd stick by you. That's what he wanted from everybody.'[8]

Clough rebuked Eric about his 'big mouth', which was akin to the pot calling the kettle black. He'd fine him the next time he argued with a ref. The boss was good to his word following Harrison's next booking. As with Cliff, the lighter pay packet convinced him to conform in the future.[9]

In a similar vein, Barry Ashworth says Clough threatened to dock his wages if he questioned authority on the pitch. 'The referee is always right. He will not change his mind,' said the boss.[10]

It was always Clough rather than Taylor who'd confront you, Barry Ashworth told me. He viewed Taylor as 'shrewd' and a bit of a dressing room spy, to the point of being 'snidey' and 'sly'. They were sure he was feeding information back to the boss. Barry found Clough a lot straighter than Taylor. 'You knew where you stood with him,' he told me. 'I found him very fair.' He had 'a lot of time for Cloughie' and nothing but admiration for him personally. 'He came across as quite an intelligent fellow.' There were a few differences of opinion between them, Barry says, but at the end of the day, 'everything he said was probably right'.[11]

Eric Harrison's autobiography describes how Taylor warned players he'd take any moans straight to Clough. They therefore kept their wits about them in the dressing room.[12]

Stan Storton's take on Taylor was more akin to Barry Ashworth's. Stan used to call him 'Cloughie's informer' or 'The Creep', and didn't consider Taylor 'straightforward' to their faces. 'You had to be careful what you said as it would get back to Cloughie.'[13]

Brian Grant, an arrival in early 1966, says Clough & Taylor 'knew how to treat individuals'. If you conformed and did what you were told, you were fine. The boss 'wouldn't stand for anything less than 100 per cent'. While he was 'the disciplinarian' of the two, who could 'rant and rave' and give you a 'kick up the arse', he was 'quite a generous man'. Grant says he 'got on' with him.

He also says that before a game, you might not see them for ages in the dressing room. They'd appear and simply say, 'You practised this on Thursday. We spoke about this on Friday.' You just had to go out and do it, and if you didn't, you were out. Taylor would 'sidle up to you' in the dressing room and say, 'Do this, do that. React to what we spoke about.'[14]

Bob McLeod has pretty much the same recollection. Taylor would quietly go around the dressing room, whisper in your ear, and reassure you.[15] Brian Drysdale recalls how Taylor would approach him and other players and whisper, 'Lads. Can you put us a bet on?' While the boss would come out with Cloughisms such as, 'Young man, do your tie up.'

Drysdale remembers once crossing a ball in a game that sailed behind the goal. The next time he had a similar opportunity, he didn't cross it. But Clough tore into him, 'Do that again and you're off. I want you to go down the line. Don't ever do that again.' The boss said he didn't care whether the cross went into the box or behind. He knew somebody would sooner or later get on the end of one. You couldn't play with a fear of failure. When thinking about Clough's overall approach, Drysdale concludes, 'He was right about what he said.'[16]

Cliff Wright says that only Taylor conversed with them about non-football matters and he was great at cracking the ice of tense situations with his dry humour.[17]

Both manager and assistant, as well as a few players, were heavy smokers. The habit helped calm their nerves, although tobacco can't have helped Clough's teeth. They were already in poor shape and badly discoloured.

Peter Taylor had relocated with his family to a rented house on the Fens Estate on the southern outskirts of West Hartlepool. A second early Clough capture from Burton Albion was PT (physical training) instructor Bryan Slater, who the boss had met on a coaching course at Arsenal two years earlier. Like Taylor, he'd been at the East Midlands club for three years.[18]

Following two initial victories, Clough said he was extracting more effort from players who were 'depressed or low in spirit' on his arrival. They were now 'pulling very hard' for him in training. Sessions concentrated on speed and finished with five-a-side games.[19]

'Pools faced a different class of opposition from tail-enders Crewe, when they entertained Third Division high-fliers Workington Town in the FA Cup second round. They couldn't have been handed a much tougher tie. Clough would not be changing the training to deal with their greater threat, however. 'Your training should be good enough all the time. There is no reason for us to change it.' Neither would he be taking the squad away to the seaside for a few days in the manner of bigger clubs, as he didn't think it would do them any good.[20] They could barely afford it anyway.

The team had bagged four goals the previous weekend, so more of the same would be 'another morale-booster', wrote Clough. He also hoped to tap the area's great potential and attract bigger attendances with a successful side. The FA Cup had 'a special magic' and he wanted to give fans something to cheer about.[21] The day before the game, Clough told big Willie McPheat that he'd be moving him from inside-forward to striker. He'd yet to score in six games since arriving at the club in September. The boss demanded goals from him, and quickly.[22]

The Scotsman and Clough had shared tragic histories at Sunderland. McPheat's most glorious moment came in March 1961 when the 18-year-old, roared on by a deafening 61,000 Roker Park crowd, equalised for Sunderland in a sixth-round FA Cup tie against table-topping Tottenham Hotspur. In a spontaneous pitch invasion, hundreds of young fans swamped the home players in celebration.

From that high, McPheat hit a low from which he never fully recovered four months before Clough suffered a similar fate. With a record 23 goals for Sunderland as a teenager, a horrific challenge from Bobby Collins of Don Revie's Leeds United broke his thigh bone ten days before his 20th birthday.

Despite a long rehabilitation, he never played for Sunderland again, and moved down the coast – and the leagues – to Hartlepools in 1965. What came around for Willie McPheat went around for fellow Scotsman Bobby Collins when a Torino player broke his thigh bone with a vicious tackle in a European Fairs Cup tie. His playing career also tailed off as a result.

Willie McPheat was a rangy and deceptively quick player who kept racing pigeons at his Peterlee home. His teammates considered him a quiet and slightly daft character, who'd sit alone in the corner of the dressing room bouncing a ball. Clough's nickname for him was Lurch (a monstrously tall character in TV series *The Addams Family*).[23]

Ahead of the Workington game, Hartlepools' FA Cup challenge was made less daunting when their opponents sold Scottish forward Kit Napier to Newcastle United for £18,000. After a brisk opening, slack marking from a throw allowed the visitors to hammer home an opener on 8 minutes. But two Willie McPheat goals and a low 25-yard bullet from Bobby Brass dulled their 'gloss and polish' to give them a 'thoroughly deserved' 3–1 cup victory. Clough's first three games, two alongside Taylor, had produced three victories. Howay, howay, and howay for 'Pools!

An army of young fans invaded the pitch after goals two and three and following the final whistle. Despite loudspeaker appeals, Jack Fletcher judged 'it would have taken a battery of machine guns' to stop them.[24] As Sentinel explained, there'd recently been so little for the 'young hedgehoppers ... to jump over the walls about' that they couldn't contain their joy. They therefore blissfully ignored the tannoy appeals to 'Keep off the park.'[25] Clough was less than impressed with their lack of discipline. He warned them: 'KEEP OFF THE GRASS. If you don't, the first little boy I catch on the pitch will receive a boot in the behind from me!'[26]

After listening to Clough explain the game plan to his players on the Friday and seeing them execute it on the Saturday, Ernie Ord was thrilled: 'This manager has got what it takes – and the team's got it too.'[27] He must have been pleased as well with the 7,466 attendance. Clough was doubly 'over the moon', first with the victory, and secondly when the Football Association's velvet bag and balls produced a winnable home tie, hosting fellow Fourth Division strugglers Wrexham in the next round.

The Workington match referee had warned Assistant Manager Peter Taylor on the touchline that repeated pitch invasions could get the game called off. Clough was keen for fans to show their enthusiasm, so long as they cheered from the right side of the wall. But he was even keener to see more of them at the ground: 'I would like to see the crowds growing now that we are producing some results. I want people to hang back, take a look at us, and if we are giving value for money, I want them to come along.'[28]

Two days earlier, the club had published its accounts for the twelve months ending 31 July 1964, showing a loss of nearly £20,000. A donation of £7,000 from the Auxiliary Association had reduced the loss to £13,000.[29] Comparing the first eight league games of 1965/66 to those of the previous season, average home attendances were down by more than 3,000 (from 7,858 to 4,754). Fans' support and resulting income were more required than ever, especially if the new management duo were going to strengthen the team. Clough beseeched fans in his programme notes: 'We are offering a bargain – good football and good results for good attendances. And I would like to see a few thousand of you take it up.'[30]

Next up at the Victoria Ground were Halifax Town, who hadn't won away from home in more than twelve months. On a heavy pitch, the first half ended 1–1. But the visitors' packed defence and quick forward breaks confounded a 'Pools side with the lion's share of possession. A breakaway 67th-minute attack gave Halifax the lead and an away victory. Sentinel judged it 'a sneak win'. A disappointed Clough blamed the midfield for 'playing far too square and slowly', and not getting the ball forward. Up front, Ernie Phythian was handicapped by the mud. In defence, 'confusion and unsteadiness' led to 'bad positioning' and the visitors' winning goal.[31] Clough & Taylor had tasted their first defeat.

After Taylor and Slater's arrival in early November, 'Pools raided Burton Albion again to sign inside-forward Tony Parry and goalkeeper Les Green (for a four-figure fee). That made four arrivals from Burton – two staff and two players – in just three weeks of November. Parry became one of the Football League's few black players in this period. The 5ft 8in Green displaced Simpkins straight away. He was the shortest goalie in the Football League, but his agility, reflexes and courage largely made up for his lack of inches. His ape-length arms both stretched for saves and hurled the ball long and accurately. Les liked a practical joke and was all round a bit of a rogue. For example, one teammate told me that Les once borrowed his car and he didn't see it again for days.

Green's first game between the sticks was away to Chester, judged the most potent attacking side in the division. Their hosts had only dropped one point in nine home games that season. The Clough & Taylor plan to play it tight away from home would face its sternest test yet.

On an afternoon of high wind, rain, hail, snow and lightning, 'Pools packed their defence with eight or nine men for nearly the entire game. They held out 'courageously if not with a great deal of elegance' until conceding on 41 minutes, and again on 77 minutes.[32] Chester ended the day third, and their visitors third bottom of the Fourth Division. In Monday's *Mail*, Clough declared it 'the side's best performance' since arriving.[33]

Welshman Ken Simpkins couldn't have been happy to lose his place. He'd been a regular since manager Alvan Williams signed him from Wrexham in March 1964, playing that season's remaining thirteen games, and every league and cup game of the 1964/65 survival season. The demotion was thus his first since arriving from North Wales. The Ken versus Les ding-dong battle had begun.

While Green was the shortest, he'd replaced the league's heaviest. Former Wolves and Aston Villa 'keeper Nigel Sims had previously held the distinction, but the XL tag now hung from Ken's shirt.

Under Alvan Williams, he'd weighed in at a hefty 15 stone 8lb. As other players holidayed in the sun in the summer of 1964, the manager had summoned 20-year-old Ken to the Victoria Ground a month early to burn off extra calories. He sent him on road runs of 5 and 6 miles and stuck him on a diet. It worked because Ken lost a stone in weight and hit a rich vein of form, particularly in away games. But he still topped the scales as the Football League's heaviest 'keeper.[34] Under Clough & Taylor, Ken fought constantly to keep the no.1 shirt and to keep his weight down. The trouble was he liked a pint.

Clough got Ken's surname wrong many years later when describing 'Simpson' as 'tubby, unmarried, staying in digs and living the life of a rake'. He discovered his regular drinking hole and warned him: 'If I catch you in that pub one more time I'll kill you.' Ken therefore switched establishments.[35] Two of his favourite haunts were The Blacksmiths and The Stranton, where his favourite tipple was the local Cameron's lager. Its brewery was next door on Stockton Street.[36]

Several married players lived in the new town of Peterlee, 8 miles to the north of West Hartlepool. They included Barry Ashworth, and direct neighbours Eric Harrison and Stan Storton. The three were dressing-room buddies and knocked around together. It was the same with friends Brian Drysdale and Ernie Phythian, fans of evening greyhound meetings. The half-daft Willie McPheat lived there, too. Some said Peterlee was a bit banged up, a shot-up place, and referred to it as Mickey Mouse land.

For a while, several players lived in the same digs at 85 Thornton Street in West Hartlepool, watched over by landlady Nell Cristlow. At different times, Hugh Hamilton, Ken Simpkins, Tony Parry, Alan Fox and Cliff Wright all paid £4 a week for full board of breakfast and an evening meal at Mrs Cristlow's three-storey house in the centre of town. After a while,

Cliff gave up the digs to live back in the North Riding. At home he could put his hand in the fridge whenever he wanted. Do that in digs and 'you'd get it snapped off'.[37]

In another welcome break from the grind of league action, 'Pools faced Wrexham on the road to Wembley. An FA Cup run would be an ideal boost to the club's finances. If they could prevail on Saturday, Clough asserted, he wanted one of the big boys away in the next round in front of 'a 40,000 crowd'. Sunderland would do just fine, he'd decided. 'I'd love to be drawn against them at Roker Park – and beat them.'[38] No fan would have disagreed.

Players were training on Seaton Carew beach in the morning, with the odd afternoon session at the Victoria Ground under assistant manager/ trainer Peter Taylor. Clough promised the accent on defence would continue, but not to the same extent as at Chester. They just needed to ensure they were tight at the back and taking their chances up front.[39]

Wrexham players relaxed on the Friday at Whitley Bay. Observers at the Chester game had reported to their manager how 'Pools had played a 'nine-one system'.[40] Swathed in a sheepskin coat, Clough leaned on a blackboard to chalk out his game plan in the Victoria Ground dressing room. Players gathered around him, with Peter Taylor and Bryan Slater looking on.[41]

In Monday's *Northern Echo*, Jack Fletcher wanted to tell 'a fisherman's tale' about the Cup game. 'All credit to Hartlepools for the goals they scored,' he wrote, 'but brother, you should have seen the ones that got away!' After a stream of wasted chances, Cliff Wright finally sailed a beautiful 25-yard shot from the touchline into the far corner on 56 minutes. A surge of elated fans collapsed the Rink End barrier and they spilled – thankfully unhurt – onto the pitch. Ernie Phythian and Willie McPheat were guilty of several 'sad lapses' up front before Jimmy Mulvaney headed a second on 77 minutes. On a sour note, Wrexham goalkeeper Steve Fleet left his goal in the second half to hand the referee a large stone.[42] 'Pools had triumphed 2–0 and were one of the polished hardwood balls in the velvet bag for the third-round draw.

When Sentinel informed Clough they'd been drawn away to Second Division Huddersfield Town, he exclaimed, 'It could have been worse.' With average gates of 13,000, they wouldn't bring the fat January cheque he'd dreamt about, but he was 'not grumbling'. Only two hours away by road, Clough was sure they'd enjoy 'a good following'. He promised fans they'd give Huddersfield 'a run for their money'.[43]

12

POLISHING A DIAMOND

When Clough took the manager's job at the end of October, his wife Barbara was four months pregnant with their second child. For the remaining months of 1965 and the first months of 1966, he commuted by car to West Hartlepool from their home in Sunderland. He'd kept in contact there with the football-playing students of Sunderland Teachers' Training College.

One of these was 18-year-old Bobby McLeod from Helmsdale, Sutherland, in the north of Scotland. He'd played for Ross County Reserves, and Newcastle United and Sunderland invited him for trials after he began his teacher training studies south of the border. Clough saw him play at centre-half in a trial game for the college and was impressed by all the headers he won. He therefore invited Bobby down to play for 'Pools Reserves. On hearing good reports following his second-team debut at Oldham, Clough phoned Bobby to ask how he and certain teammates had performed. He subsequently learned that Cloughie had 'bombed' one of them out, i.e. got rid of him.[1]

Bobby was reluctant to sign on professional terms for Hartlepools because it would compromise his student grant, so he signed as an amateur soon into Clough's reign. He'd travel down to the Victoria Ground two nights a week to train alongside other part-timers and the Reserves. Clough would give him a lift home if he was driving back to Sunderland. Speaking to me decades later, Bob says about Clough, 'He was really good to me.' His wife Barbara invited him into their home for cups of tea, and Brian even tried to fix up Bobby with their babysitter.[2]

Clough asked third-year students Grant Shearer and Russ Postlewhite to bring their college players down to the Victoria Ground to provide an opposition in practice matches. Sometimes they'd play defence against attack, or attack against defence, and other times their whole college team would play against a 'Pools XI. Clough enquired about Grant and Russ signing as well, but they and their parents had made sacrifices for them to attend college. It would be very difficult to combine studies with playing for 'Pools, and they were reluctant to abandon their studies to take a punt on making it in football.[3]

On the Vic's excellent pitch, Clough & Taylor would often stop practice games mid-flow to instruct their players: 'We don't want you to do that.' 'Challenge the goalkeeper. One of them is always going to make a mistake.' 'Get into the space. Seize it before the defender.' Clough encouraged them to cross to the far post, forcing the keeper to parry the ball into a forward's path. They'd practise shooting from all angles of the box. Taylor often sat alone in the dugout, fag in hand.[4]

John Beresford, a trainee English teacher at the college, who'd play for the Hartlepools first team the following season, thought Clough was 'very impressive' as a football manager. As an ex-star forward for Sunderland, now managing in the Fourth Division, 'He knew what to say. He sounded very confident.' Grant Shearer remembers the 'Pools players ribbing them about their teacher training, asking ridiculous history questions, and saying things like, 'You don't need to worry about what you're going to do afterwards.'[5]

They also saw another side to Clough. As with Bobby McLeod, he'd give them lifts to and from Sunderland in his new gold metallic Ford Corsair. 'FLAIR EVERYWHERE,' declared advertising for the car. It boasted a 'lusty 1500cc engine … safe road-holding and disc braking … spacious comfort for five … up to 33mpg economy! In everything the new Consul Corsair has flair!' One afternoon, Russ closed his car door a bit harder than Clough liked and 'he went apeshit'. He turned Russ around by the shoulder, marched him back to the car, and gave him a lecture: 'Now open the door that you got out of. Now shut it gently and hear it click. That's how you do it, and that's the way you'll do it every time you come.'

On another occasion near Easington Village, Clough was itchy to overtake a van, but pulled out too suddenly and nearly crashed into an oncoming car. John told him, 'You're the worst driver,' and Clough didn't disagree.[6]

As well as needing outsiders to train against, 'Pools players had threadbare kit to train in. Woe betide anyone in late for training on a Monday. It was a case of 'first in, best dressed', wrote Eric Harrison, although they didn't need to pick up the kit from the boiler room where it had been left to dry. They 'just whistled for it and it walked across the room'.[7]

Clough described the training kit as a pile of assorted and ill-fitting garments dumped on the dressing-room table. Tracksuits were a luxury they'd 'seen only on television – or on other teams'. When there weren't enough socks to go around, some players trained in their own 'civvy socks'. If the laundry came back with a shirt or a pair of shorts missing, they were in big trouble.[8]

The over-boiled, shrunk, faded, ill-fitting and assorted kit was more suited to stuffing mattresses. Bob McLeod told me it was the 'biggest load of rags you have ever seen. The elastic had gone in the shorts. There were holes in the socks.'[9] Cliff Wright described it as 'ragtag and bobtail gear'. Some of it was heavy wool, not great in a hot wash, and the jockstraps gave them sweat rash.[10]

Brian Drysdale agrees they were always in first thing on Mondays to avoid the shame of unpaired socks. They'd often wash the good kit at home for fear of never seeing it again.[11]

They couldn't afford a new ball for every game. Hoping the referee wouldn't notice, they therefore lathered and polished used ones and made them last weeks. Clough & Taylor wouldn't buy new boots for players after Christmas, figuring that many would be out the door by June. Unlike other clubs, they gathered the sock tie-ups from the dressing-room floor instead of tossing them away.[12]

By late November, one month in, Clough & Taylor had transformed training, tactical preparation, and the team's method of playing. And in the absence of any scouting system, they set one up. Clough declared that all the scouts were contacts from his playing days and instead of receiving a salary, they'd be paid on results. Surely some of them were Taylor's contacts, too. The new scouting network would cover the Midlands, Sheffield and the North East. Of the three, Clough & Taylor were particularly keen to mine the 'rich seam' of local talent.[13]

The pair's defensive approach had been criticised, but Clough was unrepentant: 'We shall be using the same method, or a variation of it, for all our games this season.' He disliked the word 'defensive' anyway. In his system, every player was a defender when the opposition had the ball.[14]

With a few up and down results, Clough's statements in the *Mail* appeared to prioritise youth over experience. On 11 December, he reported himself happy with how 'really bright prospect' Tony Parry was developing and predicted the 18-year-old would be in the first team by the New Year. In truth, it would be sooner than that. Meanwhile, he'd listen to any bids for defensive trio Ashworth, Harrison and Storton, all of whom were still on the transfer list. 'If any player is dissatisfied at this club, I do not want to keep him, although we have had no offers for the players so far.' Alvan Williams at Southend was said to be considering another approach for Storton after having an early-season bid rejected.[15] Attending the club's annual meeting for the first time, Clough told the two supporters' associations that he had a job for them right away:

'Buy me some players, or find me the cash to buy players.'[16] Cash had always been short, and Ord wasn't dipping into his pocket for now.

When Clough & Taylor got their heads under the bonnet, everything told them they'd inherited a misfiring banger. There were spark plugs that weren't sparking, a fan belt that sagged, and oil that hadn't been changed in years. And they had no time or inclination for tyre kicking:

- In goal, overweight and mild-mannered Welshman **Ken Simpkins**. An ever-present in the 1964/65 season, a solid shot stopper but not the most agile.
- Versatile defender **Eric Harrison** from Hebden Bridge, West Yorkshire. Forceful and determined with a will to win, but too much to say to referees.
- Fiery red-haired **Stan Storton** from Keighley, West Yorkshire. Another ever-present the previous season, a consistent and strong right-back who liked to play out and use the ball. Could run all day.
- Overlapping left-back **Brian Drysdale**, nickname Trapper (after the *Mail*'s greyhound tipster). Just one first-team appearance before Clough & Taylor walked in but became a regular for them straight away. A quick but quiet lad with the sweetest of left foots, splendid distribution, and a flair for attacking.
- Tall Stockport-born wing-half **Barry Ashworth**. Another late Alvan Williams recruit (for £3,500). Better with the ball than without it. He'd played three games the previous season with a stitch above his eye and two toenails removed.[17]
- Charming but short-fused Irish utility midfielder **Amby Fogarty**. Wonderful ball control and positional play. Could dart into empty spaces and leave opponents for dust. His calming influence and destructive ability were great assets. Like Stan, kick him and he'd kick you harder.
- Inside-left **Cliff Wright** from Lingdale, North Yorkshire, signed from Middlesbrough. Skilful dribbler with lots of endeavour who knew where the goal was.

Scottish players later thrived under Clough & Taylor in their rise to the top. For example, Dave Mackay at Derby and the rekindled John Robertson and Kenny Burns at Nottingham Forest. Archie Gemmill and John O'Hare played for the pair at both Derby and then Forest. But after arriving at Hartlepools a third of the way into the 1965/66 season, the new management duo soon froze out four Scotsmen at the club:

- Former Ayr United outside-left **Willie Bradley** (made only ten full appearances under Clough & Taylor).
- **Willie McPheat**, signed by Twentyman from Sunderland (nine).
- Former Brighton outside-right **Jimmy Cooper** (six).
- Former Falkirk winger **Hughie Hamilton** (three).

Of course, it wasn't just Scottish players who found they no longer had a place at Hartlepools:

- Belfast-born former Oldham full-back **Billy Marshall** was a regular before Clough & Taylor arrived, but the opinionated Northern Irishman played under them just twice.
- Middlesbrough-born wing-half **Bobby Brass** made just ten early appearances.

Meanwhile, forwards they inherited and liked were:

- Inside/centre-forward **Peter Thompson**, a regular from late December 1965. Raised in Blackhall, County Durham, he'd started his career at 'Pools in 1957 and returned in October 1963 after stints at Derby and Bournemouth. A good target man with a solid shot.
- Outside-left **Jimmy Mulvaney** was a summer 1965 recruit from Northern League Whitby Town after playing and scoring in the FA Amateur Cup final at Wembley in May 1965. The pint-sized former miner and lorry driver was a front-runner with a big heart and an eye for goal. His persistence and speed were the perfect foil for defenders trying to pin down his prolific strike partner Ernie.
- Saturday sports edition copytakers easily misheard **Ernie Phythian**'s surname as Fithian, Pithien, Fynnion, and even Featherhen. They heard it often because he hit the net habitually. Phythian began on the ground staff at local Bolton Wanderers and forked the turf that Nat Lofthouse trod. When told he wouldn't make it in the First Division, Ernie joined Wrexham in part-exchange for Wyn Davies.[18] He added zing and zest to the Hartlepools front line and was an accurate shooter who knew the road to goal, but his fondness for dog racing led to large gambling debts.

When he later looked back at their early days at Hartlepools, Clough wrote about their squad: 'Our first thought was that they might respond to a bit of encouragement, but reality screamed at us that, overall, we'd been lumbered with a crap side.'[19] His deputy Peter Taylor proved indispensable:

> Never was his talent for spotting poor players and good replacements more of a priority. I can see him sitting there now, thinking, tongue in cheek, having slipped the *Sporting Life* from underneath his arm and flipped it on the table. 'Something's got to be done about this lot – and quick,' was his opening address. 'We're in the shit, good and proper. We'll be asking for re-election at the end of the season with this team.'[20]

With precious little cash to buy in talent, they'd have to nurture some.

The last time John McGovern had seen Brian Clough was when he was being stretchered from the Roker Park pitch on Boxing Day 1962. Now, weeks after his 16th birthday in late 1965, he found himself standing in line following a training session at the Victoria Ground.

Born in Montrose on Scotland's east coast, John's family had moved to Hartlepool when he was 7 years old. Living opposite an old cement works with his older brother and mother, and after passing his eleven-plus, they were knocked sideways by the news that his father had died following a road accident in Ghana. He'd been working as an engineer on a dam project in the newly independent African country.

John became a pupil at Henry Smith Grammar School, where he excelled in rugby and cricket. At home, he kept racing pigeons with his brother in a converted tea chest in the back yard. It was only during holidays back in Scotland that he kicked a round ball for the first time, aged 13. Football wasn't played at his school, although he kicked a tennis ball around in the playground with classmates after lessons. He progressed, aged 15, to playing for local side Central Park FC in the Church League.

According to McGovern's autobiography, he and friend Kenny Jessop were invited to play in a trial match at Hartlepools United because the club was 'going to start a youth team'. After both doing well, they were asked back for training two evenings a week. It was after one such session that John first saw Brian Clough face to face, three years after witnessing the Boxing Day collision that cut his playing career short.[21]

The reality was that Alvan Williams had already decided to set up a youth team at the club. Replacement manager Geoff Twentyman then inherited the initiative, and for the first time in its history, the club entered a team in the FA Youth Cup qualifying rounds early in the 1965/66 season.[22]

John McGovern and Kenny Jessop played in both Youth Cup matches, starting with a 5–0 first-round defeat of Billingham Synthonia at the Victoria Ground on Saturday, 11 September 1965, seven weeks before Clough arrived at the club.[23] In a warm-up game against Stockton prior to this, McGovern was described as the youth team's 'most effective forward'.[24] Both teenagers represented 'Pools again in the FA Youth Cup on 16 October, when visitors Montagu & North Fenham (Newcastle) knocked them out 3–2.[25] Clough's first game as manager took place at Bradford City two weeks later.

Hence the narrative that Clough & Taylor 'discovered' John McGovern is a myth. There's no doubt they recognised and developed his talent, but the truth is he was already in Hartlepools' youth team when they arrived. They therefore didn't so much as mine a diamond, as polish one already pulled from the ground.

After the aforementioned training session at the Victoria Ground, certainly no earlier than November 1965, new manager Clough asked to speak to the youth players. The young-looking man who McGovern had last seen stricken on a stretcher at Sunderland took one look at him in the line-up and exclaimed: 'Stand up straight, get your shoulders back, and get your hair cut. You look like a girl.' John had grown his hair long and unkempt because he idolised the Rolling Stones and their lead singer Mick Jagger.[26] But Clough always cringed at players who had 'hair creeping down their necks'.[27] In the football as opposed to the music world, John's heroes were Jimmy Greaves of Tottenham Hotspur and Denis Law of Manchester United, rebels in their own right. He'd filled scrapbooks with newspaper cuttings about both forwards.[28]

In berating the teenager on seeing him for the first time, Clough had established the ground rules for their relationship over the next seventeen years. Furthermore, the Football League's most outwardly confident manager had anticipated – by more than fifty years – Rule 1 of *12 Rules for Life: An Antidote to Chaos*, by clinical psychologist Jordan B. Peterson. His book provides twelve practical principles for how to live a meaningful life. Peterson's very first rule states: 'Stand up straight with your shoulders back.'[29]

The emeritus professor cites the long-established lobster kingdom, describing how victors produce high levels of serotonin in clashes of thrashing claws and swirling antennae on the seabed. Like humans, success changes their brain chemistry, making them strut and walk tall. Dominant lobsters refuse to back down when challenged.[30]

As Dr Peterson asserts, 'If you present yourself as defeated, then people will react to you as if you are losing. If you start to straighten up, then people will look at and treat you differently.' Therefore, if you want to succeed in life, whether crustacean or human, standing up straight is a good place to start. It's also not a bad idea to cut your hair.[31]

Winners stand erect. Losers slouch. Peterson adds, 'The bottom of the dominance hierarchy is a terrible, dangerous place to be.'[32] And that's where Hartlepools United found themselves in the football world. Clough was determined that they walk tall and scrape themselves off the ocean floor. And young John McGovern could help him in that ambition, if only he'd stand up straight and get his shoulders back.

Like many families in the Hartlepools, the McGovern home at 10 Arch Street had a coalhouse in the back yard. John devised a system where he'd practise striking the ball against it inches from where it met the wall, using both left and right feet for side-foot passes and control. He'd bounce the ball off the sloped roof of the coalhouse and head the rebounds. There was a windowless building adjacent to a hairdresser on a corner near his home, against which he'd smash the ball from 5–8 yards. The owner used to complain to John's mother about the incessant thudding on the wall that was disturbing her customers. Through common sense and incessant practice, John learnt the basics of football.[33]

John immediately caught the eagle eye of Peter Taylor. Clough & Taylor were keen for him to sign for the club. But there were a few obstacles to overcome. Firstly, the boy's age and the fact he was still at school. Secondly, his mother's desire – and his deceased father's wish – that he do well at school and continue with his academic studies. And thirdly, the fact that John's headmaster looked down on association football, a sport not even played at Henry Smith Grammar School.

Signed like Bobby McLeod as an amateur, John quickly progressed from the youth team to playing for the Reserves. Arriving for a game at the Victoria Ground on his bicycle one afternoon, he was initially refused entry. The man guarding the official entrance didn't consider him old enough. The same thing happened on another day to fellow teen Bobby. On 22 November, the *Mail* described the trainee teacher centre-half as 'the amateur find of the season'.[34] Bobby would make his first-team debut in February 1966, followed by John McGovern in the season's final game.

13

PARKING THE BUS

Looking back on their first steps in joint management, Peter Taylor reminisced twenty-five years later how 'it was doubly hard at Hartlepools, football's rock bottom'.[1] A month into their jobs, a fan advised the *Mail*: 'It is well known that if a team is in the bottom four at Christmas it is thereabouts at the end of the season. So look out 'Pools, you're heading for the last round up.'[2]

After the joy and distraction of progress in the FA Cup and with more than six weeks to go before the Huddersfield tie, they returned to the humdrum of league action at Lincoln City on 11 December. With winter starting to bite, the ABC cinema in West Hartlepool offered two sizzling films: *The Pleasure Girls*, about 'the gin and sin of bed-sit life'; and *The Wild Affair* with guest star Terry Thomas – 'Can a secretary say No! when her boss says Yes?'

Clough's ultra-defensive approach away from home continued at Sincil Bank. In a first half of even chances, they went ahead on 40 minutes through Willie McPheat's head. Their defence then shielded their goal with 'a ring of eight men' for almost the whole second half. Under enormous pressure and with new goalkeeper Green performing heroics, the home side equalised. Then with five minutes remaining, Green stood transfixed as a touchline cross sailed over his head into the far corner of his net.[3] The 'fluke goal' rewarded Lincoln with both points. But the visitors' defence had taken 'a fearful hammering'.[4] Clough consoled himself with the thought that 'football can laugh at you sometimes'. Les Green had performed heroically to keep them in the game, only for his unfortunate error to cost them a draw.[5]

After rising to nineteenth place and out of the re-election zone in early November following two league wins, the team was back in second-bottom place. In a desperate search for strength on the wings, they brought in 20-year-old Tony Parry at outside-right for his Football League debut in their next game at home to Colchester.[6] Clough told fans how he'd proved 'a most popular lad in the dressing room', although he'd picked him for his ability, for he was 'as a good a ball player' as any on the staff. Alongside Cliff Wright, the 'most consistent player' since the manager's arrival, he anticipated 'an abundance of "craft" between them'.[7]

On the day, however, the team fluffed their lines. 'It was chances, chances all the way' according to that evening's *Football Mail*. The best came on 10 minutes when Ernie Phythian crossed from the byline and from 6 yards out and with the goal gaping, Willie McPheat 'stumbled and fell'. Colchester's disciplined defence of seven or eight men kept them at bay until the visitors collected a half-clearance to break away and hammer home the game's only goal on 78 minutes.[8]

Jack Fletcher concluded they had enough chances to win 'at a canter'. A 30-yard Phythian lob over the keeper bounced off the crossbar early in the game. In a second-half breakthrough, McPheat misfired again, this time shooting wide with only the keeper to beat. With winter solstice a few days away, 'the shadows creeping over the ground were nothing to the gloom on the terraces'.[9]

Meanwhile, Sentinel lamented they'd once again had 'all the play and none of the goals, all the bark and none of the bite'. Firmly settled in the bottom four and facing little Christmas and New Year joy, they were in trouble. The early air that Clough & Taylor had puffed into their balloon had just as quickly hissed out. Clough's optimism about Tony Parry was also misplaced. He spent the afternoon 'looking unhappy' on the right wing.[10]

Clough was disappointed but realistic. They'd 'dominated the game from start to finish', but the opposition had stolen a goal and both points. His team had 'failed to cash in' on the many opportunities created. People might rightly ask what he intended to do about it. After all, he'd a been a forty-odd goal a season striker in his prime. The truth was that 'a manager cannot actually teach a player to put the ball in the net', he wrote. You can impart many things, but not that. 'If Jimmy Greaves is going to miss from two yards there is nothing anyone can do about it except Jimmy Greaves.'[11] And Clough would know, both as a striker himself, and an ex-England colleague of the Spurs forward.

The place to teach the players was the training ground. Only problem was, the club didn't have one. Most of the time they trained on sand rather than grass. They used the Victoria Ground if the pitch wasn't soft, but their main training venue was Seaton Carew beach. If the tide was out, Middleton Beach in Hartlepool was another option. Or, for a change, there was Crimdon Dene beach up the coast, next to Hartlepool Golf Course.

At Seaton Carew, the tide left a perfectly flat and even surface for running and five-a-sides. And its dunes were ideal in the summer for pre-season endurance and strength training. The downside with Seaton was its exposed location, and the constant wind. In the winter, it felt like it cut through you rather than going around you. And for Simpkins, fighting a constant battle to keep his weight down, Seaton was the world's worst place to get a sweat on.

Coal gatherers also depended on the tides to erode black gold from the seabed and wash it ashore on the beaches of Seaton Carew, Hartlepool, Blackhall and Easington Colliery. Commercial sea-coal gatherers worked in teams to fill their 5-ton lorries, while lone men balanced sacks of it on the handlebars and frames of bicycles they wheeled across the sands.

Clough, who was far from an outsider, deemed it 'one of the coldest spots in Britain'. You had to keep moving just to keep your circulation going.[12] Even the seagulls flew backwards to stop their eyes watering. All this might partly explain why, despite Clough's ropey knee, he got involved in games of five-a-side. Barry Ashworth remembers an occasion when the boss went through the back of him. They squared up and a scuffle ensued, but it was handbags at two paces and was sorted straight away.[13]

Several players told me that Taylor took training more often than Clough. Their early Burton Albion recruit Bryan Slater was pictured putting the players through their paces in new routines on Middleton Beach, including scrum work with a round ball.[14] He only worked in the role a short time before Clough & Taylor shipped him out. Slater's name briefly cropped up again at the end of the 1966/67 season, when he was reportedly in charge of raffle ticket sales for the Auxiliary Association.[15]

When they weren't training on the beach, Taylor often ordered the team captain to lead the players on runs from the ground. 'Take them around the docks. And on the way back, have a chat with the dockers,' he'd order. They'd stop for regular fag breaks, and ask the dockers, 'Alright lads? How're you keeping?'[16] These same men might be stood on the terraces come Saturday.

John McGovern told me how Taylor would sometimes follow in his car. He wasn't stupid and knew what they were like.[17] Cliff Wright says Taylor knew the times of the Middleton Beach tides.[18] If timings weren't convenient, he'd tell them to run to the bus station instead. Such variety!

While Taylor never exercised himself, Clough loved to lead by example and don some training kit, if he could lay his hands on any. Several players described him as a superb striker of the ball who'd show them how it was done. You could tell, says Bob McLeod, that 'he still desperately wanted to play'.[19] On other occasions he'd do bizarre things. Ken Simpkins described his 'daft habit' of picking up pebbles and flinging them towards players. He once hit Trapper on the knee. When the left-back fired back and struck

Cloughie, he didn't like it. Taylor told him it was his own fault for starting it all.[20]

In games, Clough would keep half-time instructions to their most basic. Trapper remembers one of the boss's conversations with Phythian:

'Ernie, young man. What are you doing over the halfway line?'
'I'm chasing the centre-half back.'
'Ernie. What am I paying you for?'
'Score goals, gaffer.'
'Well, if I see you over the halfway line on the offence side, I'm gonna fine you.'[21]

He told Jimmy Mulvaney before one game, 'You must be the worst player in the league. But you score goals. Never forget, that makes you priceless, like me.' It worked, because Jimmy professed that he 'would have run through fire for him'.[22]

Barry Ashworth says a pet hate of Clough's was crosses entering their box. He'd tell the full-backs, 'I don't care what you do, where it hits you. It doesn't come into the danger area.'[23] Cliff Wright says, 'You were told rather than coached.' Although there were lighter moments. He recalls Clough bringing his oldest son Simon for a tap around with the players on the pitch.[24]

Away from the ground, the docks and the beach, the club and its chairman were making front-page news for all the wrong reasons. The *Northern Echo* reported how Ernest Ord (59) of Greenbank, Manor Road, had been fined £5 by West Hartlepool Magistrates' Court and ordered to pay £17 7s costs after pleading guilty – during a court lunch adjournment – to assault. Outside the Victoria Ground on 20 October 1965, *Mail* photographer Bryan Scott had been waiting to snap a photo of Peter Gordon, soon to take up an appointment at Southend United. But instead of the trainer the chairman appeared, and punched Mr Scott 'in the stomach'. Mr Bailey, representing Mr Ord, suggested 'there are still some realms of privacy left to us in our decaying years, and one of these is whether one wants to be photographed'. He claimed Ord was within his rights, but in an altercation that was 'electrified by high emotions', like football itself, 'a squabble' had led to 'this unfortunate photographer being touched somewhere around the midriff'.[25] One wonders whether, but for his lack of inches, he'd have preferred to touch him around his jaw.

Another Ord bombshell dropped the next day on 22 December, this time on the front page of the *Northern Daily Mail*. Not for the first time, he'd resigned as chairman. His director son David (27) was quitting, too. It was almost Christmas, so the board wouldn't discuss it until their next meeting in the New Year. Given that he'd resigned a few times before, the reaction was tentative. When asked directly for his response, Clough declared: 'If he has left it is a great pity because there is no doubt that he kept the club going.' He saw no immediate danger of the club going out of existence, but his mere mention of it was a concern. Adding to the provisional nature of the announcement, he added: 'I don't know if any efforts are being made to persuade him to continue as Chairman.'[26] Jack Fletcher had been led to believe that on this occasion, Ord's departure was 'final'.[27]

On the same day, Clough confirmed his interest in Nottingham Forest defender Brian Grant, one of two or three full-backs he'd enquired about. The only problem was that he'd need to sell somebody in order to afford him. He didn't want Stan Storton to leave, but he'd expressed a desire to go. Clough would therefore not stand in his way if the board accepted Alvan Williams's recent bid.[28]

Next up straight after the Christmas and Boxing Day fixtures was a home and away double-header against North-East rivals Darlington, sitting seventh (with games in hand) in the Fourth Division. Could 'Pools pick up any points? Clough rang the changes up front. Out went McPheat and Mulvaney up top and in came Jimmy Cooper and Peter Thompson after strong performances in the Reserves. He also switched inside-forward Cliff Wright to the left wing for his first ever game there. Tony Parry was moved from that position to inside-left.[29] They needed goals, and quick.

Clough's changes brought instant reward on 'a rutted ice-rink' of a pitch. Darlington players appeared mesmerised from the kick-off as the ball moved from Amby Fogarty via Tony Parry to Peter Thompson. After a two-month absence from the team, he rammed his shot between the outcoming goal-keeper's legs to put them ahead after just 20 seconds. In front of the biggest Victoria Ground crowd of the season (9,290), including a sizeable away following, 'Pools did battle against what Clough described as 'a very good side'. The visitors had the best away record in the division, and in a derby clash full 'of incident and excitement', a 1–1 draw was a fair result. Cliff Wright was a revelation on the left wing, and Tony Parry looked a much-improved player until he ran out of puff in the second half.[30]

Part two of the Darlo v Harlo derby took place the following evening. Despite Darlington's six consecutive home victories coming into the game, 'Pools became the first team to earn a point at Feethams since August. *Northern Echo* correspondent Bob James said it was a case of 'floodlight robbery'. A performance of 'sheer guts, fighting spirit, and a liberal dash of luck' led to 'one of their cheekiest and most celebrated' raids yet on their rivals. 'Pools hadn't lost at Darlington in any of their four previous league visits.[31]

In an otherwise fine goalkeeping display, Darlington went ahead on 37 minutes when Green misjudged a cross and punched the air instead of the ball. Ernie Phythian, who hadn't scored in seven weeks, played hero eight minutes from time. With Darlington players stood appealing for offside as Parry slipped him a pass, the forward bored through the middle of their defence and shot low past the diving keeper.[32] They'd bagged two points in two games against one of the most fancied teams in the division. It's not the dog in the fight but the fight in the dog.

Tranmere Rovers away was another tough ask. They lay third in the division, with a home record of nine victories and two defeats. Although one of these reverses was their most recent home game against Notts County, when they'd gone down 3–0 in the shock result of the afternoon.

In his programme notes for the Darlington game, Clough had told fans about the seasonal sacrifices his men would be making for the greater good:

> Twelve footballers who will not be celebrating the New Year are those who play for Hartlepools United. On New Year's Day we meet Tranmere Rovers in Birkenhead, and will be travelling by coach the day before, so all the players will be nicely tucked up in bed on New Year's Eve.[33]

The *Mail* told the same story, describing how the players would be 'sleeping soundly in their Chester hotel' in preparation for their battle the next day.[34]

Brian 'Trapper' Drysdale relates something quite different about the sequence of events on New Year's Eve. He told me how they were indeed chatting over cups of tea in the hotel the night before the game, when one player declared: 'Gaffer, I'm going to bed. We've got a game tomorrow. Good night lads.'

'Get your arse down here. Don't you know it's New Year's Eve?' Clough insisted.

Trapper admitted, 'He got us half-pissed.' At one point during their drinking session a dog appeared in the lounge. Clough barked at its owner, 'Get this dog out the room.' The dog and its owner obeyed.[35]

If Clough's intention had been to relax the players, he succeeded. Green dropped a cross to concede just 24 seconds into the match and was picking the ball out of his net for a second time after Tranmere's third attack on 5 minutes. While 'Pools did have plenty of possession and hit the woodwork twice in the first half, their defence went 'very ragged' and 'fell to pieces' after the break. Following the 6–1 New Year drubbing, Sentinel declared it was 'back to square one' for Brian Clough.[36] Even the manager admitted that his 'New Year's Eve celebration "Ban" on the players didn't seem to have the required effect'.[37]

It wasn't the ideal start to 1966, the year that England hosted the World Cup.

14

TIGHTROPE

Clough stood in for Sentinel to write the first *Football Mail* column of 1966. After 'two rather testing months', the league's youngest manager told readers he wasn't going to spout hard-luck clichés about bad runs or bad breaks. He always looked football 'squarely in the face'. Indeed, his team was firmly wedged in the bottom four, a familiar predicament. So far with the players he'd inherited, all he'd done was improve team spirit and demand a little more effort. Changing tack and ever the arch-realist, he admitted frankly, 'I must tell you that everything in the garden is not rosy':

> I will not retain players who are unhappy with the club. I will not tolerate players who don't want to play for Hartlepools United. I don't want those who want to play the game any other way but mine. I want men who never complain about hard work.

The club was walking 'a tightrope', and in another 'body blow', the chairman had just resigned. When Clough learned of Ord's decision, he admitted to 'mixed feelings of regret, apprehension and disappointment'.[1] Eleven months down the line, he'd be greeting another Ord resignation with relish, anticipation and joy.

The Victoria Ground, rather than smelling of roses, hummed like its drains were blocked again. With Jeyes Fluid merely masking the problem, and the team needing a scrub with new formula Vim, he'd have to channel his inner Sinatra to make a success of it in this place. The Hartlepools were not 'New York, New York', but there were two of them just the same. Make it there, and he could make it anywhere.

Assistant Manager Peter Taylor contributed a column of his own in praise of goalkeepers. But he turned to the team's problems and their biggest priority at the end: 'We are giving the lads here a fair deal, and all we ask in return is plenty of endeavour.' He continued: 'If you don't have the right kind of foundation, a building will collapse. It's exactly the same in football. If your defence is weak, the side will crumble.'[2]

Published on – but written before – the day of their 6–1 demolition at Tranmere, Clough & Taylor's columns pointed to commitment and defence issues that needed sorting fast. Still next-to-bottom of the Football League, they were stuck in the mire. At the end of the day, it wasn't just about the fight in the dog. They needed some new dogs in the fight.

There were continued ructions in the boardroom. After a one-and-a-half-hour evening board meeting on 4 January, Ernie Ord announced his intention to continue as chairman and further finance the club. This prompted all six directors to resign, although their reasoning was unclear. There was evident chaos behind the scenes, and they gave a unanimous 'no comment' when asked about it. The *Northern Daily Mail* was given to understand that 'a late appeal' had convinced Ord to change his mind about resigning. Furthermore, he'd be providing some cash for new players, and soon.[3] It was the only salvation from re-election.

In a welcome distraction from the topsy-turvy events at the Victoria Ground, qualifying countries for the World Cup discovered who they'd be playing in July. FIFA President Sir Stanley Rous conducted the draw at London's Royal Garden Hotel. Many eyes from the sixteen competing countries fixed on ball no. 13, belonging to North Korea. The draw placed the 200–1 outsiders in Group 4 alongside Chile, Italy and the USSR, with their games to be played at Ayresome Park (Middlesbrough) and Roker Park (Sunderland). After seeing the groups, and with all England's games set for Wembley, their former skipper Johnny Haynes pronounced: 'Bobby Moore should be smiling. They look like certainties for the semi-final.' In previous World Cups, England had never progressed beyond the quarter-finals.[4]

The Beatles' double A-side 'Day Tripper'/'We Can Work It Out' began its fifth week at number one on 8 January 1966. With the end of the 1965/66 season getting nearer by the game, Clough & Taylor had to work out an escape plan.

When Sentinel next arrived at the Victoria Ground to occupy his customary place in the press box, newly reinstated Chairman Ernie Ord refused him admission at the officials' entrance. Sentinel had no other option but to stand guard-like on the terraces alongside the entrance-paying punters. Under a front-page text box that evening headed 'SENTINEL NOT ADMITTED', he informed *Football Mail* readers how he'd written his match report 'with less than normal facilities but with not less than his usual appreciation of the play'.[5] Dispensing with his typewriter, he worked open to the elements with pen and paper. Instead of dictating his report by telephone from the press box, a runner shuttled his written copy from a hole in the fence to the *Mail*'s office down Clarence Road.

Ord was good to his word and provided Clough & Taylor with some cash to splash. They travelled to the East Midlands to sign 22-year-old Brian Grant late on a Friday. Jack Fletcher described the Scottish right-back on his debut the next day as 'a stylish player' who 'tackled well and used the ball intelligently'. Clough was also keen to bring in a new centre-half. He agreed terms with Derby County to sign Ray Young, but after pondering the move, the defender decided to stay put.[6]

'Pools edged Port Vale by 2–0 in a tight home game. In Clough's verdict, 'We were never allowed any clear-cut chances, but we got the breaks.' Peter Thompson rattled a shot against the underside of the bar and into the net on 60 minutes. And with dusk making it difficult for anybody to see, Ernie Phythian headed in when a 20-yard Cliff Wright drive rebounded to him off the bar with two minutes remaining.[7]

Sentinel found reporting from 'somewhere on the terraces' a 'stimulating' experience. As well as acting as windbreaks, he described how the supporters 'know the game thoroughly and value highly the right of free speech freely expressed'. In Sentinel-speak, this meant they were forthright in their opinions and not shy to offer them. He was only sorry he hadn't taken a tape-recorder with him as well as a notebook.[8] By Saturday evening, their first league victory in more than two months had lifted them one place to third-bottom of the Fourth Division.

In arctic conditions on a frozen pitch with a carpet of light snow, the team gained a well-earned point in a 2–2 draw at mid-table Barnsley. Hot-firing Peter Thompson bagged both goals, while Stockport manager Bert Trautmann, the German former goalkeeper and wartime PoW, watched Stan Storton from the stands. York City were said to be pondering a move for Barry Ashworth. After reading news from the Victoria Ground about director resignations, reporters being banned, and players wanting to leave, fans wondered in the *Football Mail* whether someone had lost the plot. Could supporters not get back the happy and respected club of Fred Westgarth's days?[9]

Clough stayed strictly on message in the press, and many matters didn't make it into the *Mail*. For example, his office phone ringing before five o'clock each afternoon, with nobody on the other end.[10] Or the chairman

invading the inner sanctum of their dressing room. Summer of '66 recruit
Tony Bircumshaw said he'd enter after games to talk to some players, miss
a few, and then talk to others. Cliff Wright concurs, saying that Ord had
spies all around town, and he'd tell individuals they'd been seen out drinking.
Clough & Taylor loathed the interference from upstairs and barred him. But if
Bircumshaw remembers it happening, the dressing room ban must have come
late into Ord's reign.[11]

Cup fever gripped the town ahead of the third-round tie at Huddersfield
Town. More than 3,000 fans planned to travel by road and rail. One option
was a 700-seat excursion train from West Hartlepool station. Peter Taylor
and a black dog led wrapped-up players on a training run across the sands
of Seaton Carew beach, while Clough sought out wingers to strengthen his
team's chances in the league. He also had a plan to nullify Huddersfield's free-
scoring forward line. It involved using the double centre-half barrier of Eric
Harrison and Stan Storton that had worked so effectively at Barnsley.[12]

In the event, the Saturday tie at Huddersfield suffered a late postponement
due to thick fog and a half-frozen pitch. Unfortunately, fifteen of the sixteen
supporters' coaches had already departed West Hartlepool. The coach company rang ahead to Thirsk, where police flagged down the convoy. Some of
the 1,500 fans turned back, but most continued their journey to watch the
Leeds v Bury tie instead, where straw stopped the pitch from freezing.[13] Some
of the Hartlepools team travelled to Leeds, too. When their red-haired midfielder Billy Bremner spotted them queuing outside Elland Road for tickets,
he recognised some faces from their League Cup tie earlier in the season. Both
Barry Ashworth and Stan Storton told me that he got them in for free with
'comps', i.e. complimentary tickets. It was a kind gesture of solidarity from
the hard-tackling Scot.[14] Rather than join them, Clough had made hurried
arrangements to go on a scouting mission instead.[15]

The ice had thawed by the time of the rearranged game on Monday evening,
although belts of fog over West Riding nearly cancelled it again. Newly signed
Brian Grant told me that Clough took one look at his players in the dressing
room and remarked, 'You all look a bit nervous.' He slid a crate into the middle
of the dressing room floor and suggested they, 'Have a beer and relax.' A few
took him up on the offer and fortified themselves straight from the bottle.[16]

On a wet and heavy pitch, 'Pools came within four minutes of forcing
a replay in front of 1,000 travelling fans. It was a tie 'packed with drama'
in which they 'stuck to their defensive plan with tremendous tenacity and
stamina'.[17] Goalless at half-time, Clough raised his foot on a chair in the
dressing room. Pointing at Barry Ashworth, he told his players: 'If you all put

in as much effort as that lad there, we'll win this match.'[18] Peter Thompson reacted first to a corner that rebounded off the bar to put them ahead, only for them to concede within a minute through a disputed offside goal. The referee then awarded a second disputed Huddersfield goal. Ten visiting players surrounded him to insist it had never crossed the line. Clough, who normally ordered his players to never question the referee, vented his spleen, too. They wuz robbed.

The *Mail* heaped praise on Amby Fogarty and Barry Ashworth, 'the "motor" of the side'.[19] Later that year, Bertie Mee would pay Huddersfield £50,000 to take locally born defender Bob McNab to Arsenal. The attendance of 24,505 was the largest to watch 'Pools play since an FA Cup third-round tie at Burnley in January 1952.

With the days gradually getting longer, Clough had started to see a few rays of light thanks to a stronger team set-up and improved performances. The attack was no longer a blunt instrument, and they had a tighter defensive screen at the back.[20] His new playing system had nearly triumphed at Second Division high-fliers Huddersfield.

He continued his efforts to shuffle and deal his hand of cards. There was reported interest in signing England Under-23 winger Dick le Flem from 'Boro. Despite filling in well for the Cup-tied Les Green at Huddersfield, Ken Simpkins was told he could leave if another club wanted him.[21]

After their exertions and near high at Huddersfield, they suffered a double low at Southport. The Lancashire team were 'ebullient' after eliminating First Division Ipswich in the FA Cup, while their visitors looked 'slow, lifeless and lethargic'. Suffering a different type of hangover to the New Year's Day reverse, they endured 'a 90-minute pounding' and went down 4–1 at Haig Avenue.[22]

Between games, 29-year-old left-back Billy Marshall agreed to terminate his contract by mutual agreement. And 25-year-old outside-right Jimmy Cooper announced he was leaving English football to try his luck in Durban, South Africa. He had no complaints about his treatment at the club, and indeed wanted to thank Brian Clough.[23] Eric Harrison, dropped from defence, again requested a free transfer. But Chairman Ord said he'd only let him go for a fee after paying money to sign him.[24] Marshall continued to train with the club's amateurs and part-timers for two weeks until Ord barred him from the Vic without explanation.[25]

Still with only one league win since early November, they faced Wrexham at home for the second time that season. Bobby McLeod replaced Eric Harrison to make his first-team debut at centre-half. Despite Wrexham coming into the game on the back of four wins and scoring first, Hartlepools beat the

Welshmen 4–2 in a scrappy game on a heavy pitch. The rejuvenated Ernie Phythian scored a brace. Another Ernie – Chairman Ord – was at the official entrance to refuse Sentinel admission to the press box for a second time. The reporter again paid to stand on the terraces, where high winds played 'low tricks' with his copy.[26] Meanwhile, the Wrexham 'keeper complained to the referee about fans flinging missiles at him. Police officers were summoned to quieten the spectators behind his goal.[27]

In the mid-1960s era of ultra-defensive tactics, every team worth its salt had a hard man, except Leeds, who had three or more of the buggers. Arsenal had Peter Storey. Chelsea had Ron 'Chopper' Harris. Liverpool had Tommy Smith, 'The Anfield Iron'. Manchester United had Nobby Stiles. Tottenham Hotspur had Dave Mackay. While Don Revie's Leeds had Billy Bremner, Johnny Giles, and most notoriously of all, Norman 'bite yer legs' Hunter. They'd earned the moniker Dirty Leeds on merit and wore it as a badge of honour. It helped intimidate the opposition before a ball – or a shin – had been kicked.

These ankle-biting, elbow-wielding, jaw-crunching, tendon-snapping, leg-breaking masters of football's dark arts were notorious for overly hard and over-the-top tackling. Not to mention other miscellaneous off-the-ball shithousery. These pitch villains weren't necessarily built like a brick shithouse, it was their ruthlessness and exquisite timing that set them apart. Meanwhile, a guilty conscience and finesse had no place in their toolboxes.

Much lower down the Football League food chain, and on a far more modest scale, Hartlepools United boasted John Gill. Although John posed a danger to all shipping, not just the opposition.

Clough & Taylor signed centre-half Gill from Mansfield Town in February 1966 for £2,500. He met his teammates on their journey down to Kenilworth Road, where they erected their defensive wall again on a heavy and sanded pitch. But Luton finally breached it twice during seven second-half minutes. Despite a spirited final twenty-minute fightback, Luton prevailed 2–1.[28]

Melting snow led to a waterlogged pitch and a cancelled game at Bradford Park Avenue. Rearranged for the following Tuesday evening, the team was already in Bradford when an hour-long downpour postponed it for a second time. With rival teams playing, 'Pools dropped to bottom position in the league.

Like the manager, Sentinel was realistic and fair in his assessment of their situation. Clough's 'great reputation' had set hearts 'pounding healthily' in late October: 'He promised success, he promised a team, he promised the paying public what they wanted. He has been here four months and he has achieved none of these objects, and in fact seems to be further away than when he began.'

But such a view was misleading. The team were playing better, although a run of away games meant dropped points, as others around them (Wrexham, Bradford City and Aldershot) picked them up. The three new Gs – Green, Grant, Gill – had improved the defence. While Clough was prepared to hear offers for any of his players, none were forthcoming. What he really needed was a bit more cash to sharpen the team's cutting edge up front. But if his hands remained tied, they'd 'have to undergo the embarrassment of another re-election application'. A fan agreed that it was 'the same old story', with the team 'staring re-election in the face'.[29]

Clough defined the visit of fellow laggards Aldershot as one of the most vital matches of the season. Sentinel again reported 'From a Point on the Terraces', with a 'lively breeze … blowing straight down the pitch and … playing havoc with [his] notepaper'. Thankfully, they exacted 'sweet revenge' on opponents who'd whipped them 5–0 in September when Geoff Twentyman was in charge. Phythian, Fogarty (from the spot) and Thompson gave them a 3–0 victory and two very welcome points.[30]

Off the pitch, Councillor John Curry, leader of the Conservative Group on West Hartlepool Town Council, became a club director. A season ticket holder for many years, he was hoping to make 'a worthwhile contribution'. He also said that with the club in its present state, he certainly couldn't be accused of 'jumping on to the bandwagon'.[31] In other civic-related matters, it was announced that after eighty-four years of trying, the two towns of Hartlepool and West Hartlepool were finally going to amalgamate into one. Together they'd form a conurbation of around 100,000 people.

A native of West Hartlepool, John Curry (1912–92) sold pianos and sheet music after leaving grammar school and served in the RAF in Italy during the war. He met his future wife in the cafeteria she managed on Lynn Street, close to the indoor market and Ord's Welcut Tailors. Grace (of Lithuanian/Scottish descent) was a fluent Italian speaker, after years working for Italians in Glasgow and West Hartlepool. The Currys bought the cafeteria from owner Mr Rossi in 1938, and later bought outright the C&C (i.e. Constantino & Curry) café in Middlesbrough. Other local café owners of Italian origin included the Greco and Rea families.[32] Clough & Taylor had spent many weekday afternoons at Rea's cafeteria during their 'Boro days. Its owner, Camillo Rea, was the father of Middlesbrough-born singer-songwriter and guitarist Chris Rea.

For decades, the Curry cafeteria in Lynn Street was *the* place to meet in West Hartlepool, for teenagers, housewives, and some professional footballers too. Its small army of waitresses served the COFFEE and ICES advertised on the building's white-painted brick façade. They kept a hawk's eye on the spoons and took many orders for Vimto with ice cream. The discerning public of West Hartlepool also frequented Binns department store and the Grand Hotel for hot drinks and something to eat.

After Halifax Town had turned down a second bid for their winger Dennis Fidler, Torquay United informed Clough they wanted £2,000 for their ex-Chelsea winger Mick Somers. The manager told the Devon club it was beyond their means.[33]

For his first game in the press box of 1966, Sentinel welcomed having a telephone again. His tool of the trade was essential to report 'a selection of injuries, fouls, cautions, dismissals, and free-kicks' in what was 'more a tragi-comedy than a football match'. Luton welcomed back outside-right David Pleat (future manager of Luton and Spurs) for his first game since breaking a leg in week three of the season. An early clash between John Gill and Luton inside-left Bruce Rioch (a future international and football manager) left the Scotsman limping. Soon substituted, his replacement and another teammate were sent off either side of half-time. Head-butts and clutched faces characterised a fiery game in which Luton finished with nine players. But most importantly, 'Pools bagged both points to move up to fourth-bottom.[34]

Poor finishing meant Newport were very flattered to beat them 3–0 with a late flurry of goals in their next game at Somerton Park. Shots flew around, but 'Pools hit everything except the back of the net. Clough said the score gave 'a completely false impression of the match'. That didn't stop him giving the players a 'rocket' after the game. Their 'enthusiasm, endeavour, and running power' had 'simply evaporated' in the final half-hour.[35]

Ahead of transfer deadline day, both Clough and Ord were busy on the phone. Clough spoke to former Middlesbrough and Newcastle winger Billy Day at Cambridge United. A deal was agreed between the clubs but not with the player. Ord contacted Middlesbrough about their 27-year-old outside-left Eddie Holliday, but couldn't afford him. Mick Somers had travelled from Torquay to Newport to speak to Clough, but no signing materialised. Transfer deadline day came and went, and the only new face was an amateur player from Consett in the Wearside League. John Bates jacked in his job as a pattern weaver to sign. There were no further departures to reduce their wage bill.[36]

At least they were picking up maximum points at home, with four victories on the bounce at the Victoria Ground since the new year. Their next visitors were Fourth Division pace-setters Torquay United. Like 'Pools, they liked to play away from home with a solid wall of eight defenders and a twin spearhead up front. Clough made seven changes following the late collapse at Newport. He dropped Green to give Simpkins his first league game since November. Harrison returned in defence and Parry at inside-right. McPheat and Bradley made way. John Bates, the 22-year-old local amateur now turned professional, made his debut at outside-right. The band of the 1st Battalion, Durham Light Infantry provided musical entertainment before the game and at half-time.[37]

Torquay's execution of the 8-2 away system worked in a way that it seldom had for their opponents. They took an early lead and swung the gate shut on 'Pools, who never unlocked their visitors' defence and lost at home for the first time since Christmas. 'Goal-starved' wrote to the *Mail* to question Clough's defensive policy. If his 8-2 setup was winning points it might be justified. But since taking over, it had led to one win, two draws, and seven defeats away from home. He pointed out that to 'bore spectators AND to lose hardly seems worthwhile'.[38] They'd sunk next to bottom of the Football League, exactly where Clough had found them.

15

STEAM STOPPED PLAY

One of Clough's most legendary quotes dates from 1972. When asked how he'd react if a player came to him and said, 'Boss, I think you're doing this wrongly,' he responded off the cuff: 'Good, well I ask him which way he thinks it should be done, we get down to it, and then we talk about it for twenty minutes, and then we decide I was right.'[1]

Following Hartlepools' first home defeat of 1966 on Saturday, 19 March, discipline suddenly became Clough's order of the day. When he dropped three players the next morning for their Monday fixture at Port Vale, full-back Stan Storton went to ask why his name was on the list. Stan, then 25 years old, confessed he wouldn't have gone to the boss's office had he been a younger player, say 21. But during the conversation, his 'fiery temper' had come out.[2]

Next day's *Mail* quoted Stan:

I asked why I had been dropped. I said I did not think I had played badly and was by no means the worst player in the side. I was offered no explanation, and a few minutes after we finished talking, the manager told me I was suspended. I asked why, but again was given no explanation.

He was going to ask the club to release him from his contract because he didn't want to stay. Stan received a fortnight's suspension and was told not to report back until advised to do so.[3] He sent his family home to Keighley and soon followed them, cleaning windows with his brother for two weeks to cover lost income.[4]

Clough told the *Mail* that Storton had been suspended for 'disciplinary reasons'. A fortnight later, the newspaper reported a further two-week ban for the player.[5]

This happened because Ord was hanging around when Stan had spoken to Clough. The defender often spotted the chairman at the ground in a long camel coat and likened him to cartoon character Mr Magoo. When Ord had intervened in his conversation with the manager, Stan had called him 'a little shit' to his face. The chairman immediately ordered Clough to 'Make it two', and hence the double punishment. Stan says he pondered the manager's reaction 'for weeks and weeks'. 'He were quite strange' that day, he remarks. In general, he was 'the type of bloke who if he says things, they have to be final.'[6]

Stan had questioned Clough's authority, but instead of them speaking about it for twenty minutes until deciding the manager was right, he'd been suspended. The wider outcome was that he never played for Hartlepools again. Come May, his name appeared on the non-retained list.

Something must have clicked, because for the first time that season, 'Pools kept a clean sheet away from home. They didn't manage to score, but 'hard work and honest endeavour' meant they returned from Vale Park in Burslem with a well-earned goalless draw.[7]

Clough's tough approach continued later in the week when goalkeeper Les Green, dropped after the Newport defeat, failed to attend training at the ground the following Thursday. The boss hit him with a seven-day suspension 'for disciplinary reasons' the next day.[8]

No stranger to the sting of discipline under Alan Brown's cat-o'-nine-tails at Sunderland, Clough explained his tough new approach in the *Mail*:

> If I haven't got team spirit here, I've got nothing at all. On Monday at Port Vale, it was spirit and spirit alone, that brought us a point. The players grafted and ran, and spared nothing for me that night … Since I came, I have built up the spirit in the dressing room until I really believe that it is now better than it has been for a long time … What I don't like is when anyone tries to destroy what I have built up. And if I think that I am being hindered … then I will not be slow to act.

He repeated that he wanted 100 per cent effort, and if the players didn't give it, he'd find eleven that did. He worked 'hard at this club' and expected players to do the same. Everybody needed to pull together if they were to escape the drop-zone.

He didn't like suspending players, barring them from the club, or stopping their wages. But even if it made his job harder, he'd suspend six players if required from his meagre squad of fifteen.[9] And there you have it. The unsuspended players had been warned.

They travelled to Chesterfield next for a Friday evening game. Displaying 'more spirit and fight than at any time since August', they returned home with only their second away win of the season. Their only wobble came during seven second-half minutes when they conceded two penalties (one scored, one missed). Simpkins played a blinder between the posts, while Parry sealed the 3–1 victory with his first professional goal four minutes from time.[10] The renewed accent on discipline and hard work appeared to be paying off.

In World Cup year, thieves stole the £30,000 solid gold Jules Rimet trophy from a stamp exhibition. Holders Brazil had left the trophy in FIFA's safekeeping, and said it was a sacrilege that football-loving Brazilian thieves would never commit. The English thieves demanded money for the trophy but then panicked. A black-and-white mongrel dog named Pickles beat Scotland Yard to the chase by sniffing it out, wrapped in newspapers under a South London hedge.[11]

Elsewhere in the country, Prime Minister Harold Wilson increased his parliamentary majority to ninety-six seats in the 1966 general election, following a narrow win two years earlier. With a swing to his party from Edward Heath's Conservatives of between 3 and 4 per cent, it was only the second time a Labour government had been voted back into power.[12]

In cinemas, the world went mad for *Alfie*. Maurice Micklewhite (aka Michael Caine) played the title lead, while Cilla Black sang its accompanying song. Alfie was a cocksure working-class cockney in Swinging Sixties London. When he wasn't bedding women for fun, he spoke to camera with his take on the meaning of life. He turned out to have a vulnerable side.

Champagne celebrated the opening of the George Best Boutique on Cross Street in Sale, and with it, the arrival of Carnaby Street style in Manchester. The 19-year-old Northern Irish winger said the fashion on offer would appeal to 'the extrovert male', but he wasn't expecting his Manchester United teammates to buy much of it. 'They are a bit old for this kind of stuff,' he added.[13]

The 1965/66 season still remained in the balance, but Clough & Taylor were already laying the foundations for 1966/67. They'd compiled a shortlist of five players they deemed essential for success. With minimal difference between top and bottom sides in the division, Clough saw 'no reason … why we shouldn't have a good go'. The ace up his sleeve was increased crowds. He was confident a well-performing side would draw gates of 10,000.[14]

Peter Taylor had made a recent scouting mission to view a game between two upcoming opponents: Crewe and Notts County.[15] Despite 'Pools performing well at Gresty Road in another Friday night game, three defensive errors in the first half hour gifted Crewe the points on a pitch resembling the

Somme. They struck a second when a Parry back pass stuck in a sheet of water to leave Simpkins stranded in no-man's-land.[16]

The April Fools' Day result was a bad start to the month, which needed to get better if they were to escape the re-election trapdoor. Following eight further games in April, only four more remained in May. The month would go a long way to deciding their season.

Starting on 8 April, they played the first of three games in four days, two of them at home. The run began well with a 2–1 Good Friday win over Stockport County at the Vic. Goals 15 minutes in and 15 minutes from the end gave the 'uncertain' hosts two more precious points. Stockport scored when Simpkins caught and dropped a cross. Despite his protests, the referee said it had crossed the goal line.[17] One down, two bank holiday weekend games to go.

They welcomed Notts County as their visitors the following afternoon to do battle on a mist-shrouded pitch. Steam from a resting locomotive flooded across Clarence Road onto the Victoria Ground pitch, turning visibility so poor the referee halted the game. When Mr Payne restarted action with a bounce-up, and Harrison had a word, the man in black booked him. A much-improved performance from the previous day meant they overcame County 'firmly and convincingly', with Fogarty and Thompson scoring in the 2–0 victory.[18]

They travelled to Edgeley Park on Easter Monday to face Stockport for the second time in quick succession. Sentinel judged that the secret of their success was once again a superb defensive action. They first contained, then subdued, and finally 'put Stockport to flight'. Typifying their fight and effort were Gill, who 'took a lot of punishment', and 'willing work-horse' Phythian.[19] Mulvaney hit their winner twenty seconds from time, meaning he'd bagged two goals against Stockport in four days. The *Northern Echo* reported how their defence had enjoyed some 'outrageous luck', including accidental blocks and inches-wide misses.[20]

Despite a strong Stockport handing them their 'biggest towsing' of the season away from home, Clough judged that 'spirit and fight' had shone through. He declared himself more pleased with how they'd won both points than the points themselves. The team liked to sing after away victories on the coach home, and this was surely such an occasion.[21]

Clough deflected criticism about changing a winning team. Not changing a side that had played badly (i.e. in the first Stockport game) was 'the cowards' way', he said. He picked players for certain situations, and after Friday's poor showing, his strategy had worked twice.[22]

What a weekend it had been. Instead of nailing themselves to the cross at Easter, the players had earned the club some temporary salvation. A maximum six points from three games had propelled the team to eighteenth, three places above the danger zone.

Next up was another Friday evening game, this time at Halifax Town. An unseasonal cold spell made for a Christmas card scene at The Shay, with thick falling snow leaving an inch-deep white carpet on the pitch. The game was pretty to watch but unpleasant to play in, particularly for Jimmy Mulvaney. He lost three front teeth when he collided with teammate John Gill. Ken Simpkins, who kept warm through regular and efficient handling of the ball, could not prevent a 7th-minute 15-yard shot skidding under his diving body. A rival Rugby League game and the snow meant just 1,403 hardy souls turned out, the lowest attendance of their season. The 1–0 victory and two points lifted fellow strugglers Halifax above them in the table.[23]

Because of double postponement in February, they visited Bradford Park Avenue the following Tuesday evening, where the Football League's leading scorer posed a sizeable threat. Leeds-born Kevin Hector had scored 38 goals in 40 games so far that season. They were goal stats to match Clough in his prime. Unfortunately, he added two more to his impressive record, the second a penalty after being fouled. The game soon turned into 'a masquerade' as Bradford PA's 'free-wheeling forwards' attacked in wave after wave to create havoc in the visitors' defence. The 4–1 drubbing sent Hartlepools tumbling back into the re-election zone.[24]

Brian Clough's personal life underwent important changes. After commuting by car from Sunderland for five and a half months, the Clough family moved into a three-bed semi-detached house on Kesteven Road, built by Yuill Homes on the new Fens Estate in West Hartlepool. Identical to Taylor's a minute's walk away on the same street, The Stranton (one of five designs) boasted a garage, a fully fitted kitchen, and Parkray 77 heating with five radiators. According to Taylor, the pair no longer socialised together or visited each other's homes.[25] This was strange, given their previous closeness at 'Boro.

'That will put an end to a lot of travelling,' the manager said, relieved, in mid-April. 'I have never seemed to have five minutes to myself since I took over here.' And he'd been enjoying even less sleep since Barbara gave birth to a 7½lb boy on 19 March 1966. Picturing the beaming parents and their new-born in Sunderland's Royal Infirmary, the prophetic headline in the *Northern Daily Mail* asked if the babe in arms would be 'Tomorrow's Soccer Star?'[26] Brian and Barbara named their second child Nigel.

Bums were twitching again as Hartlepools entered the final stretch. They could at least look forward to a straight run of four home games to end the season in May. But they needed points desperately in what remained of April. And Chester, who'd dropped away from the promotion places but played with an eight-man defensive barrier, were next to visit the North East.

'Pools laid siege to Chester's rear-guard after the opening 15 minutes, and but for wasteful finishing, would have won more comfortably than 2–0. Their performance left Jack Fletcher scratching his head. Why were they still entangled with the 'foot-of-the-table hoi polloi' on this form? The man from the *Northern Echo* was so impressed that he'd stake his typewriter against two World Cup tickets they'd be safe at the end of the season. Skipper Amby Fogarty was the 'life and soul' of the party, setting up Phythian for his goal, and then back-heeling one of his own from 2 yards. He made Chester's defensive blanket look as if moths had got in it. Meanwhile, Drysdale and Grant had a 'spanking match' in defence.[27] The win yo-yoed them back to eighteenth spot.

The 'up-and-coming' outside-right Johnny [*sic*] McGovern made his debut for the Reserves on 27 April. With Brian Clough looking on, his left foot pro-voked panic in the Darlington defence with a series of well-placed corners. All that incessant practice in his back yard and neighbouring streets had evidently paid off. Reserves correspondent North-Easterner reported in the *Mail*: 'He is a most promising player and gave the visitors' experienced full-back Curley a testing time.'[28]

The boot was on the other foot when the first team visited Rochdale mid-week. Conceding twice in the first nine minutes gave them a mountain to climb. Their defence looked particularly fragile in the air as they succumbed 3–1.[29]

Four days later at Notts County, Les Green replaced the injured Ken Simpkins. Both teams prioritised defence on a hot sunny day. The action played out on a bone-hard surface whose bare patch stretched down the middle from goalmouth to goalmouth. 'Pools packed their defence with eight men, but in first-half injury time, four players mis-kicked clearances to gift County a goal. The main entertainment of the game was a long 'running battle' between centre-half John Gill and opposing centre-forward Ron Still. According to Sentinel, they were both guilty of 'manoeuvres not in the rule book'. Minutes from time, Gill and Still clashed again on the edge of County's 6-yard box. With Still on the ground holding his face, the referee consulted his linesman and ran half the length of the pitch to order Gill from the pitch. He refused to walk, as his teammates surrounded the referee for two minutes. When he finally marched off, Clough and a policeman escorted Gill into the away dugout as fighting broke out in the baying crowd behind it. 'Pools ended the bruising afternoon with zero points.[30]

Clough analysed the team's deficiencies at both ends of the pitch. Players were no good to him sat in the bath, so he gave Gill a lesson in controlled aggression. Sometimes his centre-half became too absorbed in games. His manager liked his 'natural game', but he shouldn't take his hardness too far. Up front, their chances-to-goals ratio was poor. Alan Brown used to 'pound it' into them at Sunderland that missing chances didn't matter so long as they got there in the end. In Clough's opinion: 'This is the only part of the game that you cannot practice. You cannot teach a man to steady down in front of goal, it is just a matter of natural ability.' A natural goalscorer was high on the Clough & Taylor summer wish list.[31]

Ahead of two home games in quick succession over the May bank holiday weekend, Clough gave his players a day off from their usual Thursday training session. Most of them relaxed with a round of golf at Castle Eden.[32] Lincoln City arrived on the Saturday with a defence that had not conceded in five matches. 'Pools upset their record after first unlocking their stubborn defence with a gem from Jimmy Mulvaney on 27 minutes. He met a Thompson pass on the run to hit a glorious left-foot drive into the far corner. 'I'd have been proud of that one myself,' Clough told him later. Mulvaney added another on 82 minutes to seal a 3–1 win.[33]

Mulvaney had switched from outside-left to inside-right following an injury to Peter Thompson that ended his season. Peter Taylor said about the switch: 'He did so well there that we had no hesitation at giving him a further run-out in that position.' His next opportunity came in their Monday game at home to Barrow. Heavy and constant pressure again produced three goals, with Mulvaney scoring the third near the end.[34] Another perfect bank holiday weekend had netted them a maximum four points to move them three places above the drop-zone. Their safety margin was two points with two games to go.

With no match the following Saturday, Sentinel predicted that 'catastrophes and minor miracles apart', they were now certain to avoid a re-election application again. If so, a 'long and sad' chapter in the club's history would be forgotten.[35]

Clough defined their penultimate game at home to fellow re-election 'warriors' Rochdale as a 'VITAL GAME'.[36] By the end of it, they'd 'stuttered and stumbled' to almost certain safety with a goalless and uninteresting draw. When they most needed some goals, Mulvaney, Phythian and Wright all left their scoring boots at home.[37]

'Safe at last' is how Clough began his final programme notes of the season. Notts County had defeated Bradford City on Wednesday to definitively save

Hartlepools' bacon. He said the team's home record had been their salvation, because their away form was as bad as anybody's.[38]

Their opponents for their final game of the season at the Vic on 21 May were the aforementioned Bradford City, who'd hosted Clough's first game in late October. While they'd been losing in Nottingham on Wednesday and thus saving Hartlepools, John McGovern had been winning the Church League Junior Cup Final with Central Park Juniors at the Victoria Ground. Now safe from re-election, Clough & Taylor gave the 16-year-old his first-team debut at outside-right. The manager said he deserved his chance and they had 'every confidence in his ability'.[39]

They'd signed forward Joe Livingstone from Carlisle United on Friday evening. The previous season's Friday night transfer, ex-Hartlepools player Alan Fox, gifted Livingstone a debut goal when he mis-kicked a defensive clearance. As McGovern had stood on the halfway line awaiting his debut, the opposing Bradford full-back remarked, 'Good luck today son. But if you go past me I'll break your fucking leg.' The youngster was largely starved of service in the game and had to go looking for the ball. In Jack Fletcher's opinion, he was 'a boy with the right ideas. His time will come.'[40]

In a wind-spoiled and 'ragged' match, Bradford equalised to go home with a point thanks to a late disputed offside goal. Before that, Wright and Phythian made awful misses from 6 yards. The game summed up Hartlepools' misfiring but ultimately salvaged season.[41]

That very evening, around 40,000 spectators watched Muhammad Ali (formerly Cassius Clay) defeat Henry Cooper to retain the boxing world heavyweight title at the Arsenal Stadium in Highbury, north London. The referee stopped the fight in the sixth round after Britain's 32-year-old white hope suffered a deep gash over his left eye. The feet-shuffling, fast-punching 24-year-old black American could again proclaim, 'I am the greatest!'[42] Brian Clough was a big fan.

Middlesbrough striker Brian Clough,
21 April 1958 at Fulham.
(PA Images/Alamy Stock Photo)

Following his injury, Clough finds solace
in Sinatra at his Sunderland bungalow,
January 1964. (MirrorPix)

Clough suffers a career-curtailing knee injury at Roker Park on Boxing Day 1962. (Unknown)

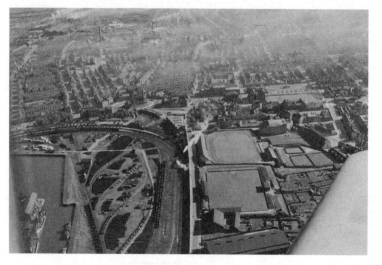

Looking south in 1945, the Victoria Ground (foreground), the Greyhound Stadium and West Hartlepool town centre (beyond), with railway and docks (left). (Reproduced with permission of Hartlepool Borough Council)

Peak post-war attendances. Fans queue on Clarence Road for (h) Darlington in the FA Cup third round, 8 January 1955. (Cultural Services, Hartlepool Borough Council)

Clough (second right) meets Hartlepools United chairman Ernest Ord (left) on 25 August 1965, two months before replacing manager Geoff Twentyman (second left). FA coach Joe Burrows (right). (North News and Pictures Ltd)

Day 1 of Brian Clough's (right) management career, 29 October 1965. Left to right: Brian Drysdale, Eric Harrison, Jimmy Cooper, Peter Thompson, Jimmy Mulvaney. (Northern Echo)

Clough coaches striker Ernie Phythian at the Victoria Ground. (Jim Larkin)

Recently retired star striker Clough (far right) leads by example during beach training. Left to right: Peter Thompson, Cliff Wright, Ernie Phythian, Tony Parry, Ambrose Fogarty. (Jim Larkin)

Clough chalks tactics in early December 1965. Left to right: Peter Taylor (partially hidden), [unknown], Brian Clough, Les Green, coach Bryan Slater, Eric Harrison, Ernie Phythian, Brian Drysdale, Amby Fogarty, Tony Parry. (North News and Pictures Ltd)

Clough helps repair and paint the ramshackle Victoria Ground in the summer of '66. (Unknown)

Taylor (left) and Clough (middle) confer with captain Amby Fogarty, 25 July 1966. (North News and Pictures Ltd)

Two Taylor-made East Midlands recruits bookend retained players. Left to right: Terry Bell, Amby Fogarty, Cliff Wright, Jimmy Mulvaney, Ernie Phythian, Mick Somers, 6 August 1966. (North News and Pictures Ltd)

Digging a hole for floodlight installation alongside the rusty Rink End roof in October 1966. (Northern Echo)

As an economy measure, Clough learned to drive the team coach, 18 October 1966. (Rex Features; ANL/Shutterstock)

Brian Clough leads publicity for the Save the Club campaign, 18 November 1966. (Northern Echo)

The Town/Greyhound Stadium End after floodlight installation, 5 January 1967. (North News and Pictures Ltd)

Taylor & Clough alongside Derby County chairman Sam Longson and football fixer Len Shackleton in summer 1967. (Derby Evening Telegraph)

Hartlepool player/manager (and former Sunderland defender) Len Ashurst in front of the 'temporary' main stand, c. 1972. (Unknown)

Obeying Clough's advice – to stand up straight, get his shoulders back, and get his hair cut –
brought John McGovern many rewards, including two European Cups at Nottingham Forest
(1979 and 1980). (Rex Features; Colorsport/Shutterstock)

PART III:
THE SUMMER OF '66

16

SUMMER JOBBING

Even stark realist Clough had underestimated the enormity of the challenge at Hartlepools United. Five months after his all is 'not rosy' New Year statement, he penned an end-of-term report on the season's 'long, hard and at times disheartening struggle': 'I'm not joking when I say that if I live to be 90 and stay in football management for another 40 years, I will never experience a period so difficult and worrying as the season which finished this week. It was as bad as that.'

By his own admission he'd begun as a novice manager, knowing only a little but 'prepared to listen and learn a lot more'. But he'd never expected problems as constant and complex as those he encountered.

He held up his hands to not achieving what he'd set out to do. His biggest obstacle had been a lack of cash, with the cupboard 'almost bare'. They'd only broken the deadlock of underperformance by spending a few thousand on the three Gs: Green, Grant and Gill. Along with Drysdale, they'd stiffened the side sufficiently to escape trouble, but only just. Another setback was the players who wanted to leave but nobody wanted to buy: Storton, Ashworth and Harrison. Clough couldn't sell any of them so 'it was stalemate' again. Another challenge was getting the players to do what he wanted on the field, something only achieved at the season's end. And then there was player discipline. It was his view that players could do what they liked off the field, so long as they gave their all for ninety minutes on a Saturday. But he'd been 'forced to take measures merely to enforce a standard of discipline which is NORMAL at all clubs'. He'd suspended two players and fined another.

But his greatest surprise of all was 'the obsession everyone – players, Press and public – had about escaping re-election'. Not just at the end of the season, but back in October, November and December! It must have been a legacy of past failure, he judged. But it was so 'contagious' that even he'd been infected. That's how bad it was. Anyway, next season would 'banish' all thoughts of re-election. 'You have seen Hartlepools United in the bottom four for the last time while I am manager,' he promised.

He'd continue to rely on Peter Taylor, and paid tribute to him for sharing the worries and responsibilities of co-managing the team. They were both looking forward to 'a much happier time' the following season.[1] Clough would particularly depend on his assistant manager for summer recruitment.

When Tyne Tees Television sports editor George Taylor interviewed Clough around this time, the manager was at turns immodest and modest, but above all realistic. Asked if he missed the big-time atmosphere, he confessed he missed 'playing the game' enormously and was indeed 'conscious of it all the time'. Regarding lessons learnt so far about football management, Clough declared:

> There's no easy way. Whether you're Manchester United or whether it be Hartlepools United, it's hard work all along the line. Mind you, the things that are hard work to other managers are not hard work to me – the discipline side of it and the judging of players, the training, the coaching … these are not problems as far as I'm concerned. Our problem at Hartlepools, my board and myself – gates, cash, etcetera, etcetera – they're our problems. We can cope with everything else.

He expanded on the question of cash, or rather the lack of it. They'd been 'restricted', because they couldn't spend £20,000 or £40,000 on players like other clubs.

Yet he was confident about the immediate future because they'd have everything needed to make a manager's job 'reasonably easy'. New players for a start. Improved gates would follow. It was 'being shaped' and would 'continue to be shaped'. Furthermore, 'We won't have to apply for re-election, and we'll be having you down here every other week next season because you'll be wanting to come along.'

He was right about the Tyne Tees cameras. They'd visit the Victoria Ground as never before.

Clough had also mentioned how the Hartlepools board was perhaps 'the best in the country because what we're spending is their money'.[2]

Back in January, when it appeared that Ord had resigned and wouldn't be returning, the manager had written that the 'easiest part' of his job had been his dealings with the club directors. 'They have given me freedom to tackle our joint problems as I see fit. No manager can ask more than that.' Indeed, he affirmed that without men like Ord and 'the love they have for the game', football in the country would struggle to survive.[3]

He also praised the board and their complete commitment to making the club a success in his end-of-term report in May, writing:

> I could not be more sincere when I say that they are as fine a set of directors as exist anywhere in the country, and in the past have accepted responsibilities far beyond those of the normal club director. I know they will back me in the future as they have done in the past.[4]

No hint here of any trouble between Clough & Taylor and the board, particularly the club chairman. Although in what sense had directors' responsibilities gone above and beyond their normal call of duty? And would they continue to back him?

Having got the re-election monkey off their backs after months of make-do and mend, Clough & Taylor set about a summer rebuild. Like all football managers, their first task was the end-of-season retained list. Who was staying and who'd be shown the door? When Sentinel saw the list, he remarked there were, 'No shocks, not even a surprise.' Nailed-on certainties to leave were Stan Storton, Eric Harrison and Barry Ashworth. They'd all contributed to avoiding re-election in both the 1964/65 and 1965/66 seasons, but their earlier transfer requests indicated a shaky commitment to the club. Joining them in the departure lounge were Duncan Robertson (without a single appearance), Bobby Brass, Willie Bradley, Willie McPheat and Hughie Hamilton.

Remaining at the club were: goalkeepers Les Green and Ken Simpkins; full-backs Brian Grant and Brian Drysdale; half-back John Gill; John Bates, Tony Parry, Ernie Phythian, Ambrose Fogarty, Cliff Wright, Joe Livingstone and Jimmy Mulvaney.

With twelve players retained, and following Peter Thompson's retirement, Sentinel expected four or five new close-season signings. At least two would be wing-halves, considering that the squad lacked even one. Clough had two in his sights, so it was now just 'a question of cash'.[5]

Reading the pages of the *Northern Daily Mail* and the *Northern Echo* between May and August 1966, there was no hint of discord between Chairman Ord and Clough & Taylor. However, it soon became clear that relations between them were not all sweetness and light.

Speaking more than three decades later, Clough recalled:

> My chairman at Hartlepools was a little bastard. He sacked me twice. He said: 'Right, you're sacked.' Now I am prone on occasions to lapse into Anglo-Saxon

language, so I said: 'You can fuck off – you're sacked.' And he said: 'I own
this club.' I said: 'Do you? You can still f-off. I ain't going anywhere. Only
the police can move me, they can have me for trespassing.' Six weeks later he
sacked me again. So I told him to f-off again.[6]

In 1974, Peter Taylor described a slightly different version of events. He'd
apparently talked Clough out of quitting a few times during their nineteen
months at Hartlepools. On leaving the boardroom after one confrontation and
sacking, Clough had raged, 'Let me go back and hit him.' Taylor stopped him
and counselled that they simply stayed put.[7]

In more measured tones in 1972, the first of a four-part account of Clough's
managerial career thus far recounted the sequence of summer '66 events at
Hartlepools. It described how Clough & Taylor were dismissed nine months
after being hired at Hartlepools, but no reason was offered, or any excuse
made. The sacking wasn't made public at the time simply because Clough
refused to accept it. He resolved to stay and fight:

> Sacked and I still don't know why. We'd been there nine months and were
> doing well. The team had improved and we'd lifted the club off the bottom. It's
> a long time ago now but it is still the worst moment I've ever had as a manager.

Little did he know it, but Clough & Taylor's worst moment in management
would come the following year at Derby, in 1973.

In October 1965, of course, Ord had proudly announced the appointment
of the league's youngest manager. But 'the chemistry for a successful partnership was not right. They were both dominant, both firm in their belief that
there could be only one boss – and it didn't work.' While their association
was 'smooth' at first, 'the power struggle' soon started. It intensified until
there was only one answer – one of them had to go.[8] The summer of 1966
was not quite that moment. With neither man budging, the tension found
other outlets.

Still more behind-the-scenes details from the 1965/66 season would come
out years after the events. In a ghostwritten article, Clough said there were
'three or four hearts' not in the job when he arrived at Hartlepools. But with
a small squad, he was forced to play them.[9] For some players, he wrote, the
club was 'a bit of a holiday camp'. They'd go drinking on Friday nights, but he
put a stop to it. On away trips he gave them a choice between the pictures or
television, both supervised, with lights out at 10.30 p.m. But some still stepped
out of line. One pair slipped out in the middle of a James Bond film (surely

Thunderball, released in late December 1965). Another 'had to be restrained from assaulting a director'. One can only speculate as to which player and board member they were.[10]

He cited the example of Les Green, who failed to report for training because he'd run 'into a spot of personal bother'. His goalkeeper was his own worst enemy, he'd decided, so he threatened to cancel his contract for this breach of discipline.[11] In the event, of course, he suspended him for seven days.

With the soccer season over, North-East football news turned scarcer on the back pages of the local press, as athletics, cycling, cricket, flat racing, golf and tennis started to fill column inches in the summer of '66.

Australian jockey Scobie Breasley won the Epsom Derby on Charlottown (5/1) by a neck. Thirty-year-old Lester Piggott rode Epsom Oaks winner Valoris (11/10 favourite). Four years before it disappeared forever, there was midweek evening racing around the tight 'frying pan' at Ally Pally (Alexandra Palace). Closer to home, there was flat racing at Stockton Racecourse next to the Tees. Manuel Santana (Spain) and Billie Jean King (USA) won the Men's and Women's Singles titles at Wimbledon. Jack Nicklaus (USA) held the Claret Jug aloft in The Open Championship at Muirfield, his first of three in an illustrious golfing career. The West Indies tourists beat England 3–1 in the summer Test Match series, with one match drawn.

Many 'Pools players had part-time jobs in the summer months. Brian 'Trapper' Drysdale had a milk round, with early morning starts for six weeks at Owton Manor.[12] The always smartly turned out Ambrose Fogarty continued to flog carpets through his carpet-fitting business. To earn a few bob, John McGovern mowed cricket pitches and marked athletics lanes on grass for the local council. Tony Parry manhandled beer barrels at Cameron's Brewery. A fan with connections obtained work for Brian Grant as a welder at the Redcar Steelworks. Awaiting a move, and before departing for Tranmere, Stan Storton and Barry Ashworth delivered bathroom suites for a local building company. Hughie Hamilton did some plumbing on the side. Striker Ernie Phythian sold cars at a local dealership. He also batted and bowled for West CC. He'd previously played for Lancashire's Minor Counties side.[13]

Following a brief two-day holiday, Clough was back at his desk at the Victoria Ground on 9 June. He told the *Mail* that once he knew how much cash was available, developments could be expected about the end of the month.[14]

His trip to see the Third Test at Trent Bridge (Nottingham) in early July turned instead into a day of triple-transfer business. Clough's cricketing friends Geoffrey Boycott and Lance Gibbs were playing for England and the West Indies, but he failed to see a single ball being bowled.

He spent the afternoon instead at the White Post Inn near Farnsfield (between Mansfield and Newark), where alongside Taylor, they signed three but not quite four new players. New director Councillor Curry travelled too in his Humber Super Snipe to help get the deals over the line. Following nearly four hours of talks, they signed outside-left Mick Somers from Torquay, inside-forward Terry Bell from Nuneaton, and full-back Tony Bircumshaw from Notts County. Doncaster had nearly whipped Bircumshaw from under their noses with a last-minute offer. Notts County wing-half John Sheridan requested additional time to consider the move. Four days later, Clough met him halfway to sign his contract at a Post House Hotel on the A1. Both outside-right targets fell through – Gerry Carver (Notts County) and John Price (Stockport).[15]

It was more than evident that all the signings came about thanks to Peter Taylor's little black contacts book. They had all either played for Notts County or had lived in Nottingham. As David Pleat told me, Taylor was friendly with 'a little clique of players from Sherwood', a neighbourhood in his hometown Nottingham.[16] Terry Bell was from Sherwood itself. Mick Somers had played with Peter Taylor's brother Tony in Nottingham. It was Tony who'd first had a word with Mick Somers at Torquay about Clough & Taylor's interest in him.[17] Bircumshaw and Sheridan were both Notts County players. Therefore, all the summer '66 signings were Taylor-made.

17

ENGLAND'S WORLD CUP

England didn't become a committed FIFA member until after the war and entered its first World Cup in 1950. Unfortunately, part-timers the USA handed them a fluke but humiliating 1–0 defeat in Brazil. Hungary then taught England a harsh lesson in short passing by thrashing them 6–3 at Wembley in 1953, before stuffing them 7–1 in Budapest the following year. During decades in which England had looked down on foreign football, the foreigners had surpassed them at their own game.

Johnny Foreigner also chipped away at the British Empire after the war, as colony after colony declared independence. With sport more than ever a vehicle to project and defend national honour, and the England team a metaphor for British greatness, there was no better opportunity than hosting the 1966 World Cup.[1]

The previous tournament in Chile in 1962 had turned into a negative spectacle of brutal tackling and countless injuries. So violent was the clash between hosts Chile and Italy that it was named the Battle of Santiago. Spitting, punching and general brawling interrupted any attempt to play football. Their next encounter was in a Group 4 game at Roker Park on 13 July 1966.

The Football Association decided to split group game venues into geographical pairings in London, the Midlands, the North West and the North East. Two allotted stadiums were later withdrawn – Arsenal's Highbury, because its pitch was too small, and due to local wrangling in Newcastle, St James' Park was replaced by Middlesbrough's Ayresome Park.[2] At 46,000, it was the only sub-50,000 capacity ground in the tournament.

A decade after the Suez Crisis, when Great Britain's roar turned into a whimper and prime minister Anthony Eden resigned with his tail between his legs, the tournament's official mascot was a furry lion named World Cup Willie. He sported a Union Jack jersey, white shorts and black football boots.

The '66 surprise package was North Korea. They'd qualified by defeating Australia in a two-leg play-off in Cambodia, after most of the Afro-Asian-Oceanian block had walked out in a huff, angry at competing for just one World Cup place.

Fear and ignorance of the unknown led to patronising comments and stereotyping of the 'inscrutable' North Koreans (average height 5ft 5in). While *Soccer Star* reminded readers that their visitors hadn't landed from Outer Mongolia or Outer Space, the magazine said Han Bong Jin sounded like 'an incitement to revolution'.[3] The team from north of the 38th Parallel had apparently lived celibate lives in barracks under military discipline for two years ahead of the tournament.[4]

Once on the ground in England, they attracted wide sympathy and support. Teesside folk couldn't dislike a team who played in red, just like their beloved 'Boro.

All Group 4 teams received special invitations to a World Cup conference on sporting fitness at the Easington Road TA Centre, West Hartlepool, on 7 July. The Italians told organisers they couldn't make it, while the Soviets and Chileans simply failed to show. The only delegates who attended were five North Koreans, welcomed by Mayor George Groves. It's a shame Brian Clough couldn't make it. Academic papers on 'Rehabilitation of the Footballer after Injury' and 'The Footballer's Knee' might have struck a chord.[5]

Evidently keen to escape their newly built team hotel at Teesside Airport, the Koreans made a 50-mile round trip one evening to 'spy' on the Soviets at Durham City. Their Cold War comrades broke off from training to give them bearhugs. After the Soviets resumed their workout, the besuited visitors in sunglasses stayed to watch more.[6]

Following an opening match defeat to the USSR, and a draw against Chile, the fast-learning North Koreans set the tournament alight in their third group game. Their 1–0 sinking of Italy produced the biggest World Cup shock since England had lost by the same scoreline in Belo Horizonte, Brazil. Dentist and part-time footballer Pak Doo Ik from Pyongyang did the damage. For Europe's most expensive team, it was their blackest showing ever. Their summer turned red when irate Italian fans pelted them with rotten tomatoes on their premature return home. Questions were asked in parliament about the 'national humiliation'.[7]

North Korea's triumph over Italy qualified them for a quarter-final game against Portugal at Goodison Park. Racing into a 3–0 lead after 25 minutes, Eusebio then tore them apart with four goals (including two penalties) to send them packing 5–3.

One local football fan who didn't attend any World Cup games at either Roker Park or Ayresome Park was Brian Clough. There was of course some history between Clough and the England set-up, particularly its establishment at Lancaster Gate. Friction between the two would continue into the 1970s and beyond.

In Clough's mind, his playing career had been stolen from him. And even when he was banging in goals for fun at Middlesbrough and Sunderland, the bunch of amateurs at the FA had largely – and ignorantly – overlooked him. In his two capped games in 1959, away to Wales and at home to Sweden, he was flanked by Jimmy Greaves and Bobby Charlton, in nothing like his normal role. He played deep, and England's attack never got going. The FA's international selection committee overlooked him for the Chile World Cup in 1962. Four years later and 31 years old, did he secretly picture himself alongside Jimmy Greaves that summer?

Before a single ball had been kicked in anger, Clough declared, 'There are certainly some great teams in the competition, but I don't think we've got any of them in the North-East.' Never short of an opinion, and never shy to express one, he didn't consider the football on offer to be worth watching. According to him, you'd have to go elsewhere in the country to see the cream sides.

Indeed, he reckoned the fare on offer in the North East would increase crowds at the start of the new league season. Not because it was so good, but because it was so bad. He concluded that regular supporters would be 'so fed up' with the standard of football from 'supposedly world-class teams' that they'd flock back to grounds in August. Although the less regular fireside fans, he judged, might be put off football 'for good'.[8]

It's a pity the *Northern Daily Mail* readership for his colourful views was so limited. Fast-forward four years to 1970, when Mexico hosted the competition, and the BBC would be paying him handsomely to voice his forthright opinions as a TV pundit. He'd switch channels to ITV to pass judgement on 1974's World Cup in Germany. By then, a national TV audience of millions could enjoy the tart opinions emanating from Cloughie's big mouth.

Ipswich Town manager Alf Ramsey had inherited the England job from Walter Winterbottom three years before the World Cup. Ramsey and Clough were chalk-and-cheese characters, but they did have a few things in common. Both men were self-conscious about their lack of school qualifications and lived and breathed football. They both believed in simple tactics and quick decisions, and neither suffered fools gladly.[9] For relaxation and social bonding, they liked their players to take in a film on the eve of games. And have them tucked up in bed by 10 or 10.30 p.m. They felt their teams needed to feel rested and relaxed to reach peak performance (although Clough was more prepared to allow his players a drink or two ahead of games). Players under the two managers both admired and feared them.

Yet while Ramsey was quiet and taciturn, Clough was loud and brash. This was evident when it came to their relationship with the press, where they were streets apart. While Alf Ramsey abhorred TV cameras and microphones, Brian Clough lapped them up. If Ramsey had an antagonistic relationship with the football press, Clough and the media were a match made in heaven.

Ramsey was sensitive about his working-class origins and paid for elocution lessons to take the rough edges off his Estuary English. He hailed from Dagenham in Essex, right next to the River Thames. The lessons worked only up to a point, as they left him sounding strangulated and still dropping a few aitches. Clough would never dream of disowning his roots or toning down his North Riding of Yorkshire nasal drawl. If anything, he ramped it up. It helped that TV impressionist Mike Yarwood later turned 'Hey, young man' into a national catchphrase.

Luck and home advantage aided England in the 1966 World Cup. Drawn in the weakest group, they played all their group games at Wembley. The Argentina captain Antonio Rattin was sent off against them in the quarter-final. He showed dissent and verbally abused the referee, a bald tailor from Stuttgart. The country's no.10 took ten minutes to walk off the Wembley pitch, a few more than John Gill had taken at Notts County.

After their 1–0 victory, Ramsey physically prevented George Cohen from swapping shirts with an opponent, and likened Argentine behaviour to 'animals'. It wasn't as bad as the Battle of Santiago, but was an awful advert for world soccer nevertheless.

Not much better was Brazil's suffering at the feet of Bulgaria and their former colonial masters Portugal. They kicked the South American giants and their star man Pele out of the competition at Goodison Park. While Portugal's star striker Eusebio ended the World Cup with nine goals and the tournament's Golden Boot, Pele limped out under a blanket.

England's semi-final against Portugal was due to be played at Goodison Park but was switched to Wembley thanks to a FIFA-approved loophole.[10] In one of the tournament's better games, England won 2–1. The Portuguese players were models of sportsmanship, congratulating Bobby Charlton on his hammer-struck second goal that sent them home. After gracefully accepting defeat at the final whistle, Eusebio melted into tears.

It was England v West Germany in the final. The crowd at Wembley, many of them irregular football fans, sang 'Land of Hope and Glory' rather than 'Abide with Me'. Most carried Union Jacks instead of the Cross of St George. The match ball was a twenty-five-panel orange Slazenger Challenge 4-Star.

A global TV audience of 400 million saw no.7 Alan Ball buzz around the pitch for 120 minutes, but did Geoff Hurst's first extra-time goal cross the line? The linesman from Azerbaijan nodded, pointed to the centre spot, and yelled, 'Da!'

Hurst sealed a hat-trick as match commentator Kenneth Wolstenholme uttered his immortal words. Jack Charlton slumped on his haunches, while Ramsey sat emotionless on the bench. Captain Bobby Moore ascended Wembley's thirty-nine steps, dried his clammy hands on his shorts and the Royal Box's velvet cloth, and shook the Queen's lily-white gloved hand. A gleaming Jules Rimet trophy made England football champions of the world and left toothless Nobby Stiles to jig on the pitch. England fans rejoiced at Wembley, in the fountains of Trafalgar Square, and around the country. 'Ee aye addio, we've won the cup.' Spare a thought for poor Jimmy Greaves, though, sidelined by a shin injury and replaced by Geoff Hurst.

Despite all the media doubters, England's teamwork, effort and firepower had prevailed. It was Alf's 'wingless wonders' wot won it. As for Brian Clough, he was nowhere to be seen, not even at Ayresome Park.

18

TAYLOR-MADE

Labour Party leader Harold Wilson heralded a 'white heat' of scientific revolution in 1963, but it was slow to arrive at the Victoria Ground. A 'devilish glow' had lit up a summer evening bank holiday game at the Vic on 30 August 1954. Its origin was a major conflagration at the North of England Match Company some 500 yards away on Swainson Dock. It began at 4 p.m. and was well alight by kick-off at 6.30. The blaze in the factory and warehouse peaked at 7 p.m., but millions of safety matches were still raging at 10. The 8,000+ spectators at the 'Pools v York City fixture were easily distracted from the action on the pitch. Embers, explosions and billowing smoke filled the air as 100-feet-high flames bathed West Hartlepool in Halloween-orange.[1] 'Gotta light, mister?'

In the mid-1950s, after decades of resistance, the Football Association finally dropped objections to football under artificial light. Carlisle played Darlington in a floodlit Cup replay at Newcastle's St James' Park in November 1955. The Football League followed suit and First Division Portsmouth hosted Newcastle under lights at Fratton Park in February 1956. Manchester United fans saw light at Old Trafford for the first time in March 1957. During the next decade, all league clubs installed floodlights at their grounds with two exceptions – Hartlepools and Chesterfield.

Down the road from West Hartlepool, even non-league Billingham Synthonia had embraced the future at their Central Avenue Stadium. The 'Synners' played their first Northern League game under lights in January 1966, leaving professional Hartlepools United in the dark age.[2]

An illuminating piece of news in the summer of 1966, therefore, was the announcement that West Hartlepool Council and the football club's directors had agreed to install floodlights at the Victoria Ground. The council would finance the £15,000 cost of the lights and their installation, while the club would renounce its 'option' to repurchase the ground. Their annual rent would also increase from £280 to £1,000. The aforementioned mayor George Groves declared, 'We talked the matter out fully, and we came away the best of friends.' The completion date for the project was set for November.[3]

There was no mention of civic pride, but it was surely wounded by the fact that the town's football club was bereft of floodlights. The amalgamation of Hartlepool and West Hartlepool was set for 1967, so the lights would add to the local spirit of progress, albeit rather delayed.

The announcement set local tongues wagging. With a population of around 100,000 and an average Victoria Ground attendance of 4,000–5,000, there were evidently many locals who weren't fans. To what extent should rate-payers be subsidising the football club? Detractors wanted their rate money spent on more widely used local infrastructure. Supporters, meanwhile, wanted the council to go the whole hog and concrete over the muddy approach to the Mill House side of the ground.[4]

As the debate continued, Clough & Taylor were photographed in shorts on the Victoria Ground pitch, with rakes in hand under a baking sun. Clough was shirtless, while groundsman Bill Bousfield handled a full wheelbarrow. Bill and Brian were all smiles, but Peter took his raking more seriously.[5]

A groundsman (possibly Bousfield himself) later recalled how Clough asked him: 'How would we go if this ground was our own house? How would we get it painted if we had no money? We'd do it ourselves, okay? So that's what, we'll do it ourselves.'[6]

Alongside a faithful band of fans, they picked up brushes to give the ground a fresh lick of paint. Clough declared: 'It strikes me that we must have a better set of supporters than Liverpool if they are prepared to sacrifice their leisure to help us without getting paid for it.' He also wanted the grass in as good condition as possible because the team wouldn't be out of the top half of the table 'all season', and more people would be watching them.[7]

That was confidence for you. The hearts and minds campaign that began with their arrival would now continue in earnest for their first full season in charge. Convince their hearts and minds, the thinking goes, and their feet will follow. More people through the turnstiles would lead to a win–win. More gate money potentially meant more cash to buy players. Success would breed success. That was the plan.

Middlesbrough endangered a key part of their strategy for success over the summer by making an approach for John McGovern. This came to nothing when they discovered that Hartlepools had registered the youngster as an amateur player, meaning they couldn't touch him. But it did galvanise Clough & Taylor into protecting their fledgling outside-right from other predators.

They made several visits to the McGovern family home on Arch Street over the summer. John's mother Joyce was keen for him to continue his studies, as his father would have wanted. Fortunately, his grandmother came to stay, and Clough charmed her into submission over cups of tea and servings of cake. She was persuaded that her grandson's future lay in the hands of these two ambitious men, and she in turn convinced Joyce.[8]

Clough also needed to win over John's headmaster at Henry Smith Grammar School. Mr Georgson had already given John a rollicking. At Henry Smith they played rugby football, not the code of association football. Disdain for the round-ball game sounded like a social class issue. John had captained both the school's cricket and rugby teams. Why on earth was he wasting his time with football, and not concentrating on his studies? John felt this was unfair, given the sporting success he'd brought to the school. His name had been mentioned in assembly.

At 16, he was at a crucial stage of his schooling. The truth was, he had indeed been distracted by football. Unlike his brother, who was in B-stream classes, John was predominantly in the top stream. But football distractions led him to only get two O-levels, while his brother achieved five.[9]

Clough didn't pass his eleven-plus, so hadn't gone to a grammar school. He wouldn't have wanted Mr Georgson to know that. Indeed, the headmaster would only have needed to ask his visitor which Middlesbrough school he'd attended to find out. Once the manager had the headmaster's permission for John to play for his team, he exited his office, and sharpish.[10]

When players reported back for pre-season training on 25 July, five days before the World Cup Final, it was Chairman Ord who did most of the talking. Looking forward to the new season, he had 'greater optimism than ever before'. For a start, the dressing-room spirit would be 'much better'. Given the right players and a little luck, they might be 'running for promotion'. There were four new faces, but the squad needed building up further. They'd have to spend money but wouldn't be rushed into buying unsuitable players. Still with only one recognised wing-half, Clough had two or three options in mind for the position.[11]

But nothing changed as July turned into August. 'Pools spent no money and no more players arrived. For some reason, Ord had changed his mind about giving Clough & Taylor cash to spend.

Clough appeared almost resigned to having no dosh at his disposal when he spoke to the *Mail* on 4 August. With two wing-halves, they'd 'fear no side' in the division, he said. But with just one, there were 'reservations' about their prospects. Clough was managing expectations, and perhaps sending a message to Ord.

Despite the limitations, Clough said there were 'no dissatisfied players this time'. They all wanted to play for the club and give maximum effort. He stressed mindset. 'Re-election and Hartlepools United must never be mentioned in the same breath again.' They 'must get away from the depression'. Instead, Clough & Taylor's efforts were focused on building a successful side. It was 'long over-due – to the club, town and supporters'. And he extinguished any thought of abandoning their defensive approach away from home. Players would only be let off the leash at home, where they'd be 'in an attacking mood'.[12]

Clough had plans for Ken Simpkins over the summer, and the goalkeeper had plans for himself. He'd once been the heaviest 'keeper in the league but planned to shed a further stone over the summer and hit the ground bouncing at around the 13 stone mark. In order to observe a strict close-season regime, the club issued him with diet sheets. He had to report to the ground every other day to stand on the scales and record progress. His manager declared:

> Ken wants to take weight off, and the only effective way of doing this is by dieting. You can do all the hard work you like and lose pounds, but you can put most of it back on again by eating the wrong food.[13]

In a new departure under Clough & Taylor, pre-season training concen-trated on building up stamina. Back in Ray Middleton's day, the manager had accompanied players on morning runs around Elwick and Hart villages.[14] Not anymore. According to Peter Taylor, roadwork 'shatters the legs'. He replaced it with lots of running on sand and grass, with sand the 'real "killer"'. There was also a new accent on speed, both off the mark and over 30 to 40 yards. They'd be weighing all players and putting some on diets. All because fitness told in the final fifteen minutes of a game.[15]

As Brian Grant told me, 'Taylor could train you hard.' He did indeed make them 'run up and down the sand dunes'.[16] Cliff Wright says the assistant manager barked instructions like a broken record, 'In and out, round and round, right we're off.' The sand blew in their eyes when the wind got up at Seaton Carew.[17] But it was summer, so they could brave a dip in the waves. Another novelty was a weekly golf day. They'd experimented with it the pre-vious season, but team bonding at the golf course would be compulsory in 1966/67.[18] This was the future.

Clough & Taylor arranged five pre-season friendlies. The first three were a sandwich of two homes with an away filling. Neighbours Middlesbrough visited for the opening 'limb-loosener'. Fans paid four bob at the Vic on a sunny Saturday evening to get their first glimpse of three newcomers: Sheridan ('industrious and clever'); Somers (knows 'the short cut to goal'); and Bell ('a decided acquisition'). The hosts won 2–1.[19]

After playing at even closer neighbours Billingham Synthonia on the Monday, they hosted a weakened Leeds United team the following Saturday afternoon. Clough & Taylor shuffled players around to get a good look at all of them. With no second wing-half signed, they had to invent one. After disappointing slightly in seven league appearances in his first season, they experimented with Tony Parry in the position. He performed so effectively that the dressing room nicknamed him 'Coluna', after Portugal's tireless World Cup captain Mario Coluna.[20]

Only 1,083 fans turned out at the Vic to watch the Leeds friendly on a rain-soaked afternoon. On the evidence seen, Sentinel saw no reason to forecast a season of 'champagne and oysters', but young McGovern's 'shining promise' did offer a possible solution to unfilled space on the wing. Phythian scored the game's only goal from the penalty spot.[21]

For their first league game of the new season 'Pools travelled to Aldershot, where they'd conceded twelve goals in their previous three visits. Clough said his players faced the season with bags of confidence, particularly in defence, and theirs wasn't a 'stupid confidence'.[22]

For the pre-season team photo, royal blue shirts with white round-neck and cuffs were unchanged from the previous season. As were their white shorts. But blue-and-white hooped stockings replaced the red socks with white turnover. Fans would be disappointed that the new management team hadn't revived the beloved blue-and-white striped shirts of old.

Clough & Taylor had every reason to be confident ahead of their first full season together. They'd discarded the less than 100 per cent committed players to sign four replacements. The squad wasn't quite as strong as they'd planned and was particularly lacking in the wing-half department. But they had faith in the blend they'd put together.

Clough had banished all mention of re-election. It was no longer in the club's vocabulary. Failure had been habitual. Now success would be infectious. It was mostly in the mind.

At the Victoria Ground, preparatory work for floodlight installation had begun. The pitch's bare patches had been seeded, and the grass brushed, cut and rolled. New lines on the turf had been marked, and the smell of fresh paint was in the air. It was still summer and warm, so hopefully the drains were running clear.

In the music charts, The Beatles' double A-side 'Yellow Submarine'/'Eleanor Rigby' promoted their new album *Revolver*. The single was enjoying its first of four weeks at number one. Up periscope. Liverpool's Fab Four were riding so high on success they'd even let Ringo sing a song.

Clough's golden tongue and mind games had dovetailed with Taylor's nous and Nottingham contacts to truly begin the process of alchemy. They'd wheeled and dealt in the transfer market without spending a penny. Players were fighting fit thanks to the latest science in dieting, training and relaxation. Clough had even managed the fans' expectations and frame of mind. With all the stars aligned for a successful season, what could possibly go wrong?

PART IV:
THE 1966/67 SEASON

19

MISSION STATEMENT

Calamity struck in the first minute of the season's first game when first-choice goalkeeper Les Green fractured his left thumb. He suffered the injury punching a clearance, only to then damage his shoulder when landing heavily on Aldershot's concrete-hard pitch. Pseudo-trainer Peter Taylor applied his sponge to no effect, while Phythian prepared to pull on Green's green jersey. He might have welcomed the breather, as August's deadening heat made Ernie physically sick during and after the game.[1]

They took the lead through Livingstone on 23 minutes. If it wasn't for his two injuries, Green reckoned he'd have saved Aldershot's equaliser six minutes from time. Holding his swollen and discoloured left hand, Clough & Taylor ferried him to hospital straight after the match.[2]

Sentinel was impressed by their 'smooth effective defensive machine'. The performance had vindicated the manager's assertion that he now had 'a TEAM', all of them prepared to work and play for Hartlepools United. New signings Sheridan and Somers made solid debuts.[3]

Unfortunately, the sunny start to the season on the pitch was tempered by grey clouds off it. Before a ball had been kicked, the directors had announced they weren't prepared to invest more cash. Indeed, the club was struggling to keep its head above water. Speaking from the team's Oxford hotel hours before the Aldershot game, Clough confirmed the 'precarious' financial position. The club would listen to offers for any of its players.[4]

The manager clarified the following week that listening to offers didn't mean the same as selling. They wouldn't be accepting buttons for their best players. Nevertheless, he said the club was living 'week to week'. Sentinel confirmed they were 'genuinely, desperately, short of cash'.[5]

With Green's thumb in plaster, the newly slimline Simpkins replaced him for the League Cup visit to Bradford Park Avenue. Clough was more than aware of their hosts' Hector threat again, the previous season's top scorer in all leagues with over forty goals. The Livingstone/Phythian spearhead notched one apiece in the tie, while Hector and Ham levelled for Bradford PA. A double sending off again punished Fogarty with an early bath. Both the player and his manager were mystified by the dismissal. 'I did nothing and I said nothing,' declared the Irishman. In a 'queer cocktail of triumph and tragedy', another battling performance earned a home replay. It also earned them an early fixture pile-up of three games in six days. The second involved a long-distance trip to Southend on a Friday.[6]

Before the cup replay, they entertained Wrexham in their opening home game. Abandoning their defensive away shield, Fogarty moved from sweeper to ortho-dox midfield. As Clough had promised, they'd be solely attack-minded at home.

Clough's opening programme notes resembled a company mission state-ment. Both he and Peter Taylor were convinced the club would enjoy its most successful season in years. The incoming players might all be free transfers, he told readers, but they'd improve the team. He assured fans they'd see 100 per cent 'effort and endeavour', as well as 'discipline and organisation and method'. These basic ingredients would be 'iced with skill and ability', he continued. He wanted the public 'to come along, watch us, see us work, judge us and make up your mind'. 'We don't demand support, we expect to earn it,' he signed off.[7] Such values sounded like they'd been forged in Yorkshire.

For a second game running, the new spearhead pairing up front both scored. Livingstone's 'build and thrust' was the perfect partner to Phythian's 'finesse'. The hosts triumphed 2–1 after Wrexham equalised from a mis-cued Simpkins punch.[8]

Meanwhile, Clough declared the club were holding a special trial for young players. They were going to make 'a real effort' in the FA Youth Cup, and thirty youngsters from local leagues had been invited along to the Victoria Ground.[9] Intensive training for all players – full-time pros, part-timers, ama-teurs – had increased stamina in both the first and reserve teams.[10]

Clough & Taylor's team no longer resembled the beat up banger of the 1965/66 season. The new blend of players purred like a Triumph TR4A. Coming in a sleek design, the British sports car possessed IRS (independent rear suspension), plenty of torque, and optional overdrive in the higher gears. You could even put its roof down and feel the wind in your hair.

Still unbeaten, they faced Bradford PA in the cup for a second time, a long trip to Southend, and Barrow at home. 'There will be no letting up,' Clough promised. 'The lads will have to give everything because anything less than that will not be enough.'[11]

Tony Parry was again tasked with the tough containment job on Kevin Hector. They were desperate for the cash that hosting Grimsby in the second round and a juicy tie in the third could bring. Yet when they needed her most, Lady Luck frowned on them. They hit the woodwork three times and had two cleared off the line. Hector pounced on a misplaced back pass for the visitors' opener, and his team triumphed 2–1. But Clough was 'delighted' because they'd played the best he'd seen in his eleven months at the club. They gave 'everything', leaving the pitch 'exhausted' and their manager 'proud'.[12] He couldn't have demanded more.

Meanwhile, new signing Terry Bell's debut for the Reserves didn't go to plan when Tony Bircumshaw's car became detached from the convoy heading to play Roker at Dawdon Colliery. After kicking off with ten men, 39-year-old trainer Tommy Johnson filled in until driver and navigator rolled up twenty minutes late.[13]

With their involvement in the League Cup over, they travelled 300 miles two days later for a Friday evening game at Southend. Following a bright opening, their defence took a prolonged pounding. Straight after the 2–0 defeat, and with no cash for a hotel, they began the long trip back home.[14] The sun was coming up when they turned off the A19 and cruised through the new Greatham bypass on the final ribbon of the A689 into West Hartlepool.

Foregoing an overnight stay did at least avoid awkward situations. Cliff Wright remembers well the occasion when an elderly waiter spilt a tray of tea over a hotel lounge table, splashing Clough's trousers. As the manager turned the air blue and tore strips off him, the players sunk into their armchairs and settees in stony silence. Once Clough was out of sight, captain John Sheridan organised a whip-round in sympathy for the old gadgie.[15]

It was a week for renewing old acquaintances: Alvan Williams and Peter Gordon at Southend on Friday; Eric Harrison visited with Barrow on Monday; and Stan Storton and Barry Ashworth returned to the North East with Tranmere the following Saturday.

After many visits to the McGovern home, the 16-year-old signed for Hartlepools United as an apprentice professional. Clough defined it as 'the best thing' to happen to the club since his arrival, announcing, 'I know this boy has real ability, and there is no reason at all why he should not go right to the top.'[16] In the Reserves' 9–0 hammering of Hylton Colliery Welfare in the Wearside League, McGovern displayed 'classy footwork, positional sense and ability to centre accurately with either foot'.[17]

Ten months after leaving the club, meanwhile, Ernie Ord invited Bill Heselton to manage the Reserves again. In a May edition of the *Mail*, the former Football League referee had shamed Clough into admitting he hadn't discovered McGovern. Heselton pointed out he'd played him in two FA Youth Cup ties, weeks before Clough & Taylor's arrival. [18]

Barrow were undefeated until their visit, and Clough and Sentinel agreed they were lucky to beat them. McGovern was making his first senior appearance of the season, the second of his career. The visitors led with eighteen minutes remaining, until a penalty gift from the referee allowed Fogarty to level from the spot. Livingstone then glided home a McGovern cross with visiting 'keeper Fred Else rooted to his line.[19] Like their first home game, the attendance was around the 5,500 mark. They sat tenth in the Fourth Division, a solid start to the season. That was a lot better than *Soccer Star* had predicted in August: 'Should succeed in keeping re-election worries at bay, but nothing more exciting than that.'[20]

A cartoon by Karr in the *Football Mail* joked that Clough was 'looking well into the future' with his youth policy. A lady wearing a shawl and holding a crystal ball discerned 'an inside-forward with 8 "A" Levels'. Meanwhile, two cloth-capped spectators watched a boy – in school cap, blazer, shorts and scarf – with a football at his feet. 'That's not his number on his back – it's his age!' one remarked.[21]

Instead of taking a full punt on a football career, Clough & Taylor and the McGovern family had found a compromise. John would continue to study for further O-levels on two mornings and two nights a week at West Hartlepool College of Further Education. He wanted something 'to fall back on', having considered studying at teachers' training college before football came along. It would be a couple of months before he really settled into the team, he predicted, but he'd already learnt a lot from the other players and Mr Clough.[22]

Having lost his own father at 11 years old, there's little doubt Clough represented a father figure. John listened to the boss intently and absorbed his football education like a sponge. Pay attention, obey, and don't question a man who's been there, done it, and is always right.[23]

Player after player told me the same thing about the manager/apprentice relationship: 'Cloughie looked after him.' They also observed that while John had the skill to get past full-backs, he didn't have the speed to get away. But what he did have was two good feet, a big engine, and an eagerness to learn.

John Beresford remembers Clough telling McGovern what to do in the simplest terms. He was sat in his office, being instructed to stay on the wing and swing it in hard to the near post. Beresford saw how he 'felt really responsible for the lad', and was 'acting as his father and his protector'.

On another occasion, he heard Clough talking to McGovern's mother at the ground. Beresford didn't consider him 'one of the best' players in the world, but he was 'reliable'. The manager spent lots of time with him.[24]

With more appearances under his belt, the apprentice explained to *Soccer Star* how Clough had helped him tremendously. Indeed, 'no one could have done more'. He added: 'I am so happy here that I cannot imagine myself doing anything else except playing football for a living. It's the finest career anyone could have.'[25] In contrast to the Victoria Ground's regular visitors from Sunderland Teachers' Training College, therefore, John didn't appear destined for a career in teaching.

Owing to improved performances and results in the league, Clough & Taylor could be content thus far. There were injury niggles to Fogarty, Phythian and Sheridan, while goalkeeper Green was still three months away from a return. Wanting to maintain a settled side, they hadn't yet played newcomers Terry Bell or Tony Bircumshaw, who – like Jimmy Mulvaney – were stuck in the Reserves. Clough asked for patience from the fans. With no money to buy a much-needed additional player, they'd just have to muddle through.[26]

After recovering from an ankle injury, Stan Storton replaced 18-year-old centre-half Roy McFarland to make his Tranmere debut, with Barry Ashworth at right-half. Like many visitors, they erected an eight-man defensive screen at the Vic. In Bob Dylan fashion, the game's two points were blowing in the wind and it was Tranmere who nabbed them, netting twice during the last ten minutes with the breeze at their backs. There was no need to panic, but defeat dampened the early season optimism.[27]

20

DRIVING THE BUS

Summer evening shadows were lengthening, although cricket fields still echoed to the smack of sixes, and tennis courts to the thwack of racquet on ball. After one draw and one defeat away from home, Clough & Taylor dispensed with their ultra-defensive system. While they'd begun the home league campaign with two victories from three games, they were leaking goals without creating them on the road. The management duo discarded collective method in defence and instead preached personal responsibility and man-to-man marking.

Grant and Parry dropped to the Reserves, and Bircumshaw and Bell (at sub) replaced them. In a 4-2-4 formation, Wright was promoted from the bench to start at inside-right, while Fogarty moved from sweeper to orthodox wing-half. John Gill took over the captaincy from the Irishman. According to Clough, the added responsibility was affecting Fogarty's game.[1]

Eleven months after beginning his management career with an away win, Clough made a less happy return to Valley Parade. The new shift of emphasis to attack 'misfired badly' and allowed Bradford City to exploit a 'brittle and exposed' defence. Their midfield appeared more in control, but forwards fluffed the newly created chances. Marking was poor, the defence was 'ripped open frequently', and they lost 3–0 to a team below them in the league. The only chink of light on a gloomy and disheartening afternoon was Bell's performance as second-half replacement for Livingstone.[2]

Out of the blue, somebody discovered some spare cash. Or so it appeared, because Clough & Taylor and the board were now fully engaged in efforts to sign a wing-half. Clough affirmed that one or two more players could turn them into a very good side.[3] But where had the new money appeared from?

On the back of two straight defeats, they welcomed Newport for a late afternoon (5.30 p.m.) Monday fixture. Terry Bell made his full debut, while

Phythian switched from centre-forward to left-half to fill in for the injured Fogarty. They dominated midfield for three quarters of the game to play neat and attractive football, but failed to convert any goal-scoring chances. The almost inevitable pay-off came when Newport broke upfield fifteen minutes from time to bury a winner and claim the points for South Wales.[4] That made it three defeats on the bounce, zero goals scored, and a slide down the Fourth Division table to seventeenth. Clough & Taylor's attacking spearhead had been severely blunted.

A fan walked into the main stand's tea room after the defeat and declared, 'Played very well, didn't they?' Those present scowled, but he carried on unperturbed: 'Well, I'd rather see them play like that and lose 1–0 than boot the ball all over the place and win 6–1.' He found no allies, but Sentinel was confident their chances-to-goals ratio was about to improve.[5]

Directors and the Auxiliary Association discussed the club's finances at an emergency meeting. Ord told supporters that cash must be found to strengthen the side. They perhaps asked themselves why he didn't search his own wallet. Beforehand, the board had spoken to Fogarty about his contract-release request. He wanted to end his playing days in Ireland, and his wife was convalescing from an operation on the Emerald Isle.[6] The player was obviously unsettled.

The board listened to Fogarty and asked him to wait a month and think things over. According to Ord, meanwhile, supporters in the meeting had decided on 'certain ideas' to bring in cash for buying players. The chairman said the board wanted to strengthen the squad and wouldn't do that by letting players go.[7] Yet only a month earlier, they'd been prepared to listen to offers for any of them. The club was sending out mixed messages.

'I must have a goal on Saturday,' insisted Clough ahead of the weekend. 'We are playing well and making chances, but we are just not scoring goals. I think Jimmy might do it for us.' Bell and Livingstone were unlucky to drop out, he admitted, but goals were of the essence.[8] It was a case of call Jimmy Mulvaney. He'd been languishing in the Reserves, but his firepower was needed in the first team.

Clough informed fans there was no way to 'legislate for forwards missing easy chances'. Tranmere should have been beaten by half-time, they'd enjoyed plenty of openings at Bradford City, and they could have banged three or four past Newport. But scoring goals was the only part of the game that a player 'cannot actually learn'. They were creating enough chances, and he had faith the tide would turn.[9]

Exeter carried erratic early season form. Despite not yet tasting victory in Division Four, they were unbeaten away from home. Something had to give, and it did. The recalled Jimmy Mulvaney added instant sharpness to the attack when he set up Phythian to score in the opening minute. Although Sheridan bossed midfield, Exeter equalised on 68 minutes, but Phythian made domination count by adding a second five minutes later. Mulvaney then sent fans home relieved and happy when his 'brisk-moving boots' made it 3–1 on 81 minutes. Jack Fletcher said that 'his enthusiasm alone' gave the home attack impetus.[10] Howay the Blues!

In a departure from listening to the latest music over the ground's loud-speakers, the Band of the 1st Battalion Durham Light Infantry provided live entertainment before the game and at half-time. But there was no pleasing everyone. While old-timers preferred the pomp of live brass, youngsters yearned for today's top hits on scratched vinyl.[11]

Sentinel had a couple of mini-scoops for *Mail* readers. Firstly, Clough had some cash to spend. Although it wasn't enough to secure his target player, the manager was confident of persuading him. The chairman had nearly always 'dipped into his own pocket deeply' in the past and was apparently doing so again. While Ord didn't want the fact made public, the news had already slipped out, so it was Sentinel's duty to report it. The chairman had scarcely been away from the ground and was working closely with Clough to strengthen the side.[12]

The fans had their tuppence-worth in the *Mail* too. A supporter of sixty years' standing, for whom Cecil Potter (player/manager, 1920–22) was not too distant a memory, recalled that the club had never used the 'no money in the kitty' excuse in their Third Division (North) days. Another thought Clough had 'plenty on his plate' and would need luck to 'get 'Pools pulled round'. A female fan added to Clough's workload with a collective complaint. She and fellow Rink-Enders were getting 'browned off!' Every time a player hit a way-ward shot it was hitting the roof and showering them with flakes of rust. Could the manager either replace the corrugated sheeting, or instruct his players to shoot more accurately? The editor added the note: 'Instructions have been passed on!'[13] Her wish would be Clough's command.

A different female correspondent lamented a week later that even when 'Pools were winning, somebody always managed to find another target for their 'misery'. They therefore picked on the ground. Personally, she wasn't bothered between comfort or discomfort.[14]

Another described their 'unique ground', which she and her friends had nicknamed the 'Gluepot'. They considered the main stand 'unfit for human habitation'. Echoing the *Mail* correspondent, she described reckless shots pranging off the Rink End roof to rain 'lumps of rust' on the fans. Meanwhile, smoke got in their eyes from passing trains at the Town End.[15]

It was Hartlepools' turn to produce a turnover when they visited fifth-placed Barrow for another Monday evening fixture. Two down at half-time, they looked every inch the beaten side. With their defensive system 'in shreds' and their goal living a charmed life, they switched from caution to aggression before the break. During seven second-half minutes after it, their forwards went on the rampage. Mulvaney started the fightback by heading in a low Phythian cross. Provider turned scorer three minutes later to plant home a Somers cut-back, before he made it two with a step-in, turn and shot from close range.[16] Barrow were undefeated against other opposition, but 'Pools returned from Cumbria with both points, three weeks after beating them at the Vic.

Sat in tenth place after nine games, five of the eight teams they'd played so far were above them in the league. Clough therefore considered their position deceptive. 'Promotion was there for the taking,' he bragged after the Barrow game. Steady on. Nobody at the Vic had uttered the P-word since the Westgarth years. The manager continued to talk a good game: 'We've got everything going here. We've always had the method, although not the players to make it work, but now we have, and we've got the spirit too. These things are a problem everywhere else, but not to us.'

Notts County had just splashed some cash, and if 'Pools had some of what they had, the sky was the limit. Sentinel estimated that Ord had put about £4,000 at Clough's disposal. He could have signed two wing-halves in the last two weeks. But the man he really wanted would cost a little more, and he was 'not going to settle for second best'. Instead, he preferred to soldier on with what he had. And what's more, there'd be no more free transfers.[17] In summary, therefore, he had a little cash but wouldn't be rash.

'Disappointed' he wrote to the *Mail* to advise that if Ord's fellow directors were unwilling to follow his example by dipping into their pockets, they'd be 'spoiling the ship for a ha'porth of tar'. Get in the two players Clough needed to make them a table-topping side and they'd get the money back from 10,000+ gate receipts.[18] Nothing ventured, nothing gained, although it wasn't the fan's money being ventured.

The Barrow win had given the side 'a tremendous amount of confidence' and had improved 'spirit in the dressing room' no end, wrote Clough ahead of their home clash with Crewe.[19] Yet the same old story played out at the Vic. They had three quarters of the play, but good goalkeeping and glaring misses from Mulvaney, Wright, Phythian and Somers meant they only had a second-half equaliser to show for their efforts. Crewe then robbed McGovern in midfield on 65 minutes to score a second and take both points.[20] It was 'an unpleasant reawakening' after the Exeter and Barrow wins, but they 'never really clicked' and prepared 'their own funeral'. They deserved a point but ended the game pointless.[21]

Despite the setback, Clough remained positive: 'We have never played better than we are at the moment, but we have no luck in front of goal. When the forwards click we'll start shooting up the table.' As for McGovern, he was 'improving all the time' and would be 'a great player'.[22]

Ernie Phythian attended his mother's funeral on the morning of their Friday evening game at York but elected to play. The *Northern Echo's* David Campbell was left unimpressed by the 'sorry story of wild shooting, aimless passing and scything tackles' from both sides. The game's most interesting early moment came when the referee changed his kit due to a clash with the visitors' 'drab blue and black'. Mulvaney was the main culprit of his side's 'slapstick efforts' in front of goal with second-half misses from 10, 7 and 2 yards.[23] He did eventually score an equaliser when he got his head onto a 30-yard Bircumshaw free-kick rocket into the box. The team motored back up the A19 with a well-earned point.[24]

They were mid-table with a quarter of the season gone. Sentinel affirmed the team was playing better than at any time in the previous season. More importantly, the new system established in April and May was now 'running smoothly'.[25]

Clough accompanied Fogarty to Sheffield for an FA Disciplinary Committee hearing into his sending off at Bradford Park Avenue in August. The fourteen-day suspension he received for 'kicking an opponent' ruled him out for three games. It gave his manager 'a bit of a problem'. Fogarty was already a stand-in wing-half, so now they'd have to find 'a stand-in for the stand-in'. The Irishman's suspension began for their game at Newport the following Monday.[26]

Clough didn't pass up the opportunity to create a national headline. He described a novel idea to the *Daily Mail*: 'I should be paying the fine, not Fogarty. I regard the discipline and behaviour of my players as my affair.' Why were clubs held responsible for their supporters' behaviour but not their players', he demanded? He suspected football was only 'scratching the surface of solving the problem of dirty play'.[27]

The same story carried a photo of Clough at the wheel of a coach with an L-plate in its windscreen. He was taking a test for a public service vehicle (PSV) licence. Apparently, he wanted the PSV qualification in order to drive the team to away matches in emergencies.[28]

It might have appeared like a cost-saving publicity stunt, but he really meant it. Even if a road trip to somewhere like Torquay in the 1960s was twelve hours there and twelve back. The real reason for seeking the licence was that he and the players were perturbed about the coach firm sending them 'a series of kamikaze drivers'. Matters had come to a head on the busy outskirts of Nottingham, when their thirty-seater coach sped through a red light at 40mph and neatly dissected two oil tankers. Ernie Phythian stormed down the steps and refused to re-board until he'd calmed his nerves. Clough had therefore determined that enough was enough. In the end, however, the coach company sent them a more level-headed driver and the manager forgot about obtaining a PSV licence.[29] Instead of driving the bus, he and the team concentrated their efforts on parking it, away from home and on their own half of the pitch.

One-from-bottom Lincoln were next up at the Victoria Ground. The home line-up was unchanged for the fifth successive time since Mulvaney's seasonal debut. They attacked the managerless visitors from the get-go. If it hadn't been for a spate of further misses and two disallowed goals, they'd have won by more than 5–0. Mulvaney scored twice, while Phythian, Fogarty (pen.) and Wright (pen.) got one apiece.[30]

With Clough reluctant to move Ernie Phythian from centre-forward to wing-half now that his attacking line was scoring goals, Brian Drysdale offered a possible solution for Fogarty's upcoming absence. He'd filled that role at Lincoln City. Bill Shankly at Liverpool had watched him at the end of the previous season and the start of this but hadn't yet tabled an offer. Blackburn were also keeping an eye on him. Sentinel judged that he'd 'fetch a fair price' in the transfer market. Meanwhile, Colchester were still keeping tabs on Phythian.[31]

Extra income from a long run in the FA Cup would boost the club's perilous finances and the wing-half budget. But the first-round draw dashed such hopes. Clough was in Newport awaiting their next league match when he received the news, and told the *Mail*: 'It's a bad draw, as bad as we could get. I don't intend to come out with any of the old clichés about Shrewsbury being a good side and about us doing our best, it's just a bad draw.'[32] Asked by the *Northern Echo*, he responded, 'We could hardly have done worse. I'm disappointed.'[33]

FA Cup opponents Shrewsbury Town sat on the fringe of the Third Division promotion zone. Progression to the second round and the big boys of the third round would be a massive ask.

21

ORD FROM THE BOARD

After he'd swallowed the FA Cup draw disappointment, Clough was forced into changing his settled side for the game at Newport. He handed a debut to 21-year-old amateur centre half John Beresford, a Sunderland Teachers' Training College graduate. Terry Bell replaced John McGovern, with the manager judging that he'd be fresher to play on the 'very heavy' ground in South Wales. It was only his second full appearance, and the pitch was only forecast to 'get heavier'.[1]

Beresford is more likely than most to remember the game because it was one of only three full appearances he made. He'd finished his studies in the summer and was now teaching in a primary school at Dawdon, a pit village near the Durham coast. His head teacher gave him time off to play. As well as football, the 6ft 3in English teacher played cricket for Durham County. The day after beating Lincoln, the team travelled by coach to stay in Gloucester on Sunday evening. He remembers Clough locking their hotel bedroom doors at 10 p.m. to prevent them sneaking out for a drink.[2]

They set up with a novel 2-4-4 formation. Clough had given the two John centre-halves – Beresford and Gill – a job to do. As Sentinel reported the next day, 'The Newport forwards continually ran straight into the blue screen thrown protectively around Simpkins; they could find no way through or round.' A tireless Mick Somers was the star performer at outside-left, when he wasn't at left-back, left-half and outside-right. The richly in-form Phythian put them ahead on 38 minutes. And with Newport unable to penetrate their defence, Sheridan sealed the points with his first goal for the club, a low 25-yard screamer into the corner of the net on 78 minutes.[3]

Ord was so happy with the result that Beresford remembers him dishing out fivers to the players on the coach. They used them to bet on card games during the long journey back to the North East.[4] The chairman surely turned even happier on viewing the league table. They'd risen to eighth.

Four days after their match in South Wales, the blackest of tragedies occurred some 20 miles away from Newport in the mining community of Aberfan in the Taff Valley. Sitting above a natural spring and after days of incessant rain, an enormous slurry heap of coal waste slipped down a hill above the village to engulf a row of houses, a farm, and a junior school where morning classes had just begun. Despite the frantic rescue efforts of local inhabitants and miners, the disaster claimed 144 lives, 116 of them children. The enormity of the loss was felt throughout the United Kingdom.

While Amby Fogarty sat out his suspension in Ireland, Stockport made a £2,500 bid for the 32-year-old. Negotiations between the clubs were ongoing, with the player himself none the wiser. The transfer income would be useful, but they'd be losing a dependable midfield player. Furthermore, Ernie Ord had forked out four times that amount to bring him to Hartlepools less than three years earlier.[5]

After its success at Newport, they wheeled out their 2-4-4 formation again at Chesterfield's Saltergate, the country's only other professional ground without floodlights. They hadn't lost away from home since the debacle at Bradford City in mid-September. Schoolteacher John Beresford continued in the no.6 shirt alongside John Gill in the centre of their defensive barrier. Unfortunately, the home side breached it on 27 minutes when a fierce drive rebounded off Simpkins's chest and the opposition no.11 rammed it home. Drysdale and Somers made all the running, but they only broke out of their 'defensive prison' in the final fifteen minutes. They went down 1–0.[6]

What followed were a very busy few weeks off the field in the life of Hartlepools United. Fans finally discovered the name of the player Clough had been targeting for the wing-half position: Mick Hopkinson of Derby County. Apparently, this was the fourth time he'd made a move for the 24-year-old. First at the end of the 1965/66 season, then at the start of this season, and again towards the end of September. The fee was still a snag. They'd offered £5,000, but Derby wanted more. Fogarty was due back from Ireland for talks with Stockport general manager Bert Trautmann. An extra £2,500 in the kitty from that deal, if clinched, would probably get the Hopkinson transfer over the line.[7]

Meanwhile, a squad of workmen with buckets and shovels had moved into the Victoria Ground. On the instruction of structural engineers, they'd broken ground in four corners to dig holes and lay foundations for the floodlight pylons. Plans were afoot to invite a First Division club for an inaugural switch-on of the lights in early December. The names Sunderland, Newcastle and Burnley were all mentioned. A Fourth Division fixture would also be rearranged to test the 'pulling power' of evening games.[8]

Table-topping Stockport County were Hartlepools' next visitors. They arrived with a record of just two defeats in thirteen games. After watching them at Bradford, Clough & Taylor had tailored their tactics towards springing the division's tightest defence. Beresford dropped to the bench, while McGovern returned.[9]

Jack Fletcher's match report began, 'Take a bow, Hartlepools.' The 'triumph,' he wrote, 'was something to set the pulses racing.' Stockport amply demonstrated what a 'formidable outfit' they were, but 'Pools 'stretched them taut in this bustling, bruising game'. The home team's 'zest was a tonic' and over 90 tiring minutes they never ceased fighting.[10] It was just as well that Ernie Phythian lashed in his 12-yard winner on 82 minutes, because Stockport responded with a ferocious offensive that nearly saw them level twice, once with an 18-yard free-kick that thundered off the bar. The home fans' roar got louder in the final minutes with each 'bigger, higher and wilder' defensive clearance. A crowd of 5,976 was the highest of the season so far. Among them was former West Hartlepool mayor and alderman John Miller. He sadly collapsed and died during all the excitement.[11]

By Monday, Clough was still happy with the result but furious with Stockport County. The Cheshire club had agreed terms with Fogarty during their visit on Saturday and promised a final decision on Sunday. They'd already promised one a week earlier. 'I have contacted Stockport this morning and told them I am not happy at being messed about like this,' he complained.[12]

Clough had said before Saturday's excellent result, 'If I had the money to buy the one or two players I want I would guarantee promotion. That's how confident I am of succeeding.'[13] The Fogarty deal was now off, and by default, so was the Derby wing-half deal too. To relax, he took his players to the Odeon Cinema West Hartlepool on Halloween to watch *Goal! World Cup 1966*, the official documentary of the July tournament.[14] Presumably, there was no repeat of the James Bond film incident, when two players had slipped out for a drink during the screening.

Something wasn't right behind the scenes, because Chairman Ord's messages were mixed in the extreme. He told the *Mail*, 'We have no money, the cupboard is bare.' They couldn't buy without selling, unless a 'fairy godmother' appeared. They'd learned from past mistakes when they'd 'wasted a lot of money', but only did so because of the trouble they were in. He judged they were now doing well, so why spend cash they hadn't got?

He was confident crowds of 10,000 and 12,000 would return. They were really going for promotion and could achieve it with the current players. Their spirit was better than he'd ever seen it: 'All the players are really going for the manager – he's the one who should take the credit. He can put it over to the players in the dressing room better than any manager I have ever seen, and I've seen a few.'

He could say that again. After Ord's glowing praise, the chairman then drenched readers with a bucket of drain water: 'I'm sorry to say it, but he won't be staying with Hartlepools United, he's bound to finish up with a big club one day.' Players were giving Clough everything because they respected him, and the new golf days were going down well. All in all, they had 'a great chance of going up'.[15]

Some – but not all – of Ord's logic appeared flawed. More worryingly, the mismatch between his recent actions and words was something to behold. One minute, Clough had money to spend. The next, he needed to sell in order to buy. He hadn't bought or sold, but now the cupboard was bare. Still, he was a great manager. So good, in fact, that he'd soon be off.

At the same time, the fans appeared over the moon with recent results and their youthful manager. One described the Stockport display as 'champagne vintage'. 'Stick at it 'Pools, and promotion is yours.' Another thought their 'grand little team' was 'fab', to use an expression of the day. An OAP, who used to pay 2*d* to watch them in the old North Eastern League, thought the team was the best since the late Fred Westgarth's days.[16] High praise indeed.

Clough made changes to ensure 'particular players' did 'particular jobs' at low-placed Rochdale on 5 November. For example, he brought in Beresford for his height and weight in the middle of defence.[17] But the plan came unstuck during nine first-half minutes when Phythian was off the field nursing a gash to his forehead. Rochdale struck three times, the second with Simpkins lying injured in a heap in his own net. Phythian returned to the action holding a sponge to his face, and they struck back through Mulvaney before half-time and Phythian on 78 minutes. But despite their late rally, they paid the price for 'inefficient marking' and playing with ten men during a game-changing twenty-minute spell.[18] They limped home having picked up a few knocks at Spotland but no points.

Assistant manager – and former 'keeper – Peter Taylor wondered afterwards, 'How could they allow a goal like that with the goalkeeper lying on the ground?' The referee had consulted his linesman and given it. The last thing Simpkins remembered was John Gill moving across to clear, and the next thing he knew he was being brought round. 'I was hit very hard by something, but

I just don't know what it was – although it felt like Cassius Clay.'[19] Neither Taylor nor the referee had the heart to tell Simpkins that the 'something' that flattened him was his teammate John Gill.

Moving on from the Fireworks Day disappointment, the club looked to the future when apprentice John McGovern signed as a full-time professional, watched over by his mother, club secretary Bill Hillan, and Ernie Ord. Clough had decided he was a future Scottish international, while Taylor added, 'This boy is really going to make the grade, make no mistake about it.' That evening he shot his club into the second round of the FA Youth Cup with a late goal at North Shields.[20]

One person watching their 3–2 steamrolling at Spotland was former manager Alvan Williams. He was reacquainting himself with the centre-forward he'd signed the day before departing Hartlepools for Southend. He'd now seen Phythian hit the net again to head the list of Fourth Division top scorers with twelve goals. Williams telephoned his old club to make an offer for the no.9. Clough told the *Mail* he knew nothing about it, and asserted, 'I am only interested in the Third Division. And that means buying players and not selling them.' Meanwhile, sections of the floodlight pylons had arrived for assembly at the Victoria Ground.[21]

It had been ten months since Ord's last resignation, so it was no surprise when it happened again. According to the *Mail*'s first report, it came during a special board meeting, held to discuss Southend's offer for high-scoring Ernie Phythian. The chairman had outlined the week's developments on the bid, and then resigned, without giving a reason. Vice-Chairman Frank Perryman then presided over what remained of the meeting. Sentinel said the announcement had come 'as a complete shock to the club's directors'.[22] The truth is they'd all been here before.

A few days later, the sequence of events became a bit clearer. The club had been threatened with a court order. Ord had gone to a bank to reach a settlement over the order. Other directors criticised him for not taking the club accountant (presumably secretary Bill Hillan). Regarding the emergency board meeting, Ord told the *Mail*, 'I was so sick that I walked out and said I wasn't coming back.'[23] In another outlet, he added, 'My resignation is due to the bad attitude of one of our directors – a troublemaker.'[24] Did he mean John Curry?

A later version of events describes Ord sacking Taylor, Clough telling him to stay, and Ord sacking Clough. The boss refused to go and carried out his threat to put the 'full facts' before a board meeting and let them decide. Ord had opened the meeting, resigned, and that was the end of it.[25]

A home clash with Fourth Division leaders Southport interrupted the behind-the-scenes turmoil. The TV cameras of Tyne Tees happened to be there for *Shoot*, now showing on Sunday afternoons between *Farming Outlook* and the film matinee. *Thunderbirds* were go at 5.05 p.m. It's a shame the cameras didn't keep rolling after the game to record the off-the-field action under the main stand.[26]

Visiting manager Billy Bingham's team erected an almost watertight eight/nine-man defence that stone-walled wave after wave of home attacks. Mulvaney breached it just once, equalising soon after Southport's late opener on 72 minutes. Watching from the main stand because of an ear-infection, and replaced by Tommy Johnson on the bench, Taylor judged the visitors 'the best side' in the division.[27] He and Clough had to be satisfied with a point.

Below deck, so to speak, Ord stormed in to demand the afternoon's gate money. His former fellow directors offered him a cheque, but he refused one, insisting on cash from the turnstile takings. On Monday, the former chairman described what had happened:

> I was treated very badly by some of the directors after the game on Saturday when I asked for the money with which I had paid the wages the previous Thursday … It was all very embarrassing, but I was only asking for money that was rightfully mine.

They did eventually persuade him to accept a cheque for £1,100 , to cover his cheque for players' wages from the week before.[28]

National newspaper the *Daily Mail* reported that gate receipts for the Southport game were £880. Ord had thrown his weight around, telling ex-colleagues: 'Either buy me out or I'll buy you out. My guarantee at the bank is bigger than the guarantees of all the other directors. I also have more shares than all theirs put together.'[29]

Ord estimated the club owed him between £13,000 and £14,000. 'I am not fussy about returning to the board. I just want my money. It's as simple as that.' There was a £6,000 bank guarantee owed to him for starters, and upwards of £7,000 in cash. 'I don't know what I will do if Hartlepools United are forced out of existence because of my demands for the money. But I have the good of the club at heart. I want to see Hartlepools United flourish, not die.'[30]

Another emergency board meeting was arranged for Tuesday morning. Ord mentioned the possibility of returning (yet again) as chairman but stressed it would be 'on his terms'. He'd manage for the meantime with just two directors – himself and son David (27). It sounded like a tighter dictatorship. He added that he had 'no quarrel at all' with manager Brian Clough. He'd done 'a wonderful job so far' and he had 'every confidence in him'. Meanwhile, the *Mail* reported no desire of his to return, and judged his seventeen-year-long association with the club as probably over.[31]

The *Northern Echo* canvassed opinion on West Hartlepool's streets about the latest goings on. One local judged that, 'Mr Ord is too domineering. He is never satisfied unless he gets his own way.' Somebody else added, 'It's common knowledge that for a long time Mr Ord has been running the show. If he's prepared to put his money in, why not let him carry on?' Others were more concerned with 'the prestige of the town' and the 'ridiculous' situation that made Hartlepools United 'a laughing-stock throughout football'.[32]

22

ON HIS BIKE

If Ord had assumed power in a bloodless revolution, he lost it in a bloody coup. The ninety-minute Tuesday morning board meeting rubber-stamped his resignation and elected Councillor John Curry as new chairman. Son David Ord would continue as director. Curry announced that any talk of Ord buying them out, or them buying him out, was just 'heat of the moment' noise. He was confident his predecessor had the good of the club at heart and wouldn't embarrass it. Immediate obligations were covered, but the board faced a critical three-week period with no home games and zero income.[1]

How would they survive financially beyond then? The answer was an immediate public appeal for donations and loans. If successful, there'd be no need to sell players for survival. 'We intend to keep faith with the manager, and not damage his efforts to build a good side,' Curry affirmed. Buying any players in the near future was 'out of the question', however. Just to break even, the club needed gates of 7,000–8,000.[2]

Brian Clough would spearhead the appeal. His job, Peter Taylor's job, and Hartlepools United's survival depended on it. He had a young family to support and occupy his time, so it was just as well they now lived in the town. He'd employ his boundless energy and all his PR skills to ensure the club didn't go under financially, as he'd done the previous season with league survival. There was no other way, and he'd get to work immediately.

Ord wasn't as amenable as Curry had hoped, at least early on. By Wednesday after the game he said he wanted his debts repaid within seven days. 'If I don't get it the matter will be put in the hands of my legal advisers.' Contradicting what he'd said two days earlier, he declared: 'I would press for my money even if the club had to close down. This is the last thing I want to happen, but I am not being unreasonable in asking for what is mine, and I will press for it.'

He admitted to still feeling 'antagonised' about the 'rudeness' he'd encountered at the ground on Saturday. Nevertheless, he confessed: 'It's a weight off my mind to be finished with the club, and I would not go back at any price.'[3] He'd been there before, as had his fellow directors. This time, however, Ord would reflect, simmer down a little, and eventually come to an arrangement with Chairman Curry over the money owed to him.

Among many letters to the *Mail*, one reader considered the club an asset to the town that the council should take over and run. A shopkeeper regretted that Ord, the club's benefactor for many years, had been treated so disgracefully. Another Ord backer thought other directors should step aside if they couldn't finance the club to the same extent. A similarly minded reader said the new set of directors had a lot of cheek in begging supporters for alms. But Ord had acted like a child in demanding his marbles back. One correspondent felt sorry for young and enterprising manager Brian Clough, who'd been caught in all the crossfire.[4]

The *Mail*'s own editorial column recognised that financial crises had been as much a part of Hartlepools United as the game of football itself. They weren't wrong. Regular supporters and business concerns should realise that a league club was a local asset. Few would disagree. And with April's forthcoming amalgamation of the two towns in mind, everybody should come together to ensure that 'the Hartlepools can be truly united'.[5] Would common sense prevail?

Sentinel judged it a good moment to analyse Clough's character and method. The reporter confessed he hadn't liked the new boss on first meeting him, couldn't help liking him a week later, and a year on, wondered why he hadn't liked him in the first place. His players would do 'anything he asked'. That included running through brick walls, or at least trying. Behind the ruthless and ambitious tough exterior was a sense of honesty and a complete frankness. It was this 'blunt integrity' that attracted journalists' respect. Taylor told Sentinel how Clough came down hard and quickly on any player who stepped out of line. When any did, everything was brought out into the open without grudges or malice and soon forgotten about.[6]

When the 'Save the Club' appeal was launched on Thursday, 17 November, Clough led by example and threw his £40-a-week salary into the kitty. Curry said it was 'a wonderful gesture', and with that spirit they couldn't go wrong. The manager pleaded with everyone to do their bit to see the club through the difficult period. While he declared himself glad to help, he didn't want to make a song and dance about it. Yet a photo in next day's *Northern Echo* pictured him riding a bicycle in a suit and tie, with a football under his arm. 'I've never been happier here than I am now,' he exclaimed.[7] The fact that Ord was gone – but not yet forgotten – might have added to his merriment.

The manager's salary sacrifice idea arose out of a brainstorming chat between Curry and Clough. They needed a gimmick to rocket-boost the public appeal. A football manager giving up his wages might do the trick, and it proved to be the case when lead stories appeared in national newspapers the following morning. He told the *Daily Express* that 'every little helps'. He was prepared to work for nothing until the club stood 'on firmer ground'. His quote for the *Daily Mail* was more personal: 'It will be a rare Christmas for my wife and two kids, but every little gesture will help the club at the moment.' Clough worked without wages for just two weeks.[8]

Instead of drips of rain, money started to fill buckets at the ground. Schoolboys collected enough coins for West Hartlepool's Schools Association to hand over £20. The RAFA Club was donating the cost of a new match ball and holding a fundraising dance at the Owton Manor Community Centre. An anonymous phone call to the ground pledged a £1,000 loan. When Clough called at a local fishmonger's, he was handed both his fish and a £5 donation for the club. Meanwhile, Curry would make a personal appeal to businessmen and promised the club would pay 4 per cent interest on any loans from shops and industry.[9]

By day two, phones at the ground were ringing incessantly and cash from 10s to £70 was raining into the repurposed buckets. Aptly named local butcher Mr Trotter purchased season tickets for the next five seasons at a cost of £32 10s. He worked on Saturdays, so wouldn't be using them, although his gesture would go some way to saving the club's bacon. The club would be asking shops in the town to place collection tins on counters. The initiative came from a young supporter who walked into the Victoria Ground and asked for a tin for the men's outfitters where he worked. An old-age pensioner and lifelong supporter arrived at the ground and handed his pension money to Clough. 'I didn't want to accept it,' said the manager. But accept it he did.[10]

While bailiffs weren't yet knocking, vultures from rival clubs were circling. A Leeds United director on business in the town had alerted Don Revie about McGovern, and the club's scouts were keeping tabs on the youngster. Walsall and Nottingham Forest were watching Drysdale. Both Chester and Colchester had joined Southend in making enquiries about Phythian. Stockport had lost interest in Fogarty, but other unnamed clubs were mulling offers. Meanwhile, Les Green was still at least another fortnight away from a return after injuring his thumb in the season's opening game. An original medical prognosis of three weeks had since turned into three months.[11]

Talking of cash, an approximate £15,000 outlay on players hadn't yet helped Notts County climb higher than fourth-bottom of the Fourth Division. A game there on 19 November was like a reunion of old friends for former County players Bircumshaw and Sheridan, and for Somers (who was born in the city). Another local lad, Peter Taylor, didn't accompany them to Nottingham but went to Peterborough instead to watch forthcoming FA Cup opponents Shrewsbury. He missed little of note at the County Ground. In a game of few chances, both sets of forwards contrived to miss them all and the game ended nil-all.

News of the Save the Club appeal had reached Doncaster. Returning from Nottingham, Clough and three directors went to settle the bill for their post-match meal on the A1, only for the owner to declare, 'Don't bother, it's all on us.' Back in West Hartlepool, businesses had so far contributed £3,000 to the fund. Meanwhile, the club's directors and Ord were struggling to schedule a date to discuss debt repayments to the ex-chairman.[12]

The club and its fans always welcomed a cup run, but desperation for a cash injection was more acute than ever. Taylor explained their approach to the tie and what he'd learned watching Shrewsbury. Their danger man was centre-forward John Manning, a recent £12,000 acquisition. A late Manning goal had helped Tranmere defeat 'Pools 2–0 earlier in the season. Clough & Taylor had spoken to the players for five or six hours that week, their normal approach before games. They'd followed their standard routine of training on the beach and at the ground, plus a leisurely round of golf. But a knee ligament injury to Mick Somers was big new blow. In addition to his attacking prowess, the outside-left performed a key defensive role, particularly away from home.[13]

On the day, Shrewsbury showed too much class and exploited an abundance of chinks and mistakes in their visitors' defence. Danger man Manning scored twice in a 5–2 rout at Gay Meadow. Playing in red shirts and white shorts, Phythian had pulled it back to 3–1. Fogarty retook and scored a penalty to make it 4–2 after toilet rolls arced onto the pitch. Clough had only given his team 'a bare chance' of forcing a replay, and admitted the following day, 'We were shown the door good and sharp.'[14] There'd be no money-spinning FA Cup run. Apart from selling players at knock-down prices, the sole remaining route to filling their financial hole was the Save the Club appeal.

23

LEAD INTO GOLD

J. W. Cameron Brewery of West Hartlepool led the way for local businesses with a novel proposal to sponsor a player's wages for twelve months at a cost of £1,200. The player in question would remain anonymous to avoid undue pressure on him to perform. Chairman and managing director Mr John Cameron made a personal appeal for other local industries to follow suit and sponsor a player.[1] None did.

One big wheel of industry had turned, while many smaller cogs made for a steady stream of callers at the Victoria Ground. Clough said the response was 'wonderful' and 'overwhelming'. He'd never dreamt there was 'so much feeling about the club'.[2] Five schoolgirls from Brierton Hill Technical High School presented the manager with a cheque for money they'd collected from their classmates. 'The cheque was not for an awful lot of money, but they had spent a lot of time collecting it, and we were very grateful,' he said.[3] The Save the Club campaign was for hearts and minds as well as money. Every little boosted morale.

Clough was also grateful to Middlesbrough manager Harold Shepherdson for assistance of a different kind in Hartlepools' hour of need. The neighbouring club agreed to offer their superior facilities for diagnosis and treatment of Mick Somers's injury. 'It's another example of how everyone is prepared to chip in when we are in trouble,' their former centre-forward said.[4]

A boon for their second visit of the season to Bradford Park Avenue was Kevin Hector's absence. Derby County had paid £40,000 for the sharp-shooter a couple of weeks after he'd helped dump 'Pools out of the League Cup. Since then, the West Yorkshire side had only won twice in thirteen games. There were some key personnel changes after the Cup hammering at Shrewsbury. Ken Simpkins lost the no. 1 shirt to the now fit Les Green, his first appearance since the season's opening game. Clough dropped the out-of-form Gill and replaced him with part-timer Bobby McLeod, for only his second first-team start since his February debut. His manager judged he'd improved a lot since then and possessed speed and plenty of courage. Tony Parry replaced Terry Bell at inside-right for his first game in nearly three months.[5]

It had been an up and down week for Ken Simpkins. First a call-up and first cap for the Welsh Under-23s against Scotland in his hometown of Wrexham on Wednesday. And then dropped by his club from its first team on Saturday. His rigid diet plan had worked because he'd plummeted from 16½ to 14 stone. Asked about his successful regime, Ken told the *Mail*: 'I've managed to get my weight down through a combination of extra training, strict dieting and tablets. It's been hard work, but it's been worth it.'

He was full of gratitude as well to Clough & Taylor for helping him with the technical side of goalkeeping, such as positioning.[6] All that effort and a long run in the team only to be dropped as soon as Les Green became fit again. It was hard to take.

On a bone-hard pitch at Park Avenue, two soft goals gave 'Pools both points when they only deserved one. Cliff Wright opened with his second goal of the season, and the other was an own goal. Clough was also over the moon to learn that the club's youth team had recovered from 2–0 down to beat Middlesbrough in the Youth Cup. If they were drawn at home in the third round, he promised they'd play it under the new floodlights. Two pylons at the Greyhound Stadium end had already been erected and they hoped for a pre-Christmas turn-on.[7] In the event, the date was put back to January.

Modest donations continued to boost the Save the Club appeal. In bow tie and tuxedo, Clough attended the annual dinner of the Hartlepools committee of the Industrial Life Offices, where a competition for premium bonds raised £20.[8] A 15-year-old handed him £15 at the ground that he'd raised by organising competitions in local clubs.[9] Supporters at the South Durham Steelworks had a whip-round to buy two new balls at £8 15s apiece.[10] Sunderland Supporters' Association promised to donate one guinea for each point their team gained during their six-match December programme.[11] On the other hand, after writing to local industry leaders and the town's prominent people, Chairman Curry confessed their lack of response was 'disappointing'. He said the greater part of the help had come from people who could least afford it.[12]

December was another action-packed month for the club and its team. Simpkins showed his disappointment at being dropped by slapping in a transfer request. He was keen to stress that he'd always been well treated at the club and there was no friction of any sort. Clough travelled 180 miles in the cold to lace up his boots for forty-five minutes in a friendly at Burton Albion, the first time he'd played a game since his testimonial. He'd been keeping up his football fitness by training with the players three times a week.[13]

Three weeks after the big boardroom bust-up, Ord was acting and sounding far more conciliatory. He would neither be pressing so urgently for the cash owed him or withdrawing his bank guarantee. The ex-chairman also pointed out that he owned £6,000 in shares and two club houses on the Fens Estate. Furthermore, he recognised that the club appeal was not meeting with the response expected (he presumably meant from businesses, not individuals).[14]

According to Taylor, Ernie Ord rolled up at the front door of the Fens Estate home he was renting to him. 'I've come to give you a warning. Your mate has finished me and one day he'll do the same to you.' It was the last time they ever saw each other.[15] The Taylor family later moved out to live in Amby Fogarty's former home in Seaton Carew.

Following a run of three away games, a run of three at home beckoned, the first against Port Vale. In a shivering wind, Wright cracked in an opener on just 30 seconds. On 30 minutes, Phythian raced in with perfect timing to head home a Sheridan cross. Jack Fletcher defined his fluid movement and classy goal as 'poetic beauty'. Somers made a fine return from injury, only to limp off on the hour mark. While Clough was disappointed with his team's performance and late capitulation, he was happy with the 2-1 win. The boss affirmed the 'confidence booster' would spread 'right through the club, crowd-wise and player-wise'. And just when they needed it.[16]

Somers headed to Middlesbrough again for further treatment on his damaged knee ligaments.[17] Clough's contacts had him up at Roker Park for a second opinion a week later. He left Sunderland with his leg in plaster.[18]

Fans were suffering from vertigo after two wins had shot the team up to an unfamiliar eighth position. It promised to be their best Christmas position since 1957. For the first time in years, they were entering the festive period looking above them in the table and not at the trapdoor below.

Clough judged it prudent to manage supporters' expectations again and offer an incentive to the faithful. He thus rated their promotion chances as 'fairly remote'. The players were producing maximum effort, but the team was 'a little short' in terms of going up. As for the fans: 'If they help us to get some cash to buy the player I want I will guarantee promotion this season. But at the moment I can only hope.'[19] With everybody pulling together, promotion was possible. Rattle your collection tins and you might begin to sniff it.

Clough and Curry were certainly doing their bit, for the club's finances and for the fans, through improving comfort levels at the ground. As well as the floodlight pylons that were literally rising on the horizon, Rink End supporters could look forward to dry and rust-free afternoons. The leaky colander of a roof was going to be scrapped for a new one. As it stood, water streamed through its holes in rivulets when it rained. The club had obtained a discounted price for roof panels from a local building company and knew it could count on its loyal band of volunteers to help fix them on.[20]

A week after his bid to rouse the fans, a few complained he was knocking their enthusiasm after some good results. But Clough was having none of it. He was simply 'facing the situation realistically'. It was opinion based on judgement, and that's what the club paid him for. The current team had got them this far, but they had to face facts. One or two extra players could make all the difference, but the money wasn't there. Curry reminded fans that the financial position was still 'precarious'. With Christmas approaching, one fan criticised 'the Scrooge-like attitude of the town's industrialists and businessmen'.[21]

There was evidently something in the dressing room air beyond liniment, sweat and tobacco smoke, because 'Pools scored on 30 seconds for the second game running. Drysdale began the move, Fogarty continued the lightning break, and Mulvaney sealed it from close range. Wright followed up with his third in three games, and Mulvaney added his second on 82 minutes. There were some late scares, but they shot down Aldershot 3–2 to rise another two places to sixth in the table. The 5,161 attendance was a tad disappointing, but there were always Saturday distractions ahead of Christmas.[22]

Clough gave 95 per cent of the credit to the players. That just left 5 per cent for him and Taylor. Their league position was 'a tribute to the lads' and he gave them Monday off for the first time that season. He was glad they'd get their bonus money before Christmas because they'd earned it. The manager was still not changing his mind about needing another player or two, though.[23] And he wanted to see 8,000 in the ground on Boxing Day.[24]

The *Northern Daily Mail* pledged to pay match fees for referees and linesmen for the season's remaining thirteen league games. The Hartlepools Divisional Police Sports and Social Club donated £50. Chairman Curry repeated his call to industrialists to come and discuss with him ways and means to help the club 'out of the red'.[25] With their headmaster's permission, two boys at Horden Day School collected £3 10s for the Save the Club appeal.[26] Clough & Taylor presented a 12-year-old schoolboy with a signed football at West Hartlepool Odeon, donated by the cinema. It was the youngster's bad luck that his parents kept him too busy on Saturday afternoons to attend any games. While Clough was sorry to lose a supporter, he wished there were more like him to help out with the housework.[27]

The multitasking manager was at the Victoria Ground on 21 December to help workmen unload asbestos sheets for the new Rink End roof. It was hoped most of it would be fixed and ready for their final winter game without floodlights – Brentford's visit on Boxing Day (kick-off 2.15 p.m.).[28]

The Rift House Social Club gave the club an early Christmas present of £120 in six monthly instalments. Clough attended alongside Curry and called the gesture 'fantastic'. And he 'meant it'. 'I simply went in, talked to the committee for 15 minutes, they discussed what I had said, and within ten minutes offered us £120.' Although volunteers had come forward to help fit the new Rink End roof, they now had the money to pay workmen and complete the task immediately.[29]

Mrs Barbara Clough wasn't seeing much of her husband at home, and neither were their two boys. Brian was leaving home in the morning and only catching the TV epilogue last thing at night. In the five days leading up to Christmas, he calculated that he'd seen his kids for a total of one hour and ruined a meal a day for the previous month. He'd been speaking practically every evening since the launch of the appeal in pubs, social clubs, working men's clubs, at dinners, at meetings. Brian said Barbara 'was not very pleased about it'. She was reluctant to comment but did admit to speaking her mind. After all, she'd been doing most of the listening now 'for seven and a half years'.[30]

Away games were a blessing, Barbara said, because at least she knew he'd be eating a square meal. Meanwhile, her hard-working husband admitted, 'I'll have to get my priorities right. It's stupid to go on like this. It's not fair to my wife and children.'[31] With a busy seasonal programme of fixtures ahead, Christmas would provide little respite.

The local fundraising circuit was relentless. Clough had visited several clubs already but intended 'to go round every one and talk'. It would take some time, he said, but if they allowed him to outline his plan for a few minutes, he was sure they'd be ready to help. The social clubs were helping Hartlepools United to its feet, and the football club would pay them back 'where it matters', i.e. on the field.[32]

Curry said he and his manager would sup half-pints outside social club committee rooms, as they awaited permission for Clough to step on stage and seduce their members with his silver tongue. The manager relished it, but returned home exhausted. In an area of high unemployment, Clough said it warmed 'the cockles of your heart' to see loyal people contribute money to a football club they considered their 'little oasis'.[33]

If fans knew about the Cloughs' sacrifices, and had read about the ground improvements, they'd surely be grateful. One wrote to the *Mail* to complain about the loudspeaker system. Announcements were impossible to comprehend, although they could just make out the pop music. Would a live brass band not be better, with local colliery bands happy to oblige? Another supporter pined for blue-and-white striped shirts instead of the 'miserable-looking' plain blue. There was no pleasing everyone, but a lone voice did give Brian Clough 'a pat on the back' for rocketing the team up the table.[34]

Clough & Taylor arrived at East Herrington half an hour late on Christmas Eve to watch their Reserve team take on Sunderland Structural Steel. Clough's half-time pep talk worked because Tony Parry scored after the break to cement their place at the top of the Wearside League.[35]

Christmas on the A1 and M1 was not everybody's idea of festive fun, but that was how Brentford and Hartlepools United were going to spend theirs. The Football League fixture boffins had presented them with two games against each other on successive days.

Amby Fogarty joined Somers in plaster following a training injury, giving Clough & Taylor a further selection headache. They tried to solve the thorny wing-half issue by bidding for Hull City left-half Norman Corner, originally from Horden in County Durham. After a week of secret negotiations, the clubs agreed on a price for the transfer-listed player, only for the Hull boss to turn it down. 'I was more than disappointed at not getting Corner. I was amazed,' admitted Clough. Now they had no option but to move high-scoring Ernie Phythian into defence.[36]

At the same time, Clough was deflecting interest from First Division clubs in John McGovern. Arsenal boss Bertie Mee had watched him at the Aldershot game. Wolves were also hovering. There had been no bids for the youngster yet, and he'd have preferred the news not to come out, but Clough was sure he could 'sell him tomorrow if he wanted'. He didn't want to, although it would be 'a different story' when the player 'realized his potential' in the next twelve months.[37]

Brentford set off for the North East by coach at 4 a.m. on Boxing Day. The 8,421 crowd, the highest of the season so far, saw 'Pools trail 2–0 after a lethargic first-half performance. Phythian moved from left-half to his customary centre-forward position at half-time. He soon won and converted a penalty. In a fierce second-half comeback, Livingstone sealed a 2–2 draw in his first game for three months.[38]

Their team coach departed at 8.30 a.m. the next morning for their 7.30 p.m. evening fixture in West London, making a vital stop on the way. Five hours ahead of his debut, 6ft 1½in centre-half Stan Aston was waiting at an M1 motorway café to meet his new teammates and sign from Burton Albion.

The 26-year-old immediately replaced Gill in central defence. Tony Parry filled in for Phythian at wing-half. They were far the superior side for most of the game, with 'perpetual motion' John Sheridan at the centre of everything. After falling behind in the second half, Phythian equalised on 76 minutes and his 'beautiful low drive' from outside the penalty area on 85 sent them back up the motorway in buoyant mood. Clough judged it their best performance of the season. Only the heroics of Brentford's teenage goalkeeper prevented a bigger win. After arriving home at 4 a.m., the manager gave himself his first day off in months. 'I think I deserve it,' he said.[39] His team were now sitting pretty in the top four of the Fourth Division.

With excitement building and demand rising at the halfway point of the season, Chairman Curry offered half-price season tickets to fans at a cost of 45*s* and 65*s*. Pensioners had already snapped up an offer of discounted tickets within an hour of them going on sale. Some incapacitated pensioners had lost out on the 'first-come first-served' offer, so the club would draw names from a hat next time round. Collection boxes were being returned and the Save the Club appeal had reached £7,000, with coins still being counted. A local department store was spending £50 on a new strip for the club, although there was no word whether it'd be any more exciting than dull-as-dishwater plain blue.[40]

Four days later, they visited the team they'd just replaced in the final promotion spot. The division's top-scorer Ernie Phythian (seventeen goals) was returning to his old club Wrexham, unbeaten at home that season. Unfortunately for their North-East visitors, the Welshmen would remain unbeaten.

Mulvaney scored an early New Year's Eve opener on 6 minutes, only for Wrexham to equalise 12 minutes later. But the Welshmen ploughed ahead with three goals in twelve second-half minutes on a heavy and draining pitch. The visiting defence cracked, with Parry undergoing a particularly 'unhappy experience'. Taylor thought they'd 'done enough to win', and Clough was 'pleased' with how the team played. They'd been well on top in the first half.[41] You can't win 'em all, and it was only their first defeat in eight matches.

Considering their plight twelve months earlier, when their chairman had walked out again with the team next-to-bottom of the Fourth Division, 1966 had not turned out too badly. Sentinel stole a soundbite from former prime minister Harold Macmillan and wrote in his Annual Review that the fans had 'never had it so good'. They could now stand under a leakproof roof and were about to watch football under lights. He paid tribute to Clough's 'leadership', Taylor's 'experience and hard work', and the 'magnificent graft' of the team. 'If everyone had increased their productivity as much as my players, the country wouldn't be in the financial mess it's in now,' the manager said in reference to Harold Wilson's Labour government. Sentinel judged there was still a long haul to reach 'solvency and success', but with Clough & Taylor now toiling under Curry, the club was on the right track. Clough confessed they didn't have the strength in depth to be optimistic about promotion. 'I'd be delighted to be proved wrong, but I KNOW that I'm right.'[42] The declaration encapsulated his whole management career.

24

LET THERE BE LIGHT

'Then God said, "Let there be light!" And there was light.'

(Genesis 1:3–27)

Floodlight installation – like pitch laying – is normally carried out during the summer close season. But this wasn't the case at Hartlepools United, where a clock was ticking on the towns' amalgamation. Winter weather hindered engineers from the start, and there were other snags and delays. Test bore holes in all four corners of the ground found suspect sub-soil, so foundations were dug deeper than planned. Sections of both the Town and Rink End roofs had to be dismantled and reassembled to manoeuvre the 100ft pylons into position. Winds were so strong they blew out torch cutters over several days and delayed the six-strong gang of steel erectors. Some concrete for the pylon bases had to be diverted to build an access road across steep and muddy ground behind the Rink End. Wiring the floodlights took place in bitterly cold December weather, 80ft up in the air. To play matches in the dark, new lighting was required over turnstiles, in the main stand, and under covered terrace roofs. In total, half a mile of electric cable was laid.[1]

After surmounting all difficulties, the Victoria Ground boasted the same floodlights as Wembley. All four pylon nests carried twenty-four lights, each of 1,500 watts. They were sufficient to light 1,000 living rooms.[2] If Blackpool had the Illuminations, the Hartlepools now had state-of-the-art floodlights. Heavens above.

Clough continued to manage expectations and praise the team's achievements. Although the lads were good enough for promotion, he said, there was no flexibility in such a small squad to cover for injured and out-of-form players. He'd been lucky because McGovern and Wright had hit rich veins of form, but there was no use kidding anyone. Something was bound to crack, as it already had. Due to limitations, he'd been forced into the 'ridiculous' fudge of playing their leading scorer at left-half in place of the injured Amby Fogarty. Tony Parry had filled in well in the game at Brentford, but Clough couldn't play him there at home. The manager accused 'stupid individuals' at the Victoria Ground crowd of 'getting at' Parry. It had affected the 21-year-old so much that he couldn't play a normal game. But he was a different player away from home, where he was free to express himself.[3]

Having said that, Parry had a stinker at Wrexham in the final game of 1966. Newspaper reports didn't mention it by name, but there was surely a racist element to some of this barracking. In the context of the time, when there were precious few non-white players in professional football, black players like Tony Parry suffered repulsive racial abuse from the terraces on a regular basis.

Given the Christmas period selection difficulties, Clough announced he was prepared to gamble on success. The directors were prepared to 'gamble' on his judgement and would put their trust in him by signing new players. If his instinct was wrong, they'd all be for the high jump, because they were 'mortgaging' the club's future. Sentinel estimated that the board had made around £4,000 to £5,000 available. What would make all the difference in the world would be gates of 8,000+, as they'd enjoyed on Boxing Day. They could then pay their own way and have some spare for new players.[4] The supporters had been told, once again.

Echoing Ord's earlier assertion, a fan agreed that Clough's potential was so 'limitless' that he was bound to be snapped up by a First or Second Division club. He was another to suggest they swap the 'drab outfits of today' for the striped shirts of yesteryear.[5]

With both teams' interest in the FA Cup having ended, and a free weekend in prospect, Friday-night specialists Southend had agreed to bring forward their April visit. They'd suffered their first ever relegation at the end of the 1965/66 season under Alvan Williams and arrived in the North East sitting eighth.

The first Victoria Ground spectacle under lights was set for Friday, 6 January 1967 at 7.15 p.m. Curry and Clough hoped for a bumper gate to surpass Boxing Day's turnout. Despite a frost-bound and snow-covered pitch, the referee's 10.45 a.m. inspection deemed conditions playable. Helpers applied tons of sand to the ice-covered terraces, and sprinkled salt on parts not covered by snow. Southend's midday train departure from London King's Cross was given a green signal.[6]

In his programme notes, Clough hoped that fans were as excited as he and the club were about the new lights. They'd now be experimenting with later kick-offs on Saturdays as well as Friday evening games to judge crowd levels.

The club aimed 'to go places', so the 'cynics' should sit up and recognise their progress. They still had a long way to go, but they were 'on the road' and 'travelling'.[7] Enjoy the ride, good people of the Hartlepools.

Maybe it was the sense of occasion. It might have been the skating-rink of a pitch, or the polar weather. Perhaps the stars and light got in their eyes. Clough surely regretted listening to fans and reverting to striped shirts.

There was no doubt Southend handled the conditions better, particularly 'on the ice-flow that was mid-field'. Sentinel saw that 'webbed feet' were required, although the visitors adapted just fine. While Somers ran and chased shadows all evening, he was not the answer to the wing-half quandary. Young McGovern never got in the game.[8] At least Phythian scored a late consolation in the 2–1 defeat. And 9,586 hardy souls turned out to watch the chilly pantomime, a combination of *Dancing on Ice* and *Football under the Stars*. There was no fairy-tale ending, and only a power cut could have saved them on a night when they didn't shine as brightly as their new lights.

When it came to Friday night football, there was no pleasing everyone. Clough had tried, learned his lesson, and consigned the striped shirts to training clobber.

Indeed, life was simpler at the Victoria Ground in the days before floodlit football. By day, fans could spot the deep mud and puddles when approaching and leaving the Mill House side. By night, wellington boots were required.[9] To make way for a pylon in one corner, the ground's only tea hut had been demolished. Working down the pit five days a week meant Friday night games were a no-go for many colliery village fans.[10] There was the old chestnut about men using Saturday afternoon football to miss shopping with their other halves. And what about the cash-starved club's soaring leccy bill?

With promotion hopes slightly dented, the board met to decide McGovern's fate. Sheffield Wednesday and Middlesbrough had joined Arsenal and Wolves in the queue of interested clubs. Directors would demand £10,000 and use the cash in an 'all-out bid' to get into the Third Division. Clough had a wing-half and an inside-forward lined up. If the money was right, he said, 'we won't stand in the boy's way'.[11] At the same time, Tranmere were 'interested' in the division's top scorer on eighteen goals: Ernie Phythian. Southend soon renewed their interest as well with a further offer.

Clough was putting McGovern through his paces on Middleton Beach as Curry announced they'd demanded £10,000 from Arsenal and Wolves for the youngster. Bertie Mee declared he was 'very much interested' in the 17-year-old but would not be drawn into an auction. Rather than plugging a financial hole, Curry insisted it was all about his playing career and making good on promises made to him and his mother.[12] The transfer didn't proceed because Arsenal only offered £7,500 and Wolves £6,000.[13]

Clough didn't play him in the FA Youth Cup third-round tie against Sunderland, and neither did Ian McColl deploy his promising wing-half Colin Todd. Both first-team managers needed their young assets fresh and fit for weekend games.[14] Sunderland won 3–1 in front of 2,313 spectators. The Wearside team went on to reach the final of the competition, where they beat Birmingham City.

Hartlepools' own poor finishing (again), and 'cast-offs' Barry Ashworth and Stan Storton, led to a horror-filled evening outing at Tranmere's Prenton Park on Friday, 13th January. Although Parry and Sheridan impressed in midfield, their forwards misfired. The home defence, with 18-year-old Roy McFarland at its heart, repelled everything thrown at it. Ashworth set up the hosts' first goal. Storton started their second with a short pass to Ashworth outside the box. Without looking, he lobbed Green with an overhead wonder-strike that tickled his fingers as both goalkeeper and ball arched into the net.[15] From rising to fourth in the table after four wins from five games in December, they'd lost three games in a row to slip to eighth in the Fourth Division.

There was little time to dwell because they hosted Sunderland three nights later for the second time in a week, although it was their first team on this occasion. At least that was the plan, for the official inauguration of the floodlights. But after ending their Saturday clash at Chelsea with eight casualties, manager Ian McColl forewarned Clough about his understrength first XI. The Hartlepools manager flew into such a rage that he considered cancelling the whole thing. After telling McColl to stuff it, he engaged in some 'swift thinking'. As he explained to the *Mail*: 'There was only one person in the whole of Britain that I knew would help me if he could … but it was what the racing men would call a 500–1 chance.'[16]

Although the person in question had given his players the day off, he rang around and discovered they were only too happy to help. With little more than twenty-four hours' notice, Sheffield Wednesday manager Alan Brown brought an almost full-strength first team to the Victoria Ground. Clough explained:

> The switching on of the lights may not mean a lot to some people, but to me, the directors, the players, and most important of all, the supporters, it's the biggest thing that has ever happened to football here.[17]

He was gilding the lily slightly. The FA Cup visit of Matt Busby's Manchester United in January 1957 surely outdid it. McColl appreciated Clough's position but said his first responsibility was to his own club. He'd only promised to send 'a team', not 'the first team'.[18]

Clough's programme notes exaggerated the perceived affront to Hartlepools United: 'The match would have been cancelled before subjecting you, the supporters to a Sunderland Reserve side after promising a game with their first eleven.'[19] Suffice it to say, Clough's relationship with the club where his playing career ended, and with its manager who'd let him go as youth team manager, was singed with molten-hot resentment. His former commanding officer at Sunderland, on the other hand, was a living legend. Brown's star ascended even further when he donated a set of training kit after the game. Notwithstanding that gesture, he merely asked his hosts to cover the cost of hiring a coach and their meal. Hartlepools' directors reciprocated by insisting on a small payment to the Wednesday players.[20]

It was no exhibition game of 'airy-fairy, tip-tapping frivolity', but rather a 'hard and fast' action-packed game to warm up the 6,421 spectators. Phythian's last-gasp deflected equaliser ended the game 3–3 and sent scores of young fans streaming onto the pitch. Given the occasion, Clough refrained from booting any of them up the backside.[21]

He had the TV cameras at the ground again for the visit of mid-table Bradford City on 21 January, kick-off 3 p.m. His programme notes contained some stern words. He was 'absolutely amazed and disgusted' at the isolated bursts of criticism aimed at new centre-half Stan Aston. How fans could judge him based on one game left him 'speechless'. He predicted he'd be 'the best centre-half in the league' with more weeks of full-time training, and warned: 'What I would like to say to all our Supporters is that "the lads" rely so much on encouragement and without your support, the achievement will be limited.'[22]

The message was clear. Button it, unless you had something positive to say.

Bell replaced Parry. McGovern was on the bench with flu. Simpkins kept his place after replacing the injured Green twenty minutes into the Sheffield Wednesday game. Back in blue again and under lights in the second half, they just about deserved the victory, sealed on 77 minutes when Phythian (again) hooked in a crossbar rebound after a Drysdale cross.[23] They'd broken their losing streak.

Amid rumours about renewed Arsenal interest in McGovern, Southend raised their £6,000 offer for Phythian to £8,000. This emboldened Curry and his fellow directors to reaffirm their confidence in Clough & Taylor by offering the centre-forward a new contract. Why break up a winning team with a fighting chance of promotion?[24]

After signing it, Ernie penned a column in the *Mail* to praise the 'tremendous, infectious spirit' and 'complete harmony' at the club. Thanks to the happy trio of Clough, Taylor and Curry, no 'stormy financial' troubles had entered the dressing room, he wrote, and he thanked the fans for sticking with them 'when the tide was against us'.[25]

They followed their Bradford win with a floodlit Monday night home victory over Chester. Still playing in blue, Phythian opened the scoring with a deft chip, a Wright 25-yard rocket put them ahead again after an equaliser, and Mulvaney headed in another to seal a 3–2 win.[26]

The team had risen to seventh in the table. A cheeky fan wrote in to suggest blaring out the new no.1 hit 'I'm a Believer' by The Monkees over the Vic's loudspeakers.[27] Before Clough & Taylor's arrival, fans thought promotion was only true in fairy tales.

Injury news was mixed. Fogarty had played his first full game in more than a month, but Clough accompanied Somers to Sunderland Accident Hospital for a cartilage operation. The skilful winger would be out of action for at least five weeks.[28] Fan opinion continued to be divided over Green or Simpkins for the goalkeeper's jersey. After an impressive return between the sticks, Clough had favoured Simpkins over fit-again Green for the first time that season. With Grimsby watching Simpkins, Green was struck down with tonsillitis.

Promotion was on people's lips and on bookmakers' boards. Oddly, one turf accountant had 'Pools at 8–1 to go up and another at 3–1. Even Clough saw grounds for optimism. He pointed out that fourteen of their seventeen remaining matches were against teams below them in the table, although that was hardly a surprise given their lofty league position.[29]

Hartlepools' team coach departed at 8 a.m. on a Friday for an overnight stay at Taunton ahead of their 4 February game at Exeter City. The Grecians awaited their first win of 1967. 'Pools discarded their defensive policy after conceding from a 34th-minute corner, but all-out attack in the second half couldn't beat inspired home 'keeper John Smout.[30] Despite throwing everything at him except the kitchen sink, Exeter survived and grabbed both points on a wing and a prayer.[31] A month later, an FA Disciplinary Committee found Peter Taylor guilty of showing dissent after the match. Its sanction was a written undertaking by the assistant manager not to repeat his 'ungentlemanly conduct'.[32]

Amby Fogarty had aggravated his ankle injury early on at Exeter. Terry Bell had replaced him at half-time and kept his place for their next game at high-flying Crewe. Clough axed Tony Bircumshaw and John Gill and replaced them with Brian Grant (without a game since September) and

Bobby McLeod (for his first game in two months). Tony Parry also returned to the side. Sentinel was gushing in his praise for Hartlepools' victory, defining it as 'a glorious illustration of harmony and planning between manager and team'. The Railmen had taken thirteen points from their previous seven league games yet were handed their first home defeat since mid-September. There were particularly impressive performances from Aston, Parry and Simpkins. Mulvaney put his team ahead after the break with a banana slice from an acute byline angle, while Wright struck with 'coolness and aplomb'. Crewe converted a late and dubious penalty consolation, but the game ended in a very well-deserved away victory.[33]

Furthermore, the team had foregone an overnight stay to complete all their travel in one day, leaving on Saturday morning and returning straight after the game. Players had spent ten out of fourteen hours sat on a coach to assist the club's money-saving efforts.[34] And despite the hardship, they'd cruised home with both points.

Big and short competition for the no. 1 jersey led to Green joining Simpkins on the transfer list. After recovering from his opening game injury, he'd never regained the brilliant form of the 1965/66 season. He'd returned to the first team only to lose his spot to Simpkins, who was now performing heroics. Green had become disillusioned with Wearside League football and wanted out. 'Pools were not going to sell both men and leave themselves without an experienced goal-stopper. Curry understood Green's frustrations, and said it was simply a case of accepting whichever offer came in first.[35]

The only change for Barnsley's visit to the Vic was McGovern coming in for Parry. Peter Taylor had seen their visitors beat Bradford PA 3–1 that week and predicted it would be 'a tough one', given their great improvement during the season. In a dull game dominated by both defences, Barnsley scored first on 30 minutes. Terry Bell equalised five minutes later with a glorious right-foot half-volley, his first ever league goal. McGovern scarcely got into the game, while Phythian missed a winner when it was easier to score just ninety seconds from the end.[36]

No business had joined Cameron's Brewery in sponsoring a player's wages as part of the Save the Club campaign, but a collective of local social clubs hoped to buy one instead. Players were helping out off the field by making one or two evening appearances a week. They'd attended a fundraising concert at the R.A.O.B. club and had visited the Rovers Quoit Club and the Owton Manor Club. Ernie Phythian said they played darts, snooker and dominoes or cards with the locals. It helped raise cash and got the fans right behind them. Clough thought the new player sponsorship was a great initiative: 'I'm hoping that it catches on among a few other organizations because I'd be over the moon if they could get together and buy me a wing-half!'[37] The wing-half problem had never gone away.

Even silver-tongued public speaker Brian Clough could not get everybody aboard the Save the Club campaign. 'Some people told me to take a running jump into the North Sea. And if Hartlepool went under, too, they couldn't care less,' he wrote later.[38] One evening, the self-declared Socialist became mired in a ninety-minute political argument with a hostile eight-man reception committee. They refused to deal with 'Tory' directors. Chairman Curry was, of course, a Conservative councillor. Clough proclaimed, 'I'm as red as any of you,' and managed to extract a few bob.[39]

Unable to obtain a wing-half, he bought an inside-forward instead. Albert Broadbent had previously terrorised Clough & Taylor's defenders alongside Kevin Hector, but Clough now travelled to Bradford to snap him up for £3,000.

It appeared odd that the confessedly cash-strapped club was spending money on players. As Clough explained: 'We can't afford him but this is an act of faith. Because of the way supporters have been rallying round the board gave me the go ahead. The chairman has been pushing for it just as much as I have.' They hadn't signed Broadbent to score goals, but to create them, as a link man between midfield and attack.[40]

His signing was a deliberate gamble to bring success on the pitch and attract more income through the turnstiles. Clough dismissed as 'nonsense' any talk that Albert was over the hill at 31. Whether '21 or 41', if a player could do the job asked of him, he was 'good enough'. The experience he'd bring to his young side would also help, and the chance was worth taking:

> I want promotion badly, so do the players. Our immediate problem here is survival. If we are successful then it will become easier to survive. Then we can start thinking about the problems that success brings.[41]

Survival the previous season had meant league survival, i.e. avoiding re-election. The fight this season was for financial survival. The Clough-Taylor-Curry trio were going gung-ho for promotion, with a gaping hole at wing-half. They had a transfer target and it was still Norman Corner, according to Sentinel. Clough said he'd sign the man in question if he became available. And he was bold about what he'd promise if it all went to plan: 'I will be prepared to put my head on the chopping block and state that we will be promoted.'[42] They'd already spent beyond their means to get Broadbent. If they went one further with Norman Corner, would the double gamble pay off?

Broadbent came straight in for Bell for their home encounter with bottom-of-the league York City. Yet it was Mulvaney who grabbed the headlines. Sporting a new all-blue strip, Jack Fletcher described jumping Jim, 'proud as a peacock, leaping with his right arm aloft to acknowledge the crowd's ovation for his hat-trick'. His first was a chip over the goalkeeper on 3 minutes. Overall, however, the team put in an 'indifferent performance'. And despite the 4–2 victory, Fletcher reported how the fans were still 'grumbling' at the final whistle. Indeed, 'they were hard at it' as he left the press box. Clough appeared to agree with them, but perhaps for different reasons. 'I wasn't at all happy with the defence. I didn't get what I expected from the wing halves.' But he was satisfied with Broadbent's performance, and believed he'd make all the difference away from home.[43]

25

DRIVE MY CAR

Norman Corner travelled to the Victoria Ground with his boots on 1 March, only to withdraw from Ambrose Fogarty's testimonial due to a last-minute hitch. Lacking insurance cover, Hull City barred him from taking part, and he watched the game from the main stand.[1] It was as close as Corner ever came to playing for Hartlepools. After Hull rejected yet another bid for him later the same week, Clough said it was pointless looking further afield. There were no wing-halves available at a price he could afford.[2]

For months, Amby had been trying to assemble a roll call of stars for his testimonial against a Charley Hurley XI. One crowd-puller he failed to attract was recent retiree (at 50) Sir Stanley Matthews, now general manager at Port Vale. Chelsea's Tony Hateley was a no-show on the day. Manchester City's ex-Sunderland inside-forward Johnny Crossan (injured) and Mike Summerbee were announced but didn't play. Other ex-Sunderland teammates of Amby's who did turn out in Hurley's team were Len Ashurst, Jimmy McNab and George Mulhall. Another one, Brian Clough, played alongside Fogarty before the break. Hartlepools director Bert Young, 57 years old, replaced him for the second half.[3]

Clough decided that a few of his players needed a rest for their visit to Lincoln City, but dropping Drysdale and Simpkins was a shock. Particularly the dependable Drysdale, a former Lincoln player.[4] Recalling Green was also a surprise, given he'd fined him £10 the previous Monday after reporting late for training. It wasn't like Clough to punish 'a breach of discipline' by recalling a player.[5] Lincoln avenged their 5–0 stuffing in October by defeating their visitors 3–0 at Sincil Bank. With their sights on a draw, 'Pools adopted 'a dour defensive set-up' but conceded twice just before the break and were largely 'ineffective'. Forwards Phythian and Mulvaney ran their socks off in the second half, Broadbent conjured some moments of good play, but it was all to no avail.[6]

'We have burnt our boats by signing Broadbent,' Curry told Sentinel. The club was 'near the breadline', and the proof came the following weekend.[7] They'd saved money on hotels for the Crewe game, as they had at Southend earlier in the season. But coaches still cost money. The journey to Lincoln and back had cost the club £50 all in, but they planned a more economical mode of transport to Barnsley. Clough explained, 'I know it may sound ridiculous, but it's not a gimmick. Our position is so desperate that we must save every penny we can.' They'd worked out they could save up to £35 by travelling less luxuriously, but it meant no card games for the players. Like a Sunday pub team, they travelled to Barnsley in a convoy of four cars, with the club covering petrol. Clough, Taylor, Curry and a friend drove their vehicles the two and a half hours each way. Thankfully, a fire engine narrowly avoided wiping out half the defence at a roundabout near Pontefract.

Clough explained:

The players accepted it because they have to. But I must add they have been wonderful. They have been subjected to a lot of pressure this season, and to a lot of tiring overnight trips simply because we can't afford hotel bills. Yet they've never cribbed or complained about it once.[8]

It didn't sound as if they had much choice.

Players packed into cars included the recalled Drysdale and McLeod, but squeezed out were the injured Fogarty and Sheridan. Parry and McGovern also had lifts to South Yorkshire. Hardship seemed to spur them on, including the strong wind in their faces in the first half and the heavy snowstorm five minutes into the game. Abandoning their normal defensive system and playing 4-2-4, Phythian crashed them into the lead from 18 yards on 20 minutes. Their hosts equalised before half-time, but Phythian flicked a second past the goalkeeper from a fine Broadbent pass to slam the car door shut on Barnsley.[9] Beep beep. Their extra win bonus was a fish-and-chips stop at Thirsk on the way home.[10]

Fogarty's contract, due to expire in June, was cancelled by mutual agreement. Dogged by a foot injury for months, and the club's highest-paid player, the decision made perfect sense all round.[11]

At 8 p.m. the following Friday, transfer deadline day, Clough made yet another effort to sign Norman Corner. He was more than prepared to travel with Peter Taylor to Hull for his signature, but they needn't bother. Manager Cliff Britton was still refusing to play ball.[12]

Ernie Phythian had endured a five-game barren spell before Barnsley but bagged another brace at home to Chesterfield. The Tyne Tees cameras were at the Victoria Ground for the third time that season to record it all. Hartlepools' fresh 4-2-4 system allowed Parry to thrive again in a freer midfield role alongside Broadbent. Aston enjoyed another outstanding game. Mulvaney repeated his now customary trick of scoring early, although this time he waited a whole eight minutes. Jimmy and Ernie were turning into a cape-less dynamic duo, with sixteen and twenty-four goals respectively.[13]

The 3–2 result flattered the visitors but didn't amuse Brian Clough. 'You can't afford to rest on your laurels. I was disappointed at the way we failed to sew it up.' They'd been coasting 3–0 with seven minutes to go, but two quick-fire goals in a minute meant Chesterfield's 'corpse had risen', although 'Pools held on for victory. Despite one of his best home displays yet, Tony Parry still had his 'knockers'.[14] Another disappointment was the 5,602 crowd.

Now sixth in the table, the economy drive continued over the Easter bank holiday weekend with three games in four days, two of them away from home. While they left the cars at home this time, there were no hotel stays for the games at Chester and Luton. Just two very early starts, two late returns, and 800 miles on Britain's A-roads, B-roads and motorways. They hosted Luton on Good Friday, departed the following morning at 7 a.m. for Chester, and arrived home at 10 p.m. on Saturday night. It was another dawn start and long round trip on Easter Monday for their return fixture at Luton.[15]

In normal times, they'd have expected to stay in a hotel in Manchester on Friday night, another in Chester on Saturday, plus a further overnight stay near London on Monday. But they couldn't afford such a round trip in their present bind, so it was 'ridiculous' to even think about it. 'We've got to do it our way,' Clough affirmed. Not Sinatra's way, but the cheap way. Hard times meant nine hours sitting on a coach on Saturday, plus a further eleven on Monday.[16]

Their win-win-win Easter in 1966 had saved their dodgy season twelve months earlier. Three bank holiday games in 1967 would either maintain their promotion push or snuff it out. They'd only lost once in the last six games, but needed a minimum of four out of six maximum points to maintain any hope of a top-four finish.

News about their travelling arrangements drew sympathy and some welcome cash. Local coach firm Richardsons of West Hartlepool donated £25, and the Bourne Hotel £20. Gold Case Travel Ltd, the company providing their coach, didn't charge them for the Monday trip to Luton and back. Such generosity meant practically all travelling expenses were covered.[17]

The dynamic duo struck again with a goal apiece at home to Luton, although Mulvaney missed a bagful before finally finding the net. Phythian struck first with a 57th-minute penalty after McGovern was brought down bursting into the box. Broadbent and Parry bossed midfield again in a wind-swept game watched by 8,442 fans.[18] Hartlepools' third successive victory kept them in sixth spot.

High wind and a rock-hard surface at Sealand Road made the ball behave like a yo-yo, but it was Chester who scored the game's only goal. The visitors' forward line performed raggedly, with Mulvaney lofting over an excellent second-half opportunity from a few yards out. They thought they'd equalised when Aston netted with his knee, only for referee Jim Finney to blow for a dubious Phythian handball.[19] Considering Chester's lowly position, it was a disappointing defeat.

They redeemed themselves against Luton at Kenilworth Road by domi-nating the game and scoring twice, although they should have netted more. The big surprise was that neither Jimmy nor Ernie increased their goals tally after squandering chance after chance. Tony Parry scored with a 20-yard half-volley on 23 minutes, and John McGovern's low drive into the bottom corner marked his first ever league goal. It was a great way to end the tough weekend. Broadbent and Parry shone again in midfield, while Mick Somers's return from injury was another cause for celebration.[20] With four points from six, they interrupted their weekend coach tour of Britain by taking in the Notts Forest v Burnley game on the way home. After all their exertions and priva-tions, Clough rewarded his players with a two-day rest.[21]

Both goalkeepers hit the front page of the *Mail* on 1 April, but it was no April Fool's joke. Clough had set the ball rolling when he dropped Green and recalled Simpkins and refused to say why. He simply announced that Green had 'not been considered for either team'.[22] He only partially cleared up the matter two days later with the shock news that Green's contract had been cancelled. 'All I am prepared to say is that I demand standards of behaviour and discipline on and off the pitch.' Clough said he hadn't arrived at the decision lightly. He was without doubt the best goalkeeper in the Fourth Division, and they could ill-afford to lose him. Chairman Curry added that the club's success was due to laying down 'certain standards'. 'Anyone who falls short of them does not fit in. We have been forced to do this because of conduct prejudicial to the good name of the club.'[23] It still wasn't clear what Green had done wrong.

The *Northern Echo* said his marching orders were related to his 'domestic affairs'. It was a hard blow for Brian Clough, considering the outside chance of promotion. But he had a code of conduct to which players must conform. The boss asserted there was 'no place' for anyone who didn't. While he was sorry to lose Green, there was no other choice.[24] He stated his moral code more bluntly years later: 'A thug at home is a thug on the pitch.' How players behaved outside football affected the way they played the game.[25]

National newspaper *The People* added still more detail to the Green affair. Clough had escorted the goalkeeper's wife Helen and their two children, 4 and 15 months, to a railway station. They'd moved out of their home in Kesteven Road on the Fens Estate (near Clough's house and opposite Taylor's former house), owned by former chairman Ernie Ord. Helen was Green's teenage sweetheart, but she and the kids were catching a train to her mother's house in Warwickshire. 'I have left my husband. I don't want to say anything about it at all,' Mrs Green said.[26]

John Curry's son shed still more light on Green's sacking. The goalie who'd broken his thumb in the season's opening game had been physically abusing his wife for a while. She'd told Chairman Curry, head of the council's Housing Committee, and he got involved. When Clough got to hear about it as well, it was curtains for their no. 1 goalkeeper.[27]

Meanwhile, Simpkins was on the *Mail*'s front page after Clough threatened him with a fine. Told he'd be playing the following Saturday, Clough insisted he had three days to shed some flab. While his teammates had been sat for endless hours on a coach the previous weekend, Ken had travelled home. Clough suspected he'd 'put on a few pounds', so gave him a written ultimatum to report back at under 15 stone. It did the trick. Ken performed extra training, stuck to a diet, and the dressing room scales proved it. Clough declared that the threat of a fine had 'spurred him on a little', with the missing pounds and ounces 'vital for his agility'.[28]

Ships' sirens and rockets over Grayfields at midnight on Friday, 31 March 1967 weren't to celebrate Simpkins' weight loss, but the amalgamation of the Ancient Borough of Hartlepool and the County Borough of West Hartlepool (after 121 years of existence). Their union into the new County Borough of Hartlepool had been eighty years in the planning.[29]

There were fewer fireworks at the Victoria Ground the following afternoon. 'Pools played with 'a jaded air' and were 'woefully out of touch' in the first half. Evidence for this was Rochdale taking the lead on 3 minutes. Thankfully their hosts sparked into life after the break, with both Somers and Broadbent scoring their first goals for the club.[30] Despite the early struggle, they were in the end full value for their two points. There were 5,952 spectators there to watch it all.[31]

26

NOT CRICKET

The gloves were off for a Monday evening 'friendly' against Hearts on 3 April to celebrate the merger of Hartlepool and West Hartlepool. Four shillings paid for a double bill that kicked off with Hartlepool Boys versus Seaham Boys. After that livener, the 3,443 crowd were treated to a main event of meaty challenges, needle and entertainment. At one point in the all-action clash, home fans chanted, 'Go home … Go home,' at their Scottish visitors. 'Pools defenders Gill, Drysdale and Bircumshaw gave as good as they got, and there was even fighting on the terraces behind both goals. The full-blooded contest ended 1–1.

The gilt was taken off Hearts' official goodwill a few hours after the final whistle when thieves stole the inscribed silver bowl they'd presented to their hosts. The heartless intruders also helped themselves to bottles of rum and gin from the boardroom, plus a commemorative World Cup statuette. In other off-the-field action, a gang of fifty local youngsters chased a small group of Hearts fans down Stockton Street. Then police rushed to deal with reports of a disturbance at a public house. It was a 'friendly' to remember, and an evening to forget.[1]

The *Thunderbirds Are Go* feature was showing at the Hartlepool Odeon. It contained a dream sequence in which Cliff Richard and The Shadows – in puppet form – performed the song 'Shooting Star'. Hartlepools United's season didn't need saving, as was usually the case come April, so International Rescue's cutting-edge equipment and Brains were not required. Instead, the club's own star was ascending and there was all to play for with seven games remaining, three at home and four away.

The first two results at Southport and Halifax would either lift or sink their promotion push. Given the different opposition, they retreated into defence in the first game and went on the attack in the second. On the afternoon that

100-1 outsider Foinavon ran off with the Grand National at nearby Aintree, 'Pools played well but lost at third-placed Southport, who'd won their previous seven at home. Clough said his team had enjoyed '65 per cent of the play', but they hit the woodwork three times on a luckless Saturday afternoon.[2] Sentinel agreed with Clough that they had 'out-ran, out-manoeuvred, and out-fought' the opposition, and the 3-1 defeat was an injustice. Furthermore, reporting from the 'tea hut ... thinly disguised as a Press box,' he was right in line with Southport's clearly offside third goal.[3]

Clough, Taylor and Curry all travelled to St James' Park in Newcastle on Monday, 10 April for an FA commission of inquiry into Les Green's sacking. The goalkeeper, also in attendance, had appealed against the club's cancellation of his contract. An FA councillor and a Football League assistant secretary ruled in the club's favour. After signing a form to officially terminate his contract, he was now a free agent to sign for another club.[4]

Hartlepools players and officials crammed into cars again for a must-win Tuesday evening game at Halifax Town. Broadbent's 16th-minute opener meant they changed their open and aggressive approach for a nine-man defensive shield in the second half. But playing more with desperation than aggression, their defence cracked to concede two goals in the 74th and 79th minutes, ending any realistic hope of promotion.[5] Their convoy of cars arrived back in Hartlepool at 2 a.m.[6]

Brian Clough was already planning to clock up thousands of miles in his brand-new Rover as he and Taylor worked on their blueprint for the following season. They'd earmarked four new players: a goalkeeper, a wing-half and two forwards. He told Sentinel there'd be 'no half measures this time'. Due to circumstances the previous summer, they hadn't signed the men they'd wanted, but he was confident the directors would back them this time. They still hadn't quite given up on the 1966/67 season. It would 'take a miracle', but they'd plough on 'at full steam' until the maths made promotion impossible.[7]

The management duo made four changes to their twice-losing team for the visit of high-spending Notts County, who were hovering around the re-election zone. John Sheridan came in and Bobby McLeod slotted into Tony Parry's position, while Jimmy Mulvaney and John McGovern replaced Cliff Wright and Joe Livingstone.

Despite their visitors pulling ahead, 'Pools wore them down sufficiently for 'cheeky chappie' Mulvaney to score twice and seal both points. Jack Fletcher found Clough 'practically lost for words' after the match. That was saying something for a manager who could 'think aloud' better than most. With so many former County and Forest men in his team, the subdued manager thought the 'family' atmosphere might explain their strained and anxious frame of mind. After this depressing show of football, Fletcher was keen for the cricket season to start.[8]

Clough & Taylor shuffled their pack again for the Friday night visit to table-toppers Stockport County, but it was all to no avail. Stan Aston returned from injury to replace John Gill, Parry replaced Sheridan, and McLeod moved to right-half. Stockport deserved their 1–0 first-half lead, but Hartlepools' spirited second-half fightback was undone by a controversial penalty decision. The referee was unmoved when a Stockport forward went down in the box under an Aston challenge, but a linesman's 'frantic flag-waving' changed his mind. The visitors took the decision so badly that a policeman had to intervene to separate the linesman from Drysdale, Phythian and Aston. The penalty was converted, and 'Pools failed to breach the home side's 'iron-defence'.[9]

Fans were also looking ahead to the summer break and the 1967/68 season. One wrote to tell the *Football Mail* that he and his friends thought Clough was 'worth every penny he gets'. They'd been a struggling side when he took over, but he'd 'worked wonders' in a short while. With his contract ending in November, Clough was adamant he wouldn't continue without one. Directors had been split on the issue. Some argued that contracts favoured managers and left clubs at a manager's mercy. Despite the opposition, Chairman Curry planned to sit down with Clough and thrash one out.[10]

There were two home games remaining, with 'Pools unbeaten at the Vic since Southend's visit under the new floodlights on 6 January. Sentinel deemed the Monday evening clash with Halifax 'the most dismal 90 minutes' the team had experienced for some time. In front of their smallest home crowd of the season (3,459), both teams seriously misfired, except for visiting centre-forward John Parks, who sealed the hosts' humiliation and his own hat-trick four minutes from the end. Mimicking his press box companion from the *Northern Echo*, Sentinel believed this poor advert for football would do the coming cricket season 'no harm at all'.[11]

Teenage winger John McGovern had played his final game of the season. His leg would be in plaster for three weeks after damaging knee ligaments against Halifax.[12] The final two games gave Ernie Phythian the chance to end his goal drought and challenge the club record for most goals in a season. He hadn't hit the net in eight league games since 24 March. Clough & Taylor gave 17-year-old amateur outside-right John Joyce (from Easington) his first-team debut against Bradford Park Avenue in the season's final home game.

Since knocking them out of the League Cup in a replay at the end of August, Bradford PA had sold their best asset, Kevin Hector, and plummeted down the table. With little to play for, apart from pride (and a new playing contract), Jack Fletcher described 'a fisherman's story' in the *Northern Echo*. 'There were two in the net, but you should have seen some of the others that got away.' The visitors defended with ten men whenever the hosts threatened, but 'were never in the same street'. The season's second-lowest crowd of 3,547 'resisted the lure' of Ayresome Park and St James' Park to see Somers score his second goal for the club. On the hour, Phythian appeared to have equalled the club record of twenty-six goals in a season when he crashed home a Joyce pass from 15 yards. He nearly surpassed it after intercepting a back pass but shot straight at the advancing goalkeeper.[13]

An anticlimactic visit to Port Vale in the Potteries remained, but local and regional newspapers had already penned their end-of-season post-mortems. Sentinel maintained that if Phythian could get one more goal, it would be 'a symbolic end to what might have been a symbolic season'. Clough, meanwhile, wouldn't be sorry to see the season end. He'd made no secret of the fact he hadn't particularly enjoyed his early taste of football management so far. 'It's been hard here, and at times I've been on the point of packing it all in, things have been so difficult,' he confessed. He'd dreamt of promotion in his first full season, so felt a sense of failure.[14]

His final programme notes declared that he and Taylor were satisfied they'd done 'as good a job as [they] could with the material available'. The players had given 'maximum effort', despite what some supporters had said. They'd 'laid the foundations' and hoped to improve in an all-out effort for Third Division football next season. He wrote, 'Peter and I know that this is "on", and if we get the players we want, we will be very confident.' With little money to work with, perhaps promotion had always been a forlorn hope.[15]

A full season of games and a lunchtime thunderstorm left the Vale Park pitch looking like a monk's tonsure, with the only grass in the corners and down the touchline. The mud-flat conditions typified a 'tedious, scrappy end of season match'. Yet when the 'perfect pass' fell at Phythian's feet, and with it his apparent chance to enter the record books, he swung and missed. Sentinel reckoned he was 'suffering from some sort of affliction' in front of goal. The game – and the season – ended in a scoreless bore draw.[16]

After a season of huff and puff they'd finished eighth, three or four wins behind the promoted sides. It was their best performance in the Fourth Division since its creation in 1958. 'But the greatest consolation,' Sentinel wrote, was that 'almost certainly, the best is yet to come.'[17] Time would tell.

Verdicts on the oh-so-near season blamed the goals leaked in defence rather than those scored. Unfortunately, when the behind-the-scenes team at the

Northern Daily Mail checked the club's records again, they discovered they'd made a mistake with their declarations about Ernie Phythian. He'd failed by one goal (twenty-six) to equal the club goalscoring record. Eric Wildon had scored twenty-seven league and cup goals in the 1950/51 season, playing three fewer games.[18]

Sentinel stressed that the goal prowess of terrible twins Phythian and Mulvaney – with forty-five league and cup goals between them – should have sealed promotion. Clough therefore had little to grumble about up front. Ernie's barren spell mimicked one of his own at Middlesbrough that lasted six weeks. They'd both experienced the 'mind-freezing tension' that builds up in a striker's mind. You can get 'apprehensive and wary' to the point that 'you don't want the chances to come along in case you miss them', he affirmed. In an improved side the following season, they could look forward to thirty goals from Ernie.[19]

A quick glance at the goals conceded column showed that Hartlepools' main problem did indeed lie in defence. Out of the division's top eleven teams, they'd let in the most goals (sixty-four). But it was still their best season since 1956/57, when they'd conceded sixty-three. Time and again away from home they'd had to pull players back to bolster a shaky defence. Detractors might have criticised the emphasis on defending, but Clough said there was no choice. Too many opposing teams had recovered from losing positions against them.[20]

Midfield had not been perfect either. There'd been 'a lack of command' there for much of the season, according to Sentinel. Unusually, they'd often played more attractively and assuredly away from home than at the Vic. Of late, however, the introduction of Albert Broadbent had remedied many matters in the centre of the park. The former Bradford PA man had formed a productive midfield partnership with Tony Parry, who'd grown in confidence. Midfield was another of Clough & Taylor's summer priorities.[21]

Signing Notts County's Gerry Carver the previous summer would have 'guaranteed promotion', according to Taylor. He'd predicted they'd struggle without this target player.[22] His football judgements were rarely wrong.

Jack Fletcher surmised it was probably just as well they hadn't achieved promotion. It would have been 'sweet', but given Darlington's relegation just twelve months after promotion from the Fourth Division, they probably weren't 'ready yet'. According to the man from the *Northern Echo*, Brian 'always the realist' Clough had never rated promotion higher than a long-odds chance anyway. Like Sentinel and the manager, he judged the defence had 'hamstrung' the team. Nevertheless, they could look back on a satisfying season that had 'bubbled with interest, enriched by hope – and that's what makes a club tick'.[23] It was miles better than mere survival.

All that remained was the unsavoury task of telling three or four players they were being let go. Clough found it 'distasteful'. But you had to 'shut your eyes to the personal aspect', he said, even if the person in question had three children. It 'has to be done for the sake of progress,' he affirmed, 'and it will be done.'[24] There's no room for sentiment in football.

Peter Taylor added his tuppence-worth too. The assistant manager had told the players their season had been 'a good mixture of joking and discipline', but now 'the joking has to stop'. He added, 'We are deadly serious now, and you all have to be prepared for what might happen.'[25] You could say that again.

A big disappointment had been home attendances. While 5,778 exceeded the previous 1965/66 season's average of 4,816, it still fell short of the 5,869 average under Alvan Williams (1964/65). Third Division Middlesbrough's promotion-achieving season on Teesside might partly explain it. Most Ayresome Park matches had coincided with games at the Vic.

The truth was that despite Clough and Curry's pleas for crowds of 8,000 to 10,000 to break even, they'd rarely achieved such gates. The 'missing thousands' of the Westgarth years had stayed missing. Now with newly installed floodlights, they'd be applying to the Football League for many more Friday evening fixtures in the 1967/68 season. Clough had concluded they were 'just throwing cash away' by playing on Saturdays.[26]

CONCLUSION

27

SNOOKERED IN SCARBOROUGH

What Shack giveth, Shack taketh away. A 'fairy godfather' had gifted Clough & Taylor to Hartlepools United, and he'd ease their exit too. Taylor had been restless for a while, weary of the club's incessant problems. Nearly seven years older than Clough and an outsider in the North East, his horizons stretched beyond the flaming chimneys of Teesside. He craved a club higher up the football pyramid with resources to build a winning team. Together they'd dragged lowly Hartlepools up to eighth in the Fourth Division, but he sought more tangible success in the form of medals and trophies.

At Taylor's behest but unbeknown to Clough, football fixer Len Shackleton acted as their unpaid go-between again. When Second Division Derby County didn't renew manager Tim Ward's contract, Shack phoned their chairman to suggest adding Clough to his shortlist. 'He's a born leader, and he's done a first-class job at Hartlepool and I'm sure he'd do one for you.' Chairman Sam Longson, a millionaire through his road haulage business, told him he'd sleep on it.[1]

Longson had seen Clough play against Derby a few times and was particularly struck in one game by how he'd barked instructions at teammates from beginning to end. This wasn't arrogance, in Sam's eyes, but leadership. After pondering his suggestion for a few hours, he rang Shack back the same evening to request a meeting.[2]

Other Derby directors baulked at the idea of heading north to meet Clough. Shouldn't the lower division manager be travelling south to meet them? Shackleton fibbed and told Longson that West Bromwich Albion were also pursuing his man.[3]

The chairman won the argument and chauffeured three fellow directors up the A1 in his Rolls-Royce the following day. A hotel near Scotch Corner in North Yorkshire was some way north of meeting Clough halfway.[4]

According to Longson, their new candidate 'never stopped talking' during the Sunday lunch interview. His confidence was off the scale, he spoke a lot of sense, and knew the football business inside out. Clough was everything the chairman had hoped for and impressed all four men.[5] Shackleton, watching from a separate table with his wife, was dismayed that Longson didn't offer to cover their meals, or even buy them a drink.[6]

By Thursday, Clough was driving south to meet the full Derby board with his family in tow. He left his two boys and heavily pregnant Barbara at Normanton Park's swings, while he went to talk business at the nearby Baseball Ground. Longson warned colleagues, 'He talks too much, he is over-confident to the point of arrogance, but I like him.' Candidate Clough dropped the bombshell that he'd only consider taking the job alongside assistant Peter Taylor, which raised a few eyebrows. After further discussion they came to agreement, an offer was made, and Clough promised them a final decision within days.[7]

Clough & Taylor treated their families to a wet weekend on the Yorkshire coast, as the pair thrashed out their futures in the snooker room of Scarborough's Royal Hotel.[8] According to Taylor, his partner didn't want to abandon his native North East. 'He was a home bird and insecure about leaving his neck of the woods.'[9] Apart from his National Service in Somerset, of course, he'd never lived away from the area.

Furthermore, Clough was reluctant to abandon the club that had given him his first chance in management. He was therefore inclined to say, 'No thanks, I want to stay with Hartlepool at least until they get up.' He pleaded with Taylor to 'see it through'.[10] But Taylor was through with all the trouble and strife.

The Yorkshireman in Clough told him not to leave a job half finished. He might have had in mind all the donations he'd extracted from working-class folk in and around the Hartlepools. Not to mention the OAP who'd arrived at the ground to hand over his 10s weekly pension. The pair had huffed and puffed without achieving their target, so should stick it out until the job was completed. Taylor couldn't wait that long. They were leaving the club in better shape than they'd found it, and there was no time like the present. He insisted they 'may never get another chance like this'.[11]

Taylor hailed from the East Midlands, born and brought up a 16-mile drive along the A52 in Nottingham. He insisted that Derby 'had tradition'. As a kid he'd seen the Baseball Ground heaving with fans after the war and was sure they could fill it again.[12]

Clough & Taylor were also protégés of Tim Ward's predecessor at the Baseball Ground, Harry Storer (1955 to 1963). His Derby side had pipped

Hartlepools United to the Third Division (North) title and promotion to the Second Division in April 1957. This was the season when Fred Westgarth led 'Pools to their highest ever league position before failing health interrupted his long reign as manager, and then ended his life.

According to Taylor, he'd extracted a pledge from Clough – as a condition of joining him in the North East – that they'd go 'all the way' together. He reminded him about the agreement, and 'he stuck to it'.[13]

Clough hadn't taken much persuading. He'd only heard about Derby's interest late the previous Saturday, the evening of Hartlepools' end-of-season game at Port Vale on 6 May. After meeting the four Derby men the next day, he'd travelled with his family to Derby on Thursday, 11 May. By late Saturday in Scarborough two days later, Taylor had worn down his resistance.[14]

Informing Chairman Curry was always going to be awkward. The three men had been through a lot together. Only days earlier, on Tuesday, 9 May, the directors had thrown further caution to the wind during a key two-hour board meeting at the Victoria Ground. Despite low cash reserves, they'd authorised Clough to make three close-season signings – a goalkeeper and two wing-halves. Councillor Curry and his directors were 'convinced' that success on the pitch would more than repay them in the long run. Clough had already identified the players he wanted, and declared, 'We are really going to have a go this time.' Furthermore, the board's confidence in their manager was such that they'd offered him a new contract. Chairman Curry called it 'more attractive' than his existing £2,000 a year deal. The day after the board meeting, Clough was reluctant to promise an immediate decision. He said there was plenty of time to think it over, with the present contract only up in October.[15] Unbeknown to Curry, he was already speaking to Derby County.

Three days later, Clough was phoning Curry from Scarborough to tell him he was leaving the club. Newspapers made the 'bombshell' announcement on Monday, 15 May. Clough told reporters he'd kept Derby's offer secret for a week, and the 'only reason' he'd delayed was Councillor Curry. Indeed, his biggest regret was 'leaving the finest chairman in the Football League'.[16] Clough recognised the announcement would 'hit them like a bomb', but he'd been working seven days a week at Hartlepools and he'd 'be a fool' to turn down Derby.[17]

Curry was the first person he rang, and as he told the *Northern Echo*, 'I didn't have a guilty conscience because this, after all, is my career. But I did have a conscience because he and I have been able to work so well together.' For his part, Curry wasn't angry with Clough:

This is, of course, a development which we knew must come. It is part of football and commercial life. Like any other young man, Brian wants to get on and it was inevitable that, sooner or later, he would be moving up the ladder. While we are sorry to lose him, we wish him every success and shall be following his career with interest.[18]

But the chairman was spitting feathers with Derby County. His manager was under contract, and they'd approached him without Hartlepools' permission: 'From a club of Derby's standing, I deplore the apparent attitude that as we are just a Fourth Division side why should they bother. It does nothing for the good name of football.'

For the moment, Clough remained the club's manager, and they'd discuss the matter at board level. They might decide to hang on to him until a replacement could be found.[19]

Curry turned his attention to Taylor. He pulled out all the stops by offering him the manager's job on Clough's salary.[20] He'd never worked under contract at Hartlepools, so it was a bit rich offering him one now. A herd of wild horses couldn't have stopped Taylor joining Clough at Derby County.

Curry failed to see how Taylor could reject his 'extremely good' offer – a £2,000 annual salary, £500 for a top-ten finish, and another £500 for promotion. Sentinel understood he wouldn't earn that much at Derby. Taylor thanked the chairman for the 'really generous offer', said it was 'difficult to refuse', and turned it down twice. He told the *Mail*, 'Brian and I have the perfect working partnership, and I feel it is only right that I should go with him.'[21] And that was the end of it.

Bill Hamilton interviewed Clough & Taylor for Tyne Tees Television after they'd accepted the 'out of the blue' offer from Derby. Clough didn't think it would be very difficult adapting from Fourth to Second Division football. They'd tackle the job the same way, albeit the players would be technically a bit different.[22]

Asked about his time at Hartlepools, he admitted he'd never have taken it on had he known how 'hard' it would be. Indeed, if experience was as valuable as people said, he'd 'had a hell of a lot'. He attributed his success to two factors – Chairman Curry and Assistant Manager Peter Taylor. In an obvious allusion to Chairman Ord, he said Curry hadn't interfered on the playing side, something of utmost importance to any manager. Derby would be hard work too, but perhaps 'not as hard' as Hartlepools. His mind was therefore 'set on football', and it made no difference whether it was Derby County or Liverpool. His approach was the same.[23]

His eyes shifting, and tongue darting inside a puckered mouth, Peter Taylor was clear about their direction of travel. He heaped praise on his partner, who'd 'fulfilled' everything he'd hoped for when joining him from Burton Albion. He intended to go with Brian 'to the top of the tree', and they'd start at Derby. He had quite a few connections in the East Midlands, but it would still be tough getting players. They'd 'set about it just the same way' as at Hartlepools. His one regret, like Clough, concerned Councillor Curry. If Derby gave them the same freedom, he was sure they'd enjoy similar success.[24]

Clough & Taylor didn't abandon the North East immediately. After accepting the inevitable and advertising the vacant manager's position, Curry asked them to stay another three weeks 'to tie up loose ends' ahead of their official departure on 3 June 1967. It was therefore Clough & Taylor who drew up the end-of-season retained list, releasing full-time players Brian Grant and Joe Livingstone, and part-timer John Bates. He hadn't made a single appearance all season. Livingstone had started it brightly until Mulvaney outshone him up front. Full-back Grant hadn't played first-team football since the end of March.[25] Meanwhile, the board reduced two dozen applications to a shortlist of five interviewees for their vacant manager's position.[26]

The Auxiliary Association organised a dance at Longscar Hall in Seaton Carew, attended by almost 300 people on Friday, 26 May. During the evening, Clough & Taylor presented Councillor John Curry with a surprise farewell gift. Their inscription on the table lighter read: 'If we stay in the game another 100 years, we will not find another chairman as good as you.'[27]

Hartlepool's parting gift to Clough was his third child, daughter Elizabeth, delivered by Barbara on 31 May 1967. She'd spent around fourteen of her husband's nineteen-month tenure at the club in a pregnant condition. On this occasion, unfortunately, a bug scare at the Grantully Maternity Home kept Brian and their two bairns from mother and baby's side.[28]

Clough's final professional act at Hartlepools United was yet another bid for transfer-listed Norman Corner. He was like a dog with a bone. But for a sixth time, Hull City weren't biting.[29]

28

TOP OF THE TREE

Absorbing some big bumps along the road, Clough & Taylor's journey from 1967 to 1980 would lead them to the promised land. At Derby, they wasted no time in applying their secret sauce, employing a ruthless but effective approach.

As luck would have it, Hartlepools United were handed a League Cup second-round tie at Derby County on 13 September 1967. Clough was 'delighted', and hoped for a gate of 30,000 for Hartlepools' sake. Taylor also wished for a big gate, and to see old friends.[1]

A week before travelling to Derby, the Vic's Rink End pitch-side barrier collapsed again when fans surged forward in anticipation of a late winner against Rochdale. Several dozen – mostly youngsters – piled forward behind visiting 'keeper Les Green, collapsing the barrier and becoming enmeshed in the goal net. After disentangling themselves, one small girl was treated for shock. Groundsman Harry Simpson and a volunteer replaced the rotted wooden posts with steel girder uprights.[2] Workmen also erected a wooden refreshment kiosk to replace the tea hut, demolished a year earlier to make way for a floodlight pylon.[3]

On a Wednesday evening in Derby, a 17,000+ crowd swelled their visitors' bank balance by £1,000. On the pitch, Clough & Taylor's new blend of players trounced them 4–0. Before departing the Baseball Ground, Clough offered his old club £4,000 for John McGovern. He'd already had two £2,000 offers turned down, the first when joining Derby in early June. The second guaranteed a further £2,000 if the youngster made the first team within two years. Curry called the new £4,000 offer 'ridiculous'. It was also a tad insulting, given that his former manager had advised him to turn down a £7,500 offer from Arsenal. He was more than familiar with Hartlepools' penniless state.[4]

In June, Curry had made a verbal agreement with Clough to inform Derby about any bids for McGovern. Now their relations became strained. Taylor explained they'd refused £7,500 from Arsenal because they'd gambled – and lost – on getting £10,000 for him. Their new £4,000 bid was 'a genuine one', and their final offer. The previous verbal agreement was now null and void.[5]

From the get-go, Clough & Taylor gave their inherited squad at Derby a hard prune, and soon only three originals remained. One was their former tormentor at Bradford Park Avenue, Kevin Hector. Clough made an early raid on Sunderland to sign his former youth team forward John O'Hare. They made a Friday night smash-and-grab on Merseyside to sign Tranmere's Roy McFarland under the noses of Everton's Harry Catterick and Liverpool's Bill Shankly. Another excellent early signing was Alan Hinton from neighbours Nottingham Forest.

When North-East football correspondent Bob Cass visited Clough early into the new season, he found a club buzzing 'like a hive of bees'. Hospitality for the press had improved, with an inexhaustible supply of tea, cakes, sandwiches, beer and other drinks. Clough told Cass he didn't invite 'good publicity', although he didn't turn it away either. Meanwhile, managing Derby was no cakewalk. 'I thought it was hard work at Hartlepool, but it was nothing compared to this,' he confessed. He turned sad when reminiscing about another team. 'I'd give a fortune to have still been playing. I loved it at Sunderland. There I had no problems. Today I've got a million.'[6]

The confession gave a clue to a large chink behind Clough's bright and busy exterior. Seeking a release from the enormous pressures and constant stresses of managing a large club, he'd seek solace in booze again. He'd first developed a predilection for it in early 1963, stuck at home in Sunderland with a career-threatening injury. But the bottle hadn't been an issue at Hartlepools, where they 'couldn't afford a glass of milk'. His single-minded drive to forge a future in management and provide for his young family provided the distractions he needed. But he developed a renewed fondness for alcohol at Derby, where it was free and free-flowing. Drink turned into an addiction that would souse his liver and provoke erratic behaviour.[7]

In December 1967, sports journalist Basil Easterbrook found 'a young man in a hurry', with a mind like 'a dynamo' and a mouth like a 'Bren gun'. Of the 'hundred battles' to be fought in the first three months, his first had come on day one. He warned the thirty players whose contracts were up, 'No one gets an extra button until I have seen what you can do and how hard you are prepared to work for this club.' Getting Derby back to the First Division would be a doddle after what he'd achieved at Hartlepools, he boasted to Easterbrook, who advised readers, 'Watch out for Mr Clough in the future. I feel his career will be worth following.'[8]

Results took a while in coming. At the end of their first season, Derby finished a place below where Tim Ward had left them in 1966/67. Although they did progress to the semi-finals of the League Cup after beating Hartlepools, only for Don Revie's Leeds United to defeat them in both legs.

Clough & Taylor's early strip down and rebuild started to reap bumper fruit in the 1968/69 season. Signing 33-year-old Scottish veteran Dave Mackay from Spurs was a large coup. Their stroke of genius was to make him sweeper, exploiting his football brain to lead from the back.

They also let bygones be bygones to bring in goalkeeper Les Green for a second time. With a stronger spine, Derby started to fire on all cylinders. They lost only five league games that season to win the Second Division Championship – and promotion to the First Division – by seven clear points.

The club built a new main stand, Clough tried to chuck smoking, and Derby finished fourth in the top flight in the 1969/70 season. In September 1970, Taylor insisted Clough rush to Lancashire and beat Everton to Archie Gemmill's signature. Sleeping over at the player's house, as he'd done with McFarland, Clough sealed the deal over bacon and eggs the following morning. The Scot provided a vital link between Derby's defence and attack.

Soon into the same 1970/71 season, Taylor suffered a mild heart attack and the team's performances and league position suffered. He gave up smoking and returned to the dugout, only to learn that Longson had given Clough a pay rise on the side. He'd already warned his partner about getting too close to the chairman. Indeed, a set-in-stone Harry Storer rule of football management was to keep the board at arm's length. They ignored the master's advice at their peril.

They went twelve games unbeaten at the start of the 1971/72 season. Couch-potato football fans saw the Rams despatch one visiting team after another on the mud-bound Baseball Ground pitch (sixteen wins, four draws, and one defeat). They kept twenty-three clean sheets home and away to bring the League Championship to a thrilling climax. Having played their final game, Clough holidayed in the Scilly Isles with his family while Taylor relaxed in Majorca with the players. They sat back as their championship rivals choked in end-of-season games to hand Derby their first ever top-tier title.

Despite this triumph, the already uneasy relations between the management pair and the board went from bad to worse. Longson turned ever more aghast at Clough's regular media appearances and tried to reign them in. The cameras and TV audiences were transfixed, but the chairman felt the work and outrageous pronouncements were distracting from his day job and jeopardising Longson's chances of joining the League Management Committee. He instructed the club secretary to lock the drinks cabinet in the manager's office.[9] To make matters worse, Clough had raided Sunderland again to sign former youth team player Colin Todd for £175,000 without seeking his chairman's prior approval.

Humiliation leading to irrationality and dire decision-making is a common feature of betrayed and jilted lovers. If Rams fans considered Clough & Taylor a gift made in heaven, most directors thought they'd become too big for their boots. Matters came to a head and the management duo dropped the biggest clanger of their careers. They handed in letters of resignation, only for the Derby board to call their bluff. Clough & Taylor hadn't learnt Ernie Ord's harsh lesson, although he was relying on precedent when he resigned for the umpteenth time. The pair put on a brave face, but they'd binned all their hard work in one moment of madness to land in a heap back at square one.

They tried to kickstart their careers at Third Division Brighton & Hove Albion, but Clough's heart and mind were only half on the job. He didn't move to the south-coast town, and Taylor found himself alone a lot of the time. At one point, Clough jetted off to New York mid-season to watch Muhammad Ali fight Joe Frazier for the heavyweight title. Showing how low the pair had sunk, amateurs Walton & Hersham dumped Brighton out of the FA Cup 4–0 in a first-round replay. A few days later, Bristol Rovers sunk the Seagulls 8–2, also at the Goldstone Ground.

If their nightmare departure from Derby wasn't bad enough, Brian Clough went one worse in 1974. When Don Revie replaced Sir Alf Ramsey as England manager, he abandoned his partner at Brighton to take over at Leeds. In sole charge of a club for the first time, Clough marched in all guns blazing and tried to stamp his authority on the high-achieving club. But their seasoned pros reacted badly, performances dipped, and the team won just one of their opening six games to drop to nineteenth in the First Division. The Leeds board sacked Clough after just forty-four days, although he did walk away with a handsome payoff. In trying to fill Revie's large shoes, he was always on a hiding to nothing. He should have listened to Taylor and stuck it out at Brighton.

When Clough arrived at Nottingham Forest in January 1975, the team lay thirteenth in the Second Division. After persuading Taylor to join him in the summer of 1976, the Forest team really started to purr. They won promotion to the First Division at the end of their first season together (1976/77). Forest then bagged two League Cups (1978 & 1979) and the League Championship (1977/78). This was Nottingham, mind, not London, Liverpool or Manchester. In Robin Hood style, Clough & Taylor were robbing silverware from the rich, established clubs. The East Midlands city had never known success like it, and likely never will again. And there was more to come.

On a balmy May evening in 1980, Clough & Taylor rose calmly from the bench at Madrid's Santiago Bernabéu Stadium to embrace. For the second season running, team captain John McGovern, wearing the red of Nottingham Forest, raised the European Cup high with outstretched arms. After fifteen years of hard work and listening to good advice, he'd dragged himself from the ocean floor at Hartlepools United to the top of the football tree. Shoulders back, upright, with short hair, he was the Continent's top lobster.

Back-to back European Cups for Nottingham Forest in 1979 and 1980 were the twin peaks of Clough & Taylor's success. Nobody could have imagined them to be the last trophies they'd win together.

Their winning relationship unravelled in tragic fashion. Taylor's book *With Clough by Taylor*, written without his partner's knowledge, was the beginning of the end. Clough found out about the book before its advance publicity began. Taylor had not even had the good grace to mention it. Something that annoyed the hell out of Clough was that his name and photo were more prominent on the cover than Taylor's. And when he read it, his anger shot up another notch. Why not concentrate on talent-spotting, instead of dissecting his partner's character flaws? It was by no means all damning about him and their partnership, but Clough fixated on a few negative passages in the book.[10]

'Brian suffers from terrible insecurity.' Ouch! 'You'll never see him alone, which is the most obvious way that he betrays his lack of confidence.' Ouch again. 'Brian was the only one [among his siblings] to fail the 11-plus examination. He was hurt again by being cast aside so hastily by England and he still feels the knee injury that destroyed his dream of First Division football.'[11] All true, but double- and treble-ouch.

Taylor announced his retirement in 1982 but changed his mind six months later to take over at Derby. After failing to persuade Clough to join him at their former club, he nabbed Scottish winger John Robertson from Forest without telling him. This incensed Clough even more.

The feeling of betrayal led to bitterness between the two former friends. Nasty words like 'rattlesnake' were uttered. Alchemy descended into acrimony as prolonged silence severed their relationship.

When Clough learned of Taylor's death in 1990, they hadn't spoken in seven years. He broke down in tears after hanging up the phone, before picking it up again to offer Taylor's wife his condolences. The chance for reconciliation was gone, a regret he carried until the end of his days in 2004. Nobody had made him laugh like his old mate Pete.

29

TURNING THE CORNER

Clough & Taylor had tried six times to sign Norman Corner. But the saga still had legs. New Hartlepools manager Angus McLean, formerly of Hull (where Corner remained), made another four bids for the wing-half/utility man. That made ten bids in all. In September 1967, the frank Welshman appeared to have given up, only for Hull to inform him a week later that Corner was available. He moved quickly to match Lincoln City's transfer bid. And hoping to trump their one-year contract offer, McLean tried to tempt the player with a two-year deal. His decision to move to Lincoln left him flabbergasted. Corner had apparently told him several times (when they were at Hull together) that he wanted to return to his native North East. But according to McLean, when he asked the player why he'd chosen Lincoln, he confessed he didn't think he'd 'get a fair deal from the crowd at Hartlepool'.[1]

Couldn't Corner have said that earlier to stop driving everyone round the bend? And was Corner really so afraid that 'townies' on the Vic's terraces would barrack him as a 'pit yacker' from the mining village of Horden?

Despite the further Corner knockback, McLean led Hartlepools to their first ever promotion in the 1967/68 season. He'd without doubt inherited a very decent squad of players, but this was only half the story. While Clough was a disciplinarian with a soft centre, square-jawed McLean was hard inside and out. His rule antagonised key players, and several soon played their last games for the club: Stan Aston (in September), Albert Broadbent and Jimmy Mulvaney (both October), and Ernie Phythian (March). Chased by the bookies due to a fat gambling debt, Ernie emigrated to South Africa.

Others who slapped in transfer requests – but didn't leave – were Cliff Wright and John McGovern. The 18-year-old detested McLean's manner, and soon found himself in the Reserves. According to McLean, he wasn't happy with reserve team football and couldn't support his mother on his earnings.[2] He was recalled in mid-December to become a regular first-teamer again.

John Gill gained a new lease of life under McLean. Given freedom to play instead of leathering the ball on sight, he began to enjoy his football again, although his discipline problems continued.[3]

Incoming 'keeper George Smith froze out Simpkins. Ken's new strategy for weight loss was a plastic sweat-suit. While he only wore the no.1 shirt once that season, he played six times in attack at no.9, even netting a winner at Port Vale.

Ashington-born former miner Bobby Cummings, an early February acquisition from Darlington for £2,000, did most of the damage up front (nine goals in eighteen starts). In an unbeaten end-of-season run beginning on 24 February, the team drew five and won eleven of their remaining matches to seal the club's first ever promotion at Swansea on 6 May 1968. A Victoria Ground bouncing with 11,000+ fans celebrated the achievement five days later. Chairman Curry handed Tony Parry the club's first player of the season award before the game.

Brian Clough was rarely surpassed, but Gus McLean managed it twice. The Welshman not only led 'Pools to promotion but went one better than his predecessor when he actually drove the team bus to away games as an economy measure.[4]

Clough & Taylor maintained their interest in McGovern, whose talent they'd developed but not discovered. The pair eventually brought him to Derby for £7,000 in September 1968, and soon turned the slow but sure-footed outside-right into a centre-midfield grafter and ball-winner.

Under their new name of Hartlepool FC, to reflect amalgamation (a year after the event), McLean's team played one year in the Third Division. It wasn't a complete disaster, but the 1968/69 season ended in relegation and a quick return to the bottom tier.

Two years after their previous encounter, they again drew Derby in the second round of the League Cup in September 1969. Chairman Curry rubbed his hands at the prospect of a full house at the Vic. Even the normally realistic *Sentinel* thought the draw might well 'tax the capacity of the ground'. The club made the glamorous tie an all-ticket affair, with a ceiling of 16,000. Secretary Bill Hillan anticipated selling 2,000 tickets to Derby. The night before the game they'd sold them 200.[5]

A special preview supplement in the *Mail* described how Clough & Taylor had transformed Derby 'from a decaying Second Division club into an exciting, modern and winning outfit'. After years 'in the doldrums', the club was now recapturing 'former glories' in the First Division.[6]

On the night, former home players Green and McGovern lined up alongside Carlin, Durban, Hector, Hinton, Mackay, McFarland and O'Hare. Just 7,778 half-filled the Victoria Ground to watch the First Division visitors bulldoze and bruise their way to a 3–1 cup victory.[7]

Twelve months after their 1969 relegation, Hartlepool reverted to their previous condition of Fourth Division re-election candidates. They repeated the feat in the following 1970/71 season.

Heavily indebted and struggling to pay players' wages in 1972, when Len Ashurst was their player-manager, Chairman Curry called in a large favour from Brian Clough. Despite not needing the player, Derby County paid £2,500 for Tony Parry to save Hartlepool from financial ruin.[8]

While Clough & Taylor were working their magic at Nottingham Forest, their old club applied for re-election in both 1976/77 and 1977/78, the second time as newly renamed Hartlepool United. They'd long since lost the extra 's'.

EPILOGUE

The age of steam ended in Hartlepool in September 1967 when British Rail called time on the old coal-hauling locos. They puffed off to the scrapyard as Thornaby-based diesels took up the strain.[1] In the same month, a new £5 million shopping centre was rising in the heart of the town. It officially opened in 1970 to eventually kill all retail trade in Lynn Street. Binns department store, a long-standing local institution next to the shopping centre, ceased trading in 1992.

Steady decline in the mining industry meant the Hartlepool docks coal trade had completely disappeared by the 1980s. Most local steelworkers lost their jobs, as did those in the manufacture of electric and nuclear power machinery.

The 1990s brought regeneration, as public and private investment transformed the once bustling docks area into a marina, housing and a historic quay – home to the National Museum of the Royal Navy. An Asda supermarket, a Mecca Bingo, and a McDonald's (with drive-thru) offer consumption where the Timber and Swainson Docks used to ply trade. A Morrisons supermarket and car park have replaced the Greyhound Stadium next to the Vic.

One might imagine Ernie Ord laughing into his porridge when reading about Brian Clough's sorry demise at Leeds United in 1974. The club chairman who sacked him, Manny Cussins, had been a close business acquaintance of Ernie's for decades. 'He was mustard,' Ord used to tell his grandson about Cussins, a Jewish businessman who'd made his millions in the Leeds furniture trade. Yet despite all the nasty things Clough said about the man who'd given him his first job in management, Ernie wasn't a person to gloat over someone's misfortune.[2] Clough's dismissal may have raised an eyebrow, but not a smile.

A year later, in 1975, Ord came out of retirement to become Hartlepool United chairman again. But after studying the club's finances, he declared he'd 'have to be a fool' to pour his money in for a second time. He resigned after twenty-one days to conclude, 'the whole place is a shambles'.[3]

Soon after taking the Hartlepools job, Clough said he could understand fanatics who wanted to climb Everest or swim the Channel. He'd harboured similar ambitions about football, until injury curtailed his playing career. He therefore confessed, 'It will be a long time before I get over the fact that I can never play again.'[4]

Clough never forgot where he came from, or the financial lifeline provided by his testimonial. When a troublesome knee curtailed Mick Somers's career at 23 years old, his ex-manager took a full-strength Derby team to his testimonial at Hartlepool in late 1969. He also brought a full Forest first-team squad to Bob McLeod's testimonial at Gateshead in 1983.[5] John McGovern never benefitted from a testimonial.

Stan Storton ended his professional playing days at Tranmere in 1970 and managed a few non-league clubs before taking the reins at Telford United. He led them to two FA Trophy Final victories at Wembley in 1983 and 1989, and FA Cup giant-killing runs that reached the fourth and fifth rounds in successive seasons.

Geoff Twentyman returned to Anfield to become Bill Shankly's chief scout in August 1967, scouring the UK for football talent until 1986. The list of household names that Liverpool signed on his recommendation in these multiple trophy-winning years included Ray Clemence, Alan Hansen, Kevin Keegan, Terry McDermott and Ian Rush. He then scouted for Graeme Souness at Rangers until his retirement in 1991.

Eric Harrison coached the Manchester United youth side for seventeen years from 1981. He was credited with producing their famous Class of '92 youth team, with players who'd enjoy highly successful first-team careers under Alex Ferguson. They included David Beckham, Ryan Giggs, Gary Neville and Paul Scholes.

Hartlepool supporters no longer endure falling flakes of rust, swirling cinder dust or a leaky terrace roof. The club remains a council tenant at the Vic, although the ground was largely redeveloped in the 1990s. The sole physical remnants of the 1965–67 era are the four floodlight pylons. More than half a century later, veterans of these sixties campaigns still reminisce about 'Trapper' Drysdale haring down the wing, and Ernie Phythian rattling them in up front.

Managers come and go, but some things never change. The North East, 'Hotbed of Soccer', awaits its first top-tier title since the war. 'Pools fans continue to dream of winning any division title. Squawking seagulls still circle the Vic, dive-bombing discarded pies and trays of chips.

Clough was always in two minds about recommending a management apprenticeship at a struggling club like Hartlepools. Soon after leaving, he defined that particular job as 'unique', given the high responsibility and hard work involved.[6] Three years later, he thought all managers could benefit from 'a stretch' at a club where nobody knew where the next shilling, let alone the next pound, was coming from.[7]

In 1972, he described learning 'how to live rough, in a managerial sense'. Life at the bottom had given him a real sense of values, but he wouldn't recommend it. Scratching for cash lumped too many distractions onto managing the team.[8] Reflecting in 1980, he was unsure if he'd 'enjoyed' his time at Hartlepools, although it had given him 'the kind of grounding' that did nobody any harm.[9]

Peter Taylor, meanwhile, said that mere mention of 'Hartlepools' put fire in his belly when he got too complacent.[10]

Clough never did boot any youngster up the backside for running onto the grass at the Victoria Ground. But in his late and lonely alcoholic years, he did swing at – and connect with – a few young men who invaded the Nottingham Forest pitch. The two parties soon met up, promised not to do it again, and parted with a kiss.

The boss dictated that it didn't matter if players liked or disliked you, 'It's when they respect you that they play for you.'[11] On winning their first League Championship in 1972, Clough told *BBC Sportsnight* that it was his partnership with Taylor combined with 'the right buys' that had produced 'the chemical reaction'.[12]

Their formula for success was simple: forge the right blend of players, motivate them, and extract their best qualities.

During nineteen roller coaster months, their first experiment in alchemy sprinkled footballing gold over Hartlepools United. Sparking together, Clough & Taylor's unique chemistry would propel Derby and Nottingham Forest to domestic and European glory.

ACKNOWLEDGEMENTS

What was always going to be a labour of love also turned into one of unprecedented challenges and frustrations when the Covid pandemic struck. Lengthy lockdowns closed libraries for many months and restricted all access to regional newspapers, an essential resource for this book. Research had to be conducted in reverse order: interviews first, newspapers second.

Detective work led me to nearly all the surviving 'Pools players from the era, as well as other key protagonists. It was a joy speaking at length on the phone – or in person – to those who were there at the beginning of the Clough & Taylor joint management story. I'm particularly grateful to Cliff Wright, with whom I talked for many hours. And to Bob McLeod, who generously connected me with his fellow graduates from Sunderland Teachers' Training College. My efforts in tracking down Richard Ord (Ernest's grandson) and John Curry's son (through Rosalind Robinson in Darlington) were also richly rewarded.

Former Hartlepool United media manager Mark Simpson did his best to assist, both before and after losing his job during the first lockdown. He connected me with Sunderland club historian Rob Mason, who provided invaluable information on Ambrose Fogarty. Geoff Wilkinson did a large favour in sending me Cloughie's official programme chatter over his nineteen-month reign.

Retired football correspondents Doug Weatherall and Arthur Pickering repaid my trust with valuable insights and information. As did Bill Hamilton, who generously detailed the match reporting and *Football Mail* production processes. I thank Dan Smith (via Cornerstones) for his support and feedback on my draft chapters, Roger Codner for his advice on Hartlepool history and images, and Adrian Davies for improving newspaper photographs.

Good friend James Clifford Kent (a Gooner) encouraged me from start to finish of this odyssey and provided feedback on many drafts. My oldest brother Jeremy (a Baggie) read a full late draft and annotated corrections and useful comments.

My dad, a faithful Derby County supporter, used to roar with laughter at Clough's bravado on the box. All football fans are fortunate that this supremely engaging – yet awkward – 'one-off' character blessed our national game.

NOTES

CHAPTER 1

1   *Newcastle Journal*, 14/12/71, p.17
2   *Cloughie: The Brian Clough Story* (ITV, 1990), presented by Brian Moore
3   Phone interview with Doug Weatherall, 06/10/20
4   *Newcastle Journal*, 27/12/62, p.1
5   Phone interview with John McGovern, 16/09/20; *Daily Mail*, 08/01/2016, p.65

CHAPTER 2

1   *Cloughie: The Brian Clough Story* (ITV, 1990); Brian Clough (with John Sadler), *Cloughie: Walking on Water* (London: Headline, 2002), pp.47–50
2   Clough, *Walking on Water*, p.51
3   Brian Clough (with John Sadler), *Clough: The Autobiography* (London: Corgi, 1995), pp.17–18
4   Johnny Rogan, *The Football Managers* (London: Queen Anne Press, 1989), p.146
5   *Newcastle Journal*, 14/12/71, p.17
6   Phone interview with Doug Weatherall, 06/10/20

CHAPTER 3

1   *Newcastle Evening Chronicle*, 27/12/62, p.1
2   Phone interview with Doug Weatherall, 06/10/20
3   Clough, *The Autobiography*, pp.48–9
4   Patrick Murphy, *His Way: The Brian Clough Story* (London: Pan, 1994), pp.49–50
5   *Newcastle Journal*, 27/12/62, p.1
6   *The People*, 15/12/63, p.1
7   *Football Echo* [henceforward: *FE*] (*Sunderland Echo* [henceforward: *SE*]), 05/01/63, p.1
8   *Sunday Pictorial*, 20/01/63, p.31
9   *SE*, 19/03/63, p.1
10 *Sunday Mirror*, 30/06/63, p.31
11 Clough, *The Autobiography*, p.49; *Northern Daily Mail* [henceforward: *NDM*], 06/11/65, p.6
12 Clough, *Walking on Water*, pp.89–90
13 Phone interview with Doug Weatherall, 06/10/20
14 *The People*, 19/01/64, pp.20–1
15 Arthur Appleton, *Hotbed of Soccer: The Story of Football in the North-East* (London: Sportsmans Book Club, 1961), pp.213–14
16 Arthur Hopcroft, *The Football Man* (London: Aurum, 1968), pp.111–19
17 *FE* (*SE*), 21/11/63, p.2
18 *SE*, 16/12/63, p.10
19 *The People*, 15/12/63, p.1
20 *Daily Herald*, 16/12/63, p.12

21 *FE (SE)*, 21/12/63, p.4
22 Ibid., p.6
23 *The People*, 15/12/63, p.1
24 *Sunday Mirror*, 22/12/63, p.33
25 *The People*, 05/01/64, pp.20–1
26 *The People*, 12/01/64, pp.20–1
27 *The People*, 19/01/64, pp.20–1
28 *SE*, 14/07/64, p.12
29 *Newcastle Journal*, 28/07/64, p.18
30 *SE*, 08/08/64, p.13
31 *Newcastle Evening Chronicle*, 14/08/64, p.20
32 *Newcastle Journal*, 15/08/64, p.1
33 *SE*, 17/08/64, p.11
34 *The People*, 16/08/64, p.18
35 *SE*, 24/08/64, p.1
36 *SE*, 29/08/64, p.9
37 *Daily Mirror*, 31/08/64, p.18
38 *Birmingham Post*, 02/09/64, p.13
39 *SE*, 01/09/64, p.11
40 *Daily Mirror*, 02/09/64, p.23
41 *SE*, 03/09/64, p.20
42 *FE (SE)*, 05/09/64, pp.1, 16
43 *SE*, 10/09/64, p.21
44 *SE*, 11/09/64, p.19
45 *FE (SE)*, 12/09/64, p.2
46 *The People*, 27/09/64, p.20

Chapter 4

1 *SE*, 06/10/64, p.1
2 *SE*, 02/11/64, p.16
3 *Newcastle Journal*, 02/11/64, p.12
4 *FE (SE)*, 14/11/64, p.1
5 'Football Legends – George Hardwick', BBC Archive, 21/10/96, www.bbc.co.uk/archive/football-legends--george-hardwick/zjpcnrd
6 *FE (SE)*, 28/11/64, p.2
7 Clough, *Walking on Water*, pp.96-7; Clough, *The Autobiography*, pp.52–3
8 Phone interview with John O'Hare, 22/01/21
9 *SE*, 11/01/65, p.11; *FE (SE)*, 06/02/65, p.2
10 *FE (SE)*, 10/04/65, p.2
11 Clough, *Walking on Water*, pp.97–8
12 Clough, *The Autobiography*, p.53
13 'Football Legends – George Hardwick', BBC Archive, 21/10/96, www.bbc.co.uk/archive/football-legends--george-hardwick/zjpcnrd
14 *Parkinson* on BBC1, 20/10/73, www.bbc.co.uk/archive/brian-clough-parkinson/zb3j47h

Chapter 5

1 *Daily Express*, 16/03/78, p.33
2 *Cloughie: The Brian Clough Story* (ITV, 1990)
3 Clough, *Walking on Water*, p.100

4   Phone interview with Grant Shearer, 02/09/20
5   Phone interviews with Grant Shearer, 02/09/20 & 17/10/20
6   Phone interviews with Grant Shearer, 02/09/20 & 17/10/20
7   Phone interview with Grant Shearer, 02/09/20
8   Phone interview with Russ Postlewhite, 03/09/20
9   *Northern Echo* [henceforward: *NE*], 03/09/65, p.18
10 Len Ashurst, *Left Back in Time* (Studley: Know the Score, 2009), p.74
11 *The Times*, 29/11/00, p.25
12 *FE (SE)*, 28/08/65, p.2; *FE (SE)*, 23/10/65, p.2; Murphy, *His Way*, p.61
13 *Newcastle Journal*, 28/10/65, p.1; *SE*, 28/10/65, p.23
14 *SE*, 28/10/65, p.23

Chapter 6

1   Reginald Smyth [pseud. Reg Smythe] (1917–98), *Dictionary of National Biography* entry by Keith Gregson doi.org/10.1093/ref:odnb/70012 (2004)
2   'The mirth and misogyny of Andy Capp', BBC News, 23/03/16, www.bbc.co.uk/news/uk-england-tees-35802880
3   Rachel Wallace, '"She's Punch Drunk!!": Humor, Domestic Violence, and the British Working Class in Andy Capp Cartoons, 1957–65', *Journal of Popular Culture*, Vol. 51, Issue 1 (2018), pp.129–51
4   *The Independent*, 14/06/98
5   British Cartoon Archive, Cartoonist Biographies – Reg Smythe, www.cartoons.ac.uk/cartoonist-biographies/c-d/RegSmythe_AndyCapp.html; 'Nationwide: Reg Smythe', BBC Archive, 1977, www.youtube.com/watch?v=rv0spE7znPQ
6   British Cartoon Archive, Cartoonist Biographies – Reg Smythe; 'Nationwide: Reg Smythe'
7   *The County Borough of West Hartlepool: Official Guide* (Gloucester: British Publishing, 1962)
8   Robert Wood, *West Hartlepool: The Rise and Development of a Victorian New Town* (Hartlepool Borough Council, 1969), p.148
9   *NDM* (supplement) 12/07/65, p.xiii
10 *West Hartlepool: Official Guide* (1962)
11 *The County Borough of West Hartlepool: Official Guide* (Gloucester: British Publishing, 1964)
12 BBC documentary, *Waiting for Work* (first broadcast 12/02/63): www.bbc.co.uk/iplayer/episode/p053r2q1/waiting-for-work
13 Geoffrey Moorhouse, *Britain in the Sixties: The Other England* (Harmondsworth: Penguin, 1964), pp.167–8
14 *West Hartlepool: Official Guide* (1964)
15 *The New County Borough of Hartlepool: Official Guide* (Gloucester: British Publishing, 1966)
16 *NDM*, 17/08/56, p.2

Chapter 7

1   *NDM*, 28/11/66, p.7
2   *NDM*, 28/06/19, p.3
3   Ibid.
4   *NDM*, 04/01/57, p.8; *NDM*, 06/09/54, p.7; *Halifax Daily Courier & Guardian*, 18/02/57, p.2
5   *NDM*, 03/01/53, p.3; *NDM*, 16/11/51, p.8

6 *NDM*, 23/01/54, p.2; *Football Mail* [henceforward: *FM*] (*NDM*), 10/01/59, p.2
7 *FM* (*NDM*), 04/04/59, p.2
8 Neil Carter, *The Football Manager: A History* (London: Routledge, 2006), p.85
9 *NDM*, 12/12/53, p.3; *NE*, 16/12/66, p.14; *FM* (*NDM*), 04/03/61, p.2
10 *Coventry Evening Telegraph*, 30/10/59, p.59
11 Ibid., 23/06/62, p.32
12 *NDM*, 13/02/57, p.8
13 *NDM*, 08/07/66, p.1
14 *NDM*, 02/03/65, p.8
15 *SE*, 27/04/64, p.7
16 *NDM*, 05/08/63, p.6; *SE*, 21 & 22/01/65, p.1
17 *SE*, 06/04/63, p.9; *Daily Herald*, 07/01/64, p.10
18 *SE*, 07/01/64, p.16
19 *NDM*, 08/06/63, p.1
20 Bill Hamilton, *Man on the Spot: A Broadcaster's Story* (Brighton: Book Guild Publishing, 2010), p.52; *SE*, 17/10/64, p.6 *SE*, 31/10/64, p.6
21 *SE*, 17/10/64, p.6
22 *NDM*, 23/04/65, p.12
23 *NDM*, 31/05/65, p.1; *NDM*, 03/06/65, p.18
24 *NDM*, 04/06/65, p.32
25 *NDM*, 10/06/65, p.20
26 *NDM*, 23/06/65, p.1; *NDM*, 28/06/65, p.12
27 *NDM*, 23/10/65, p.2
28 *NE*, 23/09/65, p.14
29 *NE*, 04/10/65, p.10
30 *NDM*, 23/10/65, p.2
31 *NE*, 23/10/65, p.16; *NDM*, 23/10/65, p.2
32 *NE*, 25/10/65, p.10

CHAPTER 8

1 'The Development of the Football Strip – Part 4' (1960s), nationalfootballmuseumstrip.com/the-development-of-the-football-strip-part-4/
2 *Newcastle Journal Weekend Magazine*, 06/11/65, p.7
3 Richard Holt, *Sport and the British: A Modern History* (Oxford: Clarendon, 1989), pp.168–72
4 *NDM*, 01/12/47, p.3
5 *FE* (*SE*), 26/09/64, p.6
6 Phone interview with Robert Ord (no relation to Ernie), 01/11/21
7 *NDM*, 29/05/67, p.9
8 *FE* (*SE*), 18/04/64, p.1
9 Bill Hamilton email to author, 11/03/20
10 Ibid.
11 Phone interview with Arthur Pickering, 15/01/21
12 Bill Hamilton email to author, 11/03/20
13 Ibid.
14 *NDM*, 26/08/65, pp.6, 10
15 *FE* (*SE*), 18/09/65, p.4
16 *NDM*, 20/09/65, p.9; *NDM*, 21/09/65, p.7; *NDM*, 17/08/65, p.16

CHAPTER 9

1 *NE*, 28/10/65, p.16
2 *NDM*, 13/09/65, p.1; *NDM*, 09/10/65, p.9
3 *NDM*, 29/10/65, p.24
4 *Newcastle Evening Chronicle*, 29/10/65, p.24
5 Phone interview with Barry Ashworth, 13/04/20
6 Interview with Brian Drysdale, Bristol, 11/09/20
7 Email from Brian Drysdale, 20/05/20
8 *NDM*, 30/10/65, p.2
9 *Newcastle Journal Weekend Magazine*, 06/11/65, p.7
10 *NDM*, 30/10/65, p.18
11 *NDM*, 01/11/65, p.18
12 Phone interview with Alan & Jean Fox, 28/04/20
13 Tony Francis, *Clough: A Biography* (London: Ebury, 2013), p.53
14 Clough, *Walking on Water*, pp.100–1
15 *The People*, 22/02/70, p.21
16 Peter Taylor (with Mike Langley), *With Clough by Taylor* (London: Sidgwick & Jackson, 1980), pp.12–13
17 *Sports Argus*, 06/11/65, p.9
18 *NDM*, 04/11/65, p.24
19 *Cloughie: The Brian Clough Story* (ITV, 1990)
20 'Victoria Ground Chatter' by Brian Clough [henceforward: 'VGC' by BC], (h) Crewe, 06/11/65
21 *NDM*, 06/11/65, p.6
22 Peter Morris, *The Team Makers: A Gallery of the Great Soccer Managers* (London: Pelham, 1971), pp.43–5
23 Ibid., pp.44–52
24 Stephen Wagg, *The Football World: A Contemporary Social History* (Brighton: Harvester, 1984), pp.51–2
25 Ibid., p.84
26 *NDM*, 29/10/65, p.24
27 'VGC' by BC, (h) Crewe, 06/11/65
28 *Observer Magazine*, 08/09/02, p.8
29 Wagg, *The Football World*, p.83
30 Carter, *The Football Manager*, p.95

CHAPTER 10

1 *NDM*, 10/08/65, p.10
2 *NDM*, 08/06/65, p.8; *NDM*, 10/08/65, p.10
3 *NDM*, 10/01/36, p.5
4 *NDM*, 24/08/43, p.2
5 *Daily Express*, 15/03/78, p.40
6 Halifax Evening Courier, 05/01/51, p.2
7 *NDM*, 14/02/51, p.7; *NDM*, 17/08/51, p.5
8 Andrew Ward & Ian Alister, *Barnsley: A Study in Football*, 1953–59 (Barton: Crowberry, 1981), p.44
9 *NDM*, 24/06/54, p.9; *NDM*, 22/12/54, p.12
10 *NDM*, 16/05/57, p.14; *NDM*, 18/06/57, p.9; *NDM*, 26/08/57, p.7
11 *Daily Mirror*, 08/08/78, p.26
12 Taylor, *With Clough by Taylor*, p.36

13 *The People*, 22/02/70, p.21
14 Clough, *The Autobiography*, p.57
15 *The People*, 22/02/70, p.21
16 Interview with Stan Storton, Eastham, 05/08/20
17 *NDM*, 16/08/57, p.14
18 Ord quoted in Francis, *Clough: A Biography*, p.53
19 Clough, *Walking on Water*, p.102
20 Phone interview with Bob McLeod, 22/06/20
21 Taylor, *With Clough by Taylor*, p.37
22 Clough, *The Autobiography*, p.53
23 Clough, *Walking on Water*, p.109
24 *NDM*, 23/08/63, p.4
25 Phone interview with Richard Ord, 19/11/21
26 *NDM*, 23/08/63, p.4; Phone interview with Richard Ord, 19/11/2021
27 *NDM*, 7/11/58, p.7
28 *NDM*, 23/08/63, p.4; *The People*, 26/09/65, p.17
29 *The People*, 26/09/65, p.17
30 *NDM*, 3 Jan. 1959, p.2
31 *NDM*, 12/06/63, p.16; *NDM*, 19/06/63, p.16; *NE*, 20/06/63, p 10
32 *NDM*, 12/06/63, p.16; *NE*, 20/06/63, p 10
33 *NDM*, 28/02/61, p.4
34 *NE*, 20/06/63, p.10; *NDM*, 19/06/63, p.16; *NDM*, 27/06/63, p.20
35 *NDM*, 30/07/63, p.13
36 *NDM*, 23/08/63, p.4
37 *Daily Mirror*, 13/08/63, p.17
38 Official programme Sunderland v Wigan FA Cup third round, 05/01/08
39 *NDM*, 02/11/63, p.12; *NDM*, 14/11/63, p.16
40 *SE*, 24/02/64, p.16
41 *SE*, 26/10/64, p.11
42 *Newcastle Evening Chronicle*, 28/10/64, p.20
43 *NE*, 29/07/65, p.6; *NE*, 13/08/65, p.16

Chapter 11

1   Interview with Brian Drysdale, Bristol, 11/09/20
2   *FM* (*NDM*), 06/11/65, pp.1, 16
3   *NDM*, 08/11/65, p.10; *NE*, 08/11/65, p.10
4   'VGC' by BC, (h) Workington, 13/11/65
5   *NDM*, 11/11/65, p.20
6   Phone interview with Cliff Wright, 06/08/20; Interview with Cliff Wright, Brotton, 10/09/21
7   Eric Harrison, *The View from the Dugout: The Autobiography of Eric Harrison* (Manchester: Parrs Wood Press, 2001), p.21
8   Interview with Brian Drysdale, Bristol, 10/09/20
9   Harrison, *The View from the Dugout*, p.17
10 Phone interviews with Barry Ashworth, 13/04/20, 24/04/20, 03/08/20, 19/02/21
11 Ibid.
12 Harrison, *The View from the Dugout*, p.18
13 Interview with Stan Storton, Eastham, 05/08/20
14 Phone interview with Brian Grant, 24/09/20
15 Interview with Bob McLeod, Burdon Village, 27/07/20

16 Interview with Brian Drysdale, Bristol, 10/09/20

17 Phone interview with Cliff Wright, 24/01/22

18 *NDM*, 08/11/65, p.16

19 *NDM*, 13/11/65, p.2

20 *NDM*, 10/11/65, p.16

21 'VGC' by BC, (h) Workington, 13/11/65

22 *NDM*, 15/11/65, p.10

23 Interview with Brian Drysdale, Bristol, 10/09/20; Phone interview with Grant Shearer, 02/09/20; Phone interview with Russ Postlewhite, 03/09/20

24 *FM (NDM)*, 13/11/65, pp.1, 16; *NE*, 15/11/65, p.10

25 *NDM*, 20/11/65, p.2

26 'VGC' by BC, (h) Halifax, 20/11/65

27 *NE*, 15/11/65, p.10

28 *NDM*, 20/11/65, p.2

29 *NDM*, 18/11/65, p.24

30 'VGC' by BC, (h) Halifax, 20/11/65

31 *FM (NDM)*, 20/11/65, pp.1, 16; *NDM*, 22/11/65, p.10

32 *FM (NDM)*, 27/11/65, pp. 1, 16

33 *NDM*, 29/11/65, p.10

34 *SE*, 31/10/64, p.6; *SE*, 05/12/64, p.6

35 Clough, *The Autobiography*, p.58

36 Interview with Ken Simpkins, Blackhall, 11/09/21

37 Interview with Hughie and Yvonne Hamilton, Seaton Carew, 27/07/20; Interview with Ken Simpkins, Blackhall, 11/09/21; *FM (NDM)*, 30/12/67, p.3

38 *NDM*, 01/12/65, p.20

39 Ibid.

40 *NDM*, 03/12/65, p.24

41 Ibid., p.1

42 *NE*, 06/12/65, p.10; *FM (NDM)*, 04/12/65, p.16

43 *NDM*, 06/12/65, p.16; *NE*, 07/12/65, p.12

CHAPTER 12

1 Interview with Bob McLeod, Burdon Village, 27/07/20

2 Ibid.

3 Phone interview with Grant Shearer, 02/09/20; Phone interview with Russ Postlewhite, 03/0920

4 Ibid.

5 Phone interviews with John Beresford, 06/02/21, 08/02/21; Phone interview with Grant Shearer, 02/09/20

6 Phone interview with Russ Postlewhite, 03/09/20; Phone interviews with John Beresford, 06/02/21, 08/02/21; *NDM*, 30/04/66, p.12

7 Harrison, *The View from the Dugout*, p.16

8 *The People*, 22/02/70, p.21

9 Interview with Bob McLeod, Burdon Village, 27/07/20

10 Interview with Cliff Wright, Brotton, 10/09/21

11 Interview with Brian Drysdale, Bristol, 10/09/20

12 *The People*, 22/02/70, p.21

13 *NDM*, 27/11/65, p.2

14 'VGC' by BC, (h) Wrexham, 04/12/65

15 *NDM*, 11/12/65, p.2

16 *NDM*, 09/12/65, p.26

17 *FE (SE)*, 24/04/65, p.4

18 *NDM*, 23/04/66, p.6

19 Clough, *Walking on Water*, pp.101–2

20 Ibid., p.101

21 John McGovern, *From Bo'ness to the Bernabeu: My Story* (Kingston: Vision Sports, 2012), p.12

22 *NDM*, 01/05/65, p.2; 'VGC' by Geoff Twentyman (h) Southport, 21/08/65

23 *NDM*, 11/09/65, p.16

24 *NDM*, 08/09/65, p.10

25 *NDM*, 16/10/65, p.16

26 McGovern, *From Bo'ness*, pp.1–14

27 Graham Denton, *Me and My Big Mouth: When Cloughie Sounded Off in TV Times* (Durrington: Pitch, 2019), p.96

28 Phone interview with John McGovern, 04/02/21

29 Jordan P. Peterson, *12 Rules for Life: An Antidote to Chaos* (London: Penguin, 2018), p.1

30 Ibid., pp.5–7

31 Ibid., p.26

32 Ibid., p.16

33 Phone interview with John McGovern, 16/09/20

34 *NDM*, 22/11/65, p.10

CHAPTER 13

1 Taylor, *With Clough by Taylor*, p.35

2 *NDM*, 27/11/65, p.2

3 *FM (NDM)*, 11/12/65, pp.1, 16

4 *NDM*, 13/12/65, p.10

5 'VGC' by BC, (h) Colchester, 18/12/65

6 *NDM*, 16/12/65, p.20

7 'VGC' by BC, (h) Colchester, 18/12/65

8 *FM (NDM)*, 18/12/65, pp.1, 16

9 *NE*, 20/12/65, p.12

10 *NDM*, 20/12/65, p.10

11 'VGC' by BC, (h) Darlington, 27/12/65

12 Clough, *The Autobiography*, pp.57–8

13 Phone interview with Barry Ashworth, 19/02/21

14 *NDM*, 8/11/65, p.16; *NDM*, 11/11/65, p.20

15 *NDM*, 21/04/67, p.24

16 Interview with Brian Drysdale, Bristol, 10/09/20

17 Phone interview with John McGovern, 16/09/20

18 Interview with Cliff Wright, Brotton, 10/09/21

19 Interview with Bob McLeod, Burdon Village, 27/07/20

20 Interview with Ken Simpkins, Blackhall, 11/09/21

21 Interview with Brian Drysdale, Bristol, 10/09/20

22 *Daily Express*, 15/03/78, p.40

23 Phone interview with Barry Ashworth, 13/04/20

24 Interview with Cliff Wright, Brotton, 10/09/21

25 *NE*, 21/12/65, p.1; *NDM*, 20/12/65, p.16

26 *NDM*, 22/12/65, p.1

27 *NE*, 23/12/65, p.10

28 *NDM*, 22/12/65, p.16
29 *NDM*, 24/12/65, p.15
30 *NDM*, 28/12/65, p.8
31 *NE*, 29/12/65, p.10
32 *NDM*, 29/12/65, p.11
33 'VGC' by BC, (h) Darlington, 27/12/65
34 *NDM*, 31/12/65, p.14
35 Interview with Brian Drysdale, Bristol, 10/09/20
36 *FM* (*NDM*), 01/01/66, pp.1, 16
37 'VGC' by BC, (h) Port Vale, 08/01/66

Chapter 14

1   *FM* (*NDM*), 01/01/66, p.2
2   Ibid., p.6
3   *NDM*, 05/01/66, p.20
4   *NE*, 07/01/66, p.16
5   *FM* (*NDM*), 08/01/66, p.1
6   *NE*, 10/01/66, pp.9, 16
7   Ibid., p.9
8   *NDM*, 10/01/66, p.10
9   *NDM*, 11/01/66, p.16; *NDM*, 15/01/66, p.2
10 Taylor, *With Clough by Taylor*, p.38
11 Neil Watson & Roy Kelly, *Up the Pools* (Hartlepool: Ords Ltd, 1991), p.58; Phone interview with Cliff Wright, 23/04/20
12 *NDM*, 17/01/66, p.16; *NDM*, 19/01/66, p.16; *NDM*, 20/01/66, p.20; *NDM*, 21/01/66, p.16
13 *NDM*, 22/01/66, p.1; *NDM*, 24/01/66, p.1
14 Phone interview with Barry Ashworth, 24/04/20; Interview with Stan Storton, Eastham, 05/08/20
15 *NDM*, 24/01/66, p.16
16 Phone interview with Brian Grant, 24/09/20
17 *NE*, 25/01/66, p.12
18 Phone interview with Barry Ashworth, 24/04/20
19 *NDM*, 25/01/66, p.10
20 *NDM*, 22/01/66, p.2
21 *NDM*, 24/01/66, p.16; *NDM*, 27/01/66, p.20
22 *NDM*, 31/01/66, p.10
23 *NDM*, 02/02/66, p.16; *NDM*, 05/02/66, p.3
24 *NDM*, 12/02/66, p.11
25 *NDM*, 16/02/66, p.16
26 *FM* (*NDM*), 05/02/66, pp.1, 16; *NDM*, 07/02/66, p.10
27 *NDM*, 07/02/66, p.16
28 *FM* (*NDM*), 12/02/66, pp.1, 16
29 *FM* (*NDM*), 26/02/66, p.2
30 *FM* (*NDM*), 26/02/66, pp.1, 16
31 *NDM*, 26/02/66, p.16
32 Phone interviews with John Curry Jr, 30/07/20, 08/11/21
33 *NDM*, 22/02/66, p.15; *NDM*, 02/02/66, p.16
34 *FM* (*NDM*), 05/03/66, pp.1, 16; *NDM*, 07/03/66, p.10
35 *FM* (*NDM*), 12/03/66, pp.1, 16; 'VGC' by BC, (h) Torquay, 19/03/66; *NDM*, 19/03/66, p.2

36 *NDM*, 14/03/66, p.16; *NDM*, 16/03/66, p.24
37 *NDM*, 18/03/66, p.19
38 *NDM*, 19/03/66, p.2

CHAPTER 15

1 BBC Archive Voices: Brian Clough on Sport Two, BBC2, broadcast on 11/08/72
2 Interview with Stan Storton, Eastham, 05/08/20
3 *NDM*, 21/03/66, p.16
4 Interview with Stan Storton, Eastham, 05/08/20
5 *NDM*, 06/04/66, p.20
6 Interview with Stan Storton, Eastham, 05/08/20
7 *NDM*, 22/03/66, p.10
8 *NDM*, 25/03/66, p.20
9 *FM (NDM)*, 26/03/66, p.2. With the departure of Fox, Cooper and Marshall, his squad of twenty full-time professionals had reduced to seventeen. Suspensions for Storton and Green had reduced that number to fifteen
10 *NDM*, 26/03/66, p.11
11 www.news.bbc.co.uk/onthisday/, 20/03/66
12 www.news.bbc.co.uk/onthisday/, 31/03/66
13 *Soccer Star*, 01/04/66, p.7
14 *FM (NDM)*, 02/04/66, p.2. In 1966 so far, all but one home attendance had been over 4,000
15 *NDM*, 30/03/66, p.20
16 *NDM*, 02/04/66, p.11
17 *NDM*, 09/04/66, p.11
18 *FM (NDM)*, 09/04/66, pp.1, 16
19 *NDM*, 12/04/66, p.11
20 *NE*, 12/04/66, p.14
21 *NDM*, 13/04/66, p.16; Brian Clough, *Brian Clough Book of Football* (Knutsford: Stafford Pemberton, 1980), p.22
22 *FM (NDM)*, 16/04/66, p.2
23 *NDM*, 16/04/66, p.11
24 *NDM*, 20/04/66, p.11
25 Taylor, *With Clough by Taylor*, p.93
26 *NDM*, 18/04/66, p.16; *NDM*, 23/03/66, p.15
27 *NE*, 25/04/66, p.12
28 *NDM*, 28/04/66, p.11
29 *NDM*, 27/04/66, p.11
30 *FM (NDM)*, 30/04/66, pp.1,16; *NDM*, 02/05/66, p.10
31 *FM (NDM)*, 07/05/66, p.2
32 *NDM*, 05/05/66, p.24
33 *FM (NDM)*, 07/05/66, pp.1, 16; *NE*, 09/05/66, p.12
34 *NDM*, 09/05/66, p.16; *NDM*, 10/05/66, p.10
35 *FM (NDM)*, 14/05/66, p.2
36 'VGC' by BC, (h) Rochdale, 16/05/66
37 *NDM*, 17/05/66, p.10
38 'VGC' by BC, (h) Bradford City, 21/05/66
39 *FM (NDM)*, 21/05/66, p.2
40 *NE*, 23/05/66, p.11; McGovern, *From Bo'ness*, p.17
41 *FM (NDM)*, 21/05/66, p.16
42 news.bbc.co.uk/onthisday/hi/dates/stories/may/21/newsid_2504000/2504777.stm

Chapter 16

1 *NDM*, 28/05/66, p.13
2 Yorkshire Film Archive, 'Clough', Record 16494, circa May 1966
3 *NDM*, 01/01/66, p.2
4 *NDM*, 28/05/66, p.13
5 *NDM*, 26/05/66, p.16
6 *Observer Magazine*, 08/09/02, p.8
7 *Daily Mail*, 23/07/74, p.31
8 *Sunday Sun*, 11/06/72, p.11
9 *The People*, 22/02/70, p.21
10 *Sunday Sun*, 11/06/72, p.11
11 *The People*, 15/02/70, p.21
12 Interview with Brian Drysdale, Bristol, 11/09/20
13 *FM* (*NDM*), 16/04/66, p.2
14 *NDM*, 09/06/66, p.20
15 *NDM*, 02/07/66, p.1; *NDM*, 06/07/66, p.16
16 Phone interview with David Pleat, 23/01/21
17 Interview with Mick & June Somers, Nottingham, 09/09/20

Chapter 17

1 Wagg, *The Football World*, pp.87–8
2 John Hughson, *England and the 1966 World Cup: A Cultural History* (Manchester: Manchester University Press, 2016), p.36
3 *Soccer Star*, 21/01/66, p.2
4 *Goal! World Cup 1966*, directed by Abidine Dino & Ross Devenish (1966)
5 *NDM*, 8/7/66, p.12
6 *NDM*, 9/7/66, p.11
7 *NDM*, 22/07/66, p.28
8 *NDM*, 10/07/66, p.2
9 Francis, *Clough: A Biography*, p.191
10 Steve Mingle, *When England Ruled the World: 1966–1970* (Durrington: Pitch, 2016), p.11

Chapter 18

1 *NDM*, 31/08/54, pp.1, 2, 11
2 *NDM*, 07/01/66, p.19
3 *NDM*, 19 /07/66, p.16
4 *NDM*, 01/08/66, p.3; *NDM*, 05/08/66, p.7
5 *NDM*, 14/08/66, p.20
6 *Daily Express*, 16/03/78, p.33
7 *NDM*, 14/08/66, p.20
8 McGovern, *From Bo'ness*, p.19; Francis, *Clough: A Biography*, p.61
9 Phone interview with John McGovern, 16/09/20
10 Clough, *The Autobiography*, p.59
11 *NDM*, 25/07/66, p.16
12 *NDM*, 04/08/66, p.8
13 *FM* (*NDM*), 16/04/66, p.2
14 *NDM*, 06/08/57, p.10
15 *NDM*, 04/08/66, p.8
16 Phone interview with Brian Grant, 24/09/20
17 Interview with Cliff Wright. Brotton, 10/09/21

18 *NDM*, 25/07/66, p.16
19 *NDM*, 05/08/66, p.11
20 *NDM*, 17/08/66, p.16. Mozambique-born midfielder Mario Coluna had helped Benfica win the European Cup in 1961 and 1962, playing alongside Eusebio in the second final
21 *NDM*, 15/08/66, p.11
22 *NDM*, 16/08/66, p.11

CHAPTER 19

1   *NDM*, 22/08/66, p.10; *FM (NDM)*, 20/08/66, p.1
2   *NDM*, 22/08/66, p.10
3   Ibid.
4   *NDM*, 20/08/66, p.10; *FM (NDM)*, 20/08/66, p.2
5   *FM (NDM)*, 27/08/66, p.2
6   *NDM*, 24/08/66, pp.12, 16
7   'VGC' by BC, (h) Wrexham, 27/08/66
8   *NE*, 29/08/66, p.12
9   *FM (NDM)*, 27/08/66, p.1
10 *NDM*, 29/08/66, p.11
11 Ibid., p.16
12 *NDM*, 03/09/66, p.2
13 *NDM*, 01/09/66, p.11
14 *NDM*, 03/09/66, p.11
15 Interview with Cliff Wright, Brotton, 10/09/21
16 *NDM*, 03/09/66, p.16
17 *NDM*, 05/09/66, p.10
18 *NDM*, 06/09/66, p.16; *FM (NDM)*, 21/05/66, p.2
19 Ibid., p.10
20 *Soccer Star*, 19/08/66, p.24
21 *FM (NDM)*, 10/09/66, p.2
22 *NDM*, 12/09/66, p.6
23 McGovern, *From Bo'ness*, p.28
24 Phone interviews with John Beresford, 06/02/21, 08/02/21
25 *Soccer Star*, 21/04/67, p.26
26 *FM (NDM)*, 10/09/66, p.2
27 *FM (NDM)*, 10/09/66, pp.1, 16; *NDM*, 12/09/66, p.10

CHAPTER 20

1   *NDM*, 16/09/66, p.10
2   *NDM*, 19/09/66, p.10
3   'VGC' by BC, (h) Newport, 19/09/66
4   *NDM*, 20/09/66, p.10
5   *FM (NDM)*, 24/09/66, p.2
6   *NDM*, 21/09/66, p.16
7   *NDM*, 22/09/66, p.24
8   Ibid.
9   'VGC' by BC, (h) Exeter, 24/09/66
10 *FM (NDM)*, 24/09/66, pp.1, 16; *NE*, 26/09/66, p.11
11 'VGC' by BC, (h) Exeter, 24/09/66; *FM (NDM)*, 15/10/66, p.2
12 *FM (NDM)*, 24/09/66, p.2

13 *FM* (*NDM*), 24/09/66, p.2
14 *FM* (*NDM*), 01/10/66, p.2
15 Carol Beresford (West Hartlepool) in *Soccer Star*, 09/09/66, p.14
16 *NDM*, 27/09/66, p.10; *NE*, 27/09/66, p.12
17 *FM* (*NDM*), 01/10/66, p.2
18 *FM* (*NDM*), 01/10/66, p.2
19 'VGC' by BC, (h) Crewe, 01/10/66
20 *NDM*, 03/10/66, p.12
21 *NE*, 03/10/66, p.12
22 *Newcastle Journal*, 04/10/66, p.14
23 *NE*, 08/10/66, p.16
24 *NDM*, 08/10/66, p.11
25 *FM* (*NDM*), 08/10/66, p.2
26 *NDM*, 14/10/66, p.28
27 *Daily Mail*, 18/10/66, p.16
28 Ibid.
29 *Sunday Sun*, 11/06/72, p.24
30 *FM* (*NDM*), 15/10/66, pp.1, 16
31 Ibid., p.2
32 *NDM*, 17/10/66, p.16
33 *NE*, 18/10/66, p.12

CHAPTER 21

1 *NDM*, 17/10/66, p.16
2 Phone interviews with John Beresford, 06/02/21, 08/02/21
3 *NDM*, 18/10/66, p.10
4 Phone interview with John Beresford, 06/02/21
5 *NE*, 20/10/66, p.16
6 *FM* (*NDM*), 22/10/66, pp.1, 16; *NE*, 24/10/66, p.11; *NDM*, 24/10/66, p.10
7 *NDM*, 24/10/66, p.16
8 *NDM*, 25/10/66, p.16
9 *NE*, 26/10/66, p.14
10 *NE*, 31/10/66, p.12
11 *FM* (*NDM*), 29/10/66, pp.1, 16; *NDM*, 31/10/66, p.10
12 *NDM*, 31/10/66, p.16
13 *FM* (*NDM*), 29/10/66, p.2
14 *NDM*, 01/11/66, p.10
15 *FM* (*NDM*), 05/11/66, p.2
16 Ibid.
17 *NDM*, 03/11/66, p.16; *NDM*, 04/11/66, p.22
18 *FM* (*NDM*), 05/11/66, pp.1, 16
19 *NDM*, 07/11/66, p.10
20 *NDM*, 07/11/66, p.16; *NDM*, 08/11/66, p.10
21 *NDM*, 09/11/66, p.16
22 *NDM*, 11/11/66, p.1
23 *NDM*, 14/11/66, p.1
24 *Newcastle Journal*, 12/11/66, p.18
25 *Daily Express*, 15/03/78, p.40
26 *FM* (*NDM*), 12/11/66, pp.1, 16
27 *NDM*, 14/11/66, p.10

28 Ibid., p.16
29 *Daily Mail*, 14/11/66, p.12
30 *NDM*, 14/11/66, p.1
31 *NDM*, 14/11/66, p.16
32 *NE*, 15/11/66, p.12

CHAPTER 22

1   *NDM*, 15/11/66, p.1
2   Ibid.
3   *NDM*, 16/11/66, p.1
4   *NDM*, 18/11/66, p.6
5   *NDM*, 17/11/66, p.2
6   *NDM*, 12/11/66, p.2
7   *NE*, 18/11/66, p.14; *Daily Mirror*, 18/11/66, p.30
8   *Sunday Sun*, 11/06/72, p.11; *Daily Express*, 18/11/66, p.18; *Daily Mail*, 18/11/66, p.16
9   *NDM*, 17/11/66, p.9
10 *NDM*, 18/11/66, p.1
11 *FM* (*NDM*), 12/11/66, p.2
12 *NDM*, 21/11/66, p.1
13 *NDM*, 25/11/66, p.16, *NDM*, 23/11/66, p.16
14 *FM* (*NDM*), 26/11/66, pp.1, 16; *NE*, 28/11/66, p.12

CHAPTER 23

1   *NDM*, 21/11/66, p.1; *Daily Mail*, 23/11/66, p.16
2   *NDM*, 23/11/66, p.1
3   *NDM*, 28/11/66, p.1
4   *NDM*, 24/11/66, p.24
5   *NE*, 02/12/66, p.18
6   *FM* (*NDM*), 26/11/66, p.2
7   *NE*, 05/12/66, p.11; *FM* (*NDM*), 03/12/66, p.1; *NDM*, 01/12/66, p.24
8   *NDM*, 01/12/66, p.5
9   Ibid., p.24
10 *NE*, 02/12/66, p.18
11 *NDM*, 02/12/66, p.24
12 *NDM*, 05/12/66, p.1
13 *NDM*, 05/12/66, p.11; *NDM*, 07/12/66, p.16
14 *NDM*, 06/12/66, p.16
15 Quoted in Francis, *Clough: A Biography*, p.60
16 *Northern Echo*, 12/12/66, p.12
17 *FM* (*NDM*), 10/12/66, pp.1, 16; *NDM*, 12/12/66, p.16
18 *FM* (*NDM*), 17/12/66, p.16
19 *FM* (*NDM*), 10/12/66, p.2
20 *NDM*, 15/12/66, p.1
21 *FM* (*NDM*), 17/12/66, p.2
22 Ibid., pp.1, 16
23 *NDM*, 19/12/66, p.11
24 *NE*, 19/12/66, p.12
25 *NDM*, 20/12/66, p.1
26 *NDM*, 22/12/66, p.20
27 *NDM*, 21/12/66, p.8

28 *NDM*, 22/12/66, p.20
29 *NDM*, 23/12/66, p.20
30 *FM* (*NDM*), 24/12/66, p.2
31 Ibid.
32 *NDM*, 23/12/66, p.20
33 Clough quoted in Francis, *Clough: A Biography*, p.56
34 *FM* (*NDM*), 24/12/66, p.2
35 Ibid., p.1
36 Ibid., p.20
37 Ibid.
38 *NDM*, 28/12/66, p.11
39 *Birmingham Post*, 29/12/66, p.9; *NDM*, 28/12/66, pp.11, 16
40 *NDM*, 30/12/66, p.16
41 *NDM*, 02/0167, p.11
42 *FM* (*NDM*), 31/12/66, p.12

CHAPTER 24

1   *NDM*, 06/01/67, p.17
2   Ibid.
3   *FM* (*NDM*), 31/12/66, p.2
4   Ibid.
5   Ibid.
6   *NDM*, 06/01/67, p.24
7   'VGC' by BC, (h) Southend, 06/01/67
8   *NDM*, 07/01/67, p.14
9   *FM* (*NDM*), 31/12/66, p.2
10 *FM* (*NDM*), 07/01/67, p.2
11 Ibid., p.16
12 *NDM*, 11/01/67, p.16
13 *FM* (*NDM*), 14/01/67, p.2
14 *NDM*, 11/01/67, p.16
15 *NDM*, 14/01/67, p.11
16 *NDM*, 16/01/67, p.16; *Daily Mail*, 16/01/67, p.12
17 *NDM*, 16/01/67, p.16
18 *Newcastle Journal*, 16/01/67, p.10
19 'VGC' by BC, (h) Sheffield Wednesday, 16/01/67
20 *FM* (*NDM*), 21/01/67, p.2
21 *NDM*, 17/01/67, p.10
22 'VGC' by BC, (h) Bradford City, 21/01/67
23 *FM* (*NDM*), 21/01/67, p.16
24 *NDM*, 25/01/67, p.16
25 *FM* (*NDM*), 28/01/67, p.2
26 *NDM*, 31/01/67, p.11
27 *FM* (*NDM*), 28/01/67, p.2
28 *NDM*, 02/02/67, p.24
29 *FM* (*NDM*), 04/02/67, p.2
30 Ibid., pp.1, 16
31 *NDM*, 06/02/67, p.10
32 *NDM*, 02/03/67, p.18
33 *NDM*, 13/02/67, p.11

34 *NDM*, 16/02/67, p.11
35 *FM (NDM)*, 18/02/67, p.2
36 *NDM*, 20/02/67, p.11
37 *FM (NDM)*, 18/02/67, p.2; Watson & Kelly, *Up the Pools*, p.48
38 *The People*, 22/02/70, p.21
39 *Sunday Sun*, 11/06/72, p.24
40 *NE*, 21/02/67, p.12
41 *FM (NDM)*, 25/02/67, p.2
42 *NE*, 21/02/67, p.16
43 *NE*, 27/02/67, p.12

Chapter 25

1   *NDM*, 02/03/67, p.18
2   *FM (NDM)*, 04/03/67, p.2
3   *NDM*, 17/02/67, p.24; *NDM*, 01/03/67, p.20; *NDM*, 02/03/67, p.18
4   *NDM*, 03/03/67, p.16
5   *FM (NDM)*, 04/03/67, p.2
6   *NDM*, 06/03/67, p.11; *NE*, 06/03/67, p.12
7   *FM (NDM)*, 04/03/67, p.?
8   *NDM*, 10/03/67, p.28; *Sunday Sun*, 11/06/72, p.24; *The People*, 22/02/70, p.21; *Coventry Evening Telegraph*, 15/04/67, p.35
9   *FM (NDM)*, 11/03/67, pp.1, 16; *NDM*, 13/03/67, p.10
10 Phone interview with Robert Ord, 29/12/20
11 *NDM*, 11/03/67, p.1
12 *NDM*, 17/03/67, p.28
13 *NDM*, 20/03/67, p.11
14 *NE*, 20/03/67, p.12
15 *NDM*, 22/03/67, p.16
16 *NDM*, 22/03/67, p.16
17 *NDM*, 23/03/67, p.24; *NDM*, 28/03/67, p.16
18 *NDM*, 25/03/67, p.11
19 *NDM*, 27/03/67, p.11; *NE*, 27/03/67, p.12
20 *NDM*, 28/03/67, p.10
21 Ibid., p.16
22 *NDM*, 30/03/67, p.16
23 *NDM*, 01/04/67, p.1
24 *NE*, 03/04/67, p.12
25 Denton, *Me and My Big Mouth*, p.276
26 *The People*, 02/04/57, p.9
27 Phone interview with John Curry Jr, 30/07/20
28 *NDM*, 01/04/67, p.1; *NE*, 03/04/67, p.12
29 *NDM*, 21/03/67, p.1
30 *NE*, 03/04/67, p.12
31 *FM (NDM)*, 01/04/67, pp.1, 16

Chapter 26

1   *NDM*, 03/04/67, p.16; *NDM*, 04/04/67, pp.1, 11
2   *NDM*, 07/04/67, p.15; *NDM*, 10/04/67, p.16
3   *NE*, 10/04/67, p.12; *NDM*, 10/04/67, p.11
4   *NDM*, 11/04/67, p.16

5 *NDM*, 12/04/67, p.19; *NE*, 12/04/67, p.14
6 *Coventry Evening Telegraph*, 15/04/67, p.35
7 *FM (NDM)*, 15/04/67, p.2
8 *NE*, 17/04/67, p.11
9 *NDM*, 22/04/67, p.11
10 *FM (NDM)*, 22/04/67, p.2
11 *NDM*, 22/04/67, p.10
12 *NDM*, 27/04/67, p.24
13 *NE*, 01/05/67, p.12; *FM (NDM)*, 29/04/67, pp.1, 16
14 *NDM*, 05/05/67, p.19
15 'VGC' by BC, (h) Bradford Park Avenue, 29/04/67
16 *NE*, 08/05/67, p.12; *FM (NDM)*, 06/05/67, pp.1, 16; *NDM*, 08/05/67, p.11
17 *NDM*, 08/05/67, p.11
18 *FM (NDM)*, 13/05/67, p.2
19 *FM (NDM)*, 29/04/67, p.2
20 Ibid.
21 *NDM*, 28/04/67, p.19
22 *Sunday Sun*, 18/06/72, p.24
23 *NE*, 01/05/67, p.12
24 *FM (NDM)*, 06/05/67, p.2
25 Ibid.
26 *FM (NDM)*, 13/05/67, p.2

CHAPTER 27

1 Taylor, *With Clough by Taylor*, p.39; Sam Longson, *Sam's Story: An Autobiography* (Chapel-en-le-Frith: Caron, 2013), p.48
2 Longson, *Sam's Story*, p.48
3 Ibid., pp.49–50
4 Ibid., pp.49–50
5 Ibid., p.50
6 Francis, *Clough: A Biography*, p.66
7 Longson, *Sam's Story*, pp.50–51; *NDM*, 15/05/67, p.16
8 *Sunday Sun*, 18/06/72, p.24
9 Francis, *Clough: A Biography*, p.67
10 *The People*, 22/02/70, p.21
11 Ibid.
12 Francis, *Clough: A Biography*, p.67
13 *Sunday Sun*, 18/06/72, p.24
14 *NDM*, 15/05/67, p.16
15 *NDM*, 10/05/67, p.16
16 *NDM*, 15/05/67, p.16
17 *NE*, 15/05/67, p.12
18 Ibid.
19 Ibid.
20 *NDM*, 15/05/67, p.1
21 *NDM*, 16/05/67, p.16
22 Yorkshire Film Archive, 'Clough', Record 16494, circa May 1967
23 Ibid.
24 Ibid.
25 *NDM*, 17/05/67, p.16; *NDM*, 26/05/67, p.24

26 *NDM*, 24/05/67, p.24
27 *NDM*, 27/05/67, p.9
28 Clough, *The Autobiography*, p.62; Birth certificate for Elizabeth Barbara Clough issued by Hartlepool Borough Council
29 *NDM*, 30/05/67, p.16

CHAPTER 28

1 *NDM*, 24/08/67, p.28
2 *NDM*, 05/09/67, p.9
3 *NDM*, 24/11/67, p.18
4 *NDM*, 14/09/67, p.22; *NDM*, 16/09/67, p.2
5 *NDM*, 23/09/67, p.2
6 *Newcastle Journal*, 04/10/67, p.12
7 Jonathan Wilson, *Brian Clough: Nobody Ever Says Thank You* (London: Orion, 2011), pp.483–6; Clough, *Walking on Water*, p.20
8 *Newcastle Evening Chronicle*, 05/12/67, p.13
9 Wilson, *Nobody Ever Says Thank You*, pp.254–55
10 Duncan Hamilton, *Provided You Don't Kiss Me: 20 years with Brian Clough* (London: Fourth Estate, 2007), pp.67–8
11 Taylor, *With Clough by Taylor*, pp.200–01

CHAPTER 29

1 *NDM*, 30/09/67, p.2; *NDM*, 07/10/67, p.16
2 *NDM*, 11/12/67, p.16
3 *NDM*, 26/09/67, p.3
4 Watson & Kelly, *Up the Pools*, p.58
5 *NDM*, 14/08/69, p.20; *NDM*, 30/08/69, p.2; *NDM*, 02/09/69, p.16
6 *NDM* supplement, 03/09/69, p.1
7 *NDM*, 04/09/69, p.15
8 *Hartlepool Mail*, 22/01/72, p.2

EPILOGUE

1 *NDM*, 11/9/67, p.8
2 Phone interview with Richard Ord, 19/11/21
3 *Newcastle Journal*, 21/10/75, p.18
4 *Newcastle Journal Weekend Magazine*, 06/11/65, p.7
5 *Newcastle Journal*, 26/04/83, p.14
6 *NDM*, 06/06/67, p.16
7 *The People*, 22/02/70, p.21
8 Brian Clough, 'Buckets in the Boardroom is no way to start,' *The Sun Soccer Annual 1972* (London: World Distributors, 1971), pp.51–3
9 Clough, *Brian Clough Book of Football*, p.22
10 Taylor, *With Clough by Taylor*, p.165
11 *Daily Express*, 17/03/78, p.43
12 *Match of the Day: Derby County* (BBC VHS, 1992)

BIBLIOGRAPHY

Newspapers and Magazines

REGIONAL (NORTH EAST)
Northern Daily Mail [*NDM*]; *Football Mail* [*FM*]; *Hartlepool Mail*
Northern Echo [*NE*]
Sunderland Echo [*SE*]; *Football Echo* [*FE*]
Newcastle Evening Chronicle
Newcastle Journal
Sunday Sun

OTHER REGIONAL
Birmingham Post
Coventry Evening Telegraph
Halifax Daily/Evening Courier & Guardian
Sports Argus (Birmingham)

NATIONAL
Daily Express
Daily Herald
The Independent
Daily Mail
Daily/Sunday Mirror
Observer
The (Sunday) *People*
Sunday Pictorial

MAGAZINES
Soccer Star

Books

Appleton, Arthur, *Hotbed of Soccer: The Story of Football in the North-East* (London: Sportsmans Book Club, 1961)
Ashurst, Len, *Left Back in Time* (Studley: Know the Score, 2009)
Carter, Neil, *The Football Manager: A History* (London: Routledge, 2006)
Clough, Brian, *Brian Clough Book of Football* (Knutsford: Stafford Pemberton, 1980)
Clough, Brian (with John Sadler), *Clough: The Autobiography* (London: Corgi, 1995)

Clough, Brian (with John Sadler), *Cloughie: Walking on Water* (London: Headline, 2002)

Denton, Graham, *Me and My Big Mouth: When Cloughie Sounded Off in TV Times* (Durrington: Pitch, 2019)

Francis, Tony, *Clough: A Biography* (London: Ebury, 2013)

Hamilton, Bill, *Man on the Spot: A Broadcaster's Story* (Brighton: Book Guild Publishing, 2010)

Hamilton, Duncan, *Provided You Don't Kiss Me: 20 years with Brian Clough* (London: Fourth Estate, 2007)

Harrison, Eric, *The View from the Dugout: The Autobiography of Eric Harrison* (Manchester: Parrs Wood Press, 2001)

Holt, Richard, *Sport and the British: A Modern History* (Oxford: Clarendon, 1989)

Hopcroft, Arthur, *The Football Man* (London: Aurum, 1968)

Hughson, John, *England and the 1966 World Cup: A Cultural History* (Manchester: Manchester University Press, 2016)

Longson, Sam, *Sam's Story: An Autobiography* (Chapel-en-le-Frith: Caron, 2013)

McGovern, John, *From Bo'ness to the Bernabeu: My Story* (Kingston: Vision Sports, 2012)

Mingle, Steve, *When England Ruled the World: 1966–1970* (Durrington: Pitch, 2016)

Moorhouse, Geoffrey, *Britain in the Sixties: The Other England* (Harmondsworth: Penguin, 1964)

Morris, Peter, *The Team Makers: A Gallery of the Great Soccer Managers* (London: Pelham, 1971)

Murphy, Patrick, *His Way: The Brian Clough Story* (London: Pan, 1994)

Peterson, Jordan P., *12 Rules for Life: An Antidote to Chaos* (London: Penguin, 2018)

Rogan, Johnny, *The Football Managers* (London: Queen Anne Press, 1989)

Taylor, Peter (with Mike Langley), *With Clough by Taylor* (London: Sidgwick & Jackson, 1980)

Wagg, Stephen, *The Football World: A Contemporary Social History* (Brighton: Harvester, 1984)

Ward, Andrew & Alister, Ian, *Barnsley: A Study in Football, 1953–59* (Barton: Crowberry, 1981)

Watson, Neil & Kelly, Roy, *Up the Pools* (Hartlepool: Ords Ltd, 1991)

Wilson, Jonathan, *Brian Clough: Nobody Ever Says Thank You* (London: Orion, 2011)

Wood, Robert, *West Hartlepool: The Rise and Development of a Victorian New Town* (Hartlepool Borough Council, 1969)

Official Documents

The County Borough of West Hartlepool: Official Guide (Gloucester: British Publishing, 1962/1964)

The New County Borough of Hartlepool: Official Guide (Gloucester: British Publishing, 1966)

Birth certificate for Elizabeth Barbara Clough (issued by Hartlepool Borough Council)

Articles

Clough, Brian, 'Buckets in the Boardroom is no way to start', *The Sun Soccer Annual 1972* (London: World Distributors, 1971), pp.48–53

Wallace, Rachel, '"She's Punch Drunk!!": Humor, Domestic Violence, and the British Working Class in Andy Capp Cartoons, 1957–65', *Journal of Popular Culture*, Vol. 51, Issue 1 (2018), pp.129–51

Interviews and emails

Telephone Interviews (2020–21)

Barry Ashworth, 13/04/20; 24/04/20; 03/08/20; 19/02/21
John Beresford, 06/02/21; 08/02/21
John Curry Jr, 30/07/20; 08/11/21
Alan & Jean Fox, 28/04/20
Brian Grant, 24/09/20
John McGovern, 16/09/20; 04/02/21
Bob McLeod, 22/06/20
John O'Hare, 22/01/21
Richard Ord (grandson of Ernest), 19/11/21
Robert Ord (no relation), 29/12/20; 01/11/21
Arthur Pickering, 15/01/21
David Pleat, 23/01/21
Russ Postlewhite, 03/09/20
Grant Shearer, 02/09/20; 17/10/20
Doug Weatherall, 06/10/20
Cliff Wright, 23/04/20; 06/08/20; 24/01/22

Face-to-face Interviews

Brian Drysdale, Bristol, 10/09/20; 11/09/20
Hughie & Yvonne Hamilton, Seaton Carew, 27/07/20
Bob McLeod, Burdon Village, 27/07/20
Ken Simpkins, Blackhall, 11/09/21
Mick & June Somers, Nottingham, 09/09/20
Stan Storton, Eastham, 05/08/20
Cliff Wright, Brotton, 10/09/21

Emails to Author

Brian Drysdale, 20/05/20
Bill Hamilton, 11/03/20

Internet

BBC News, 'The mirth and misogyny of Andy Capp', 23/03/16, www.bbc.co.uk/news/uk-england-tees-35802880
BBC Website, On This Day, www.bbc.co.uk/onthisday
British Cartoon Archive, Cartoonist Biographies – Reg Smythe, www.cartoons.ac.uk/cartoonist-biographies/c-d/RegSmythe_AndyCapp.html
Hartlepools United/Hartlepool/Hartlepool United statistics, www.inthemadcrowd.co.uk
National Football Museum, www.nationalfootballmuseumstrip.com/the-development-of-the-football-strip-part-4/
Oxford Dictionary of National Biography, www.oxforddnb.com

Television & Cinema

BBC1, *Parkinson*, 20/10/73, www.bbc.co.uk/archive/brian-clough-parkinson/zb3j47h

BBC Archive, *Nationwide: Reg Smythe*, 1977, www.youtube.com/watch?v=rv0spE7znPQ

BBC Archive, *Football Legends: George Hardwick*, broadcast on 21/10/96, www.bbc.co.uk/archive/football-legends--george-hardwick/zjpcnrd

BBC Archive Voices, Brian Clough on Sport Two, BBC2, broadcast on 11/08/72. CD: *Brian Clough in his own words* (BBC/AudioGO, 2012)

BBC documentary *Waiting for Work*, broadcast 12/02/63, www.bbc.co.uk/iplayer/episode/p053r2q1/waiting-for-work

BBC VHS, *Match of the Day: Derby County*, 1992

ITV, *Cloughie: The Brian Clough Story*, 1990, presented by Brian Moore, www.youtube.com/watch?v=LiGlFr3ooZU

Yorkshire Film Archive, end-of-season interviews with 'Clough' and Taylor, Record 16494, circa May 1966/circa May 1967

Goal! World Cup 1966, directed by Abidine Dino & Ross Devenish (UK/Liechtenstein: Frigo, 1966)

Football Programmes

Hartlepools United (1965–67), including 'Victoria Ground Chatter' (i.e. manager's notes) by Geoff Twentyman and Brian Clough

Sunderland (2008)

INDEX

The History Press

The destination for history
www.thehistorypress.co.uk